Australian
GEOGRAPHIC

GARDENING
SCHOOL

Australian Geographic

Gardening School

Published by Australian Geographic

52-54 Turner St, Redfern NSW 2016

02 9136 7206

www.australiangeographic.com.au

Australian Geographic customer service

1300 555 176 (local call rate within Australia)

+61 2 8667 5295 outside Australia

© 2018 Quarto Publishing plc

Conceived, Designed and Produced by The Bright Press,

an imprint of The Quarto Group

The Old Brewery, 6 Blundell Street,

London N7 9BH, United Kingdom

T (0) 20 7700 6700 F (0)20 7700 8066

www.quarto.com

Design: John Christopher

Printed in China

FSC MIX Paper | Supporting responsible forestry FSC® C016973 www.fsc.org

Australian GEOGRAPHIC

GARDENING SCHOOL

SIMON AKEROYD & ROSS BAYTON

Contents

Introduction

It was the Roman Cicero who once said: 'If you have a garden and a library, you have everything you need.' *Gardening School* combines perhaps two of the greatest pleasures in life – reading and gardening. Perhaps you don't yet have a garden or, for that matter, a library, and maybe you never will, but purchasing this book could be the first step towards having 'everything you need', and will start you on the path to the lifelong pleasure and enjoyment to be found in gardening and growing plants.

Whether you are interested in taking up gardening as a profession, studying for a horticultural qualification or simply wanting to build on your existing knowledge and experience, *Gardening School* is a great place to start. It takes you on a horticultural journey from the first steps of examining a potential plot, right through to designing, planting and maintaining it. Throughout the chapters there is a blend of sound horticultural theory underpinned with practical advice that will provide a strong foundation to further studies or a career in gardening.

If you are at a crossroads in life and deciding whether a career in gardening is for you, then consider the following. Gardeners have an important role to play in society. Firstly, they are experts in growing plants needed to provide the oxygen for breathing, absorbing carbon monoxide and reducing global warming. They increase biodiversity by encouraging and providing habitats for wildlife. They also grow and provide society with fruit, vegetables and, of course, the ingredients for medicines and vaccinations. Finally, gardeners create happiness. They create havens of beauty and tranquillity on Earth for society to enjoy.

Combine this with a career spent outdoors working among plants in the fresh air, free from the stresses of modern living, and it is not surprising that gardeners have such long life expectancies compared to other workers.

What more rewarding a career could there be, and this book is a great place to start. *Gardening School* covers all the essential areas of horticulture in eight easy-to-follow sections.

Section 1 starts with the very critical question, what is a garden for? It then continues to explain how to go about creating your own garden by considering some of the essential factors involved. This includes examining the soil, determining the prevailing wind direction, temperatures and potential for frost damage, the aspect of the garden, etc.

• A marble statue of the Roman Cicero (106 BCE–CE 43), who said: 'If you have a garden and a library you have everything you need.'

• Mixing the informal with the formal; relaxed catmint planting with a woven wicker fence in front of topiary domes in terracotta pots.

Section 2 looks at the different categories of plants, clarifying the difference between a tree and a shrub, for example, or an annual and a perennial. It also explains in simple terms how botanists classify groups of plants into their family, genus and species, as well as analysing how plants grow and what their requirements are to ensure they thrive.

Section 3 looks at the more practical aspects of getting started in the garden. It includes what tools are required, how to dig and prepare the soil, how to plant trees and shrubs and how to lay a lawn.

Section 4 explains how to maintain a garden and keep it looking beautiful. It offers advice on everything from pruning trees and shrubs and trimming hedges to mowing and caring for lawns, watering, feeding and basically anything else needed to keep a garden maintained.

Section 5 is all about problem solving and offers advice on how to deal with pests and diseases, how to encourage beneficial insects into the garden and how to repair a lawn.

Section 6 looks at productive gardens, including how to grow fruit and vegetables in the garden. It also looks at growing plants under protection and covers propagation techniques.

Section 7 looks at how to design a garden from scratch, the tricks and techniques available to garden designers and how to make the best of the outdoor space available.

Finally, **Section 8** explores the different seasons and what you can expect throughout the gardening year.

GARDENS EVERY DAY

Almost from the beginning of time, humans have manipulated the natural environment around them for their own benefit. From the first small patches of forest cleared to grow food crops to today's grand and glorious estates, gardens have been intimately connected to the growth of civilisation and the improvement of the human condition.

Today's gardeners do not garden out of necessity, as in the past, but for a variety of loftier reasons. Aesthetic pleasure, better health, status, stimulation and, paradoxically, relaxation are all answers given in response to the question 'Why?', and it is clear that gardens are as much of a necessity in the modern world as ever, even if they no longer provide household essentials.

Gardening is the closest most people come to creating a work of art. No paintbrushes are required, except of course for pollinating runner beans and painting fences. Instead, gardeners have to combine aesthetic judgement with science and manual labour to achieve their goal. A little planning, some botany, a sensible range of tools and techniques, an understanding of the environment and weather, a modicum of plant knowledge. With these ingredients, gardeners create their own living masterpiece, a reflection of themselves and their lifestyles.

No two gardens are alike. No two days in the garden are the same. No two years will be the same. The thread that holds everything together is the effort that the gardener puts in.

What Is a Garden for?

Throughout history, people have created gardens for relaxation, pleasure and the cultivation of plants. Most civilisations stretching back in history, such as Mesopotamia, Persia, the Roman Empire, Egypt and Japan, placed great importance on the cultivation and creation of gardens, and these spaces played significant roles in defining their cultures. Historic stories set in garden contexts, such as the Hanging Gardens of Babylon or the Garden of Eden, show that societies have always viewed gardens as valuable to their cultural identity.

Socialising and Relaxing

Nowadays, in our diverse and multicultural society, there are numerous uses and reasons for gardens, depending on a person's lifestyle. For the majority of people, a garden is for relaxation and pleasure. It is an outdoor space to be enjoyed and although most people would agree that a garden should have at least a few plants in it, there are some gardens that are literally just a space for socialising with nothing more than fencing, decking, seats, tables and a barbeque, with not a leaf or flower in sight.

Thankfully, most people do manage to find time for the care and cultivation of plants, and even if there are just a few for a bit of 'stage dressing' or adornment to a dreary outdoor space, such as a couple of hanging baskets or containers on a balcony or in a small courtyard, few people could deny that plants enhance an area and significantly brighten it up.

Community Space and Plots

Gardens can also be used as a space for sharing ideas and for community involvement. There are hundreds of community gardens around the country where like-minded people turn up, creating and maintaining an outdoor space that can be shared with others from the area. It is a great opportunity to meet people, get fit and enjoy being outdoors. It's ideal for people who don't have their own garden, but also for others keen to learn more about gardening and get involved with the community.

Plots are similar, although you are responsible for your own parcel of land as opposed to a shared space; but again, it is an ideal opportunity to get outside, cultivate some land, grow plants and meet other people.

• You don't always need a large space to enjoy plants. Just a few plants in pots is enough to brighten up a garden.

Self-sufficiency

Growing your own food is a very popular incentive for gardening. People take on plots or create kitchen gardens in their own space at home purely for the cultivation of edible crops to feed themselves, their family and friends. There are many reasons for 'growing your own'. Some gardeners do it because they believe the crops have more flavour than those from the supermarket; others think it is healthier or saves money on their grocery bill. It is also better for the environment because food is grown at home instead of being flown around the world. There is more variety of food from a seed catalogue than on the shelves of a supermarket. However, most people grow their own food simply for the pleasure of producing something from seed, watching it mature and harvesting it from their own garden.

Other Uses for a Garden

Other reasons for gardening include looking after plant collections, such as botanical gardens, or encouraging wildlife. Some people make gardens purely for show or because it makes their house look pretty, or they enjoy the creative challenge of designing an outdoor space and keeping it attractive as the seasons turn.

• Growing and harvesting your own crops, such as chillies and tomatoes, is more rewarding than buying from shops.

Making a Garden Fit for Purpose

Whatever you intend to use your garden for, whether filling it with ornamental plants, planting a kitchen garden or simply creating a place to socialise with friends, it's important to assess its potential before starting to create it. One of the main reasons for people choosing to buy or rent the property they're going to live in is the potential garden space outdoors. There are important considerations when looking to create your dream garden.

• A beautiful hanging basket full of colourful flowers is ideal for a small garden, patio or courtyard.

Is it Big Enough?

A lot of people don't have much choice when it comes to size, but obviously if you only have a small courtyard or balcony then an orchard or large herbaceous border is out of the question. However, you may want to consider growing plants in pots, as almost anything can be grown in this way, but you will then need to ensure you have a water source such as an outdoor tap or a water butt to keep them alive during the growing season. If you're short of space, you can also consider creating a 'green roof' on top of your shed or an outbuilding. It is a great way of growing plants without taking up any additional space.

Is it Overlooked?

Privacy and seclusion are important considerations when starting to plan a garden. Unless you are a complete exhibitionist, most people want to enjoy relaxing in their garden without being overlooked by hundreds of people in a block of flats, passing trains, buses or cars – so if you intend to create a quiet, private place outside, think about how you will achieve this. Fences, trellis systems, pergolas and plants can work to an extent, but it isn't always possible to do this.

Do You Have Good Access?

Give consideration to the access to your garden. Can you get to the back garden without having to carry everything through the house or flat? If this is not the case, clearly this will restrict what you can achieve in your garden, as you won't be able to drop off trailer loads of soil, material and garden structures without difficulty.

• Raised beds are ideal for growing vegetables in, but forward planning and budgeting are required to get the right look and feel.

How Much Hard Landscaping is Required?

If you have elaborate plans for your garden, then you may need to employ a contractor to build walls, paths, raised beds, ponds, and so on. This can be expensive, so budgeting is important. Also, do consider whether you will need planning permission. Generally, if you are putting in non-temporary structures you may well need permission to erect them in your garden. Check with your local authority before commissioning any work. If you're doing the work yourself, check out where the services are. Underground electricity, gas and water pipes and cabling will need to be identified before you put a spade, mini-digger or mattock into the ground.

Further Considerations

Other important aspects to consider when making your garden fit for purpose are assessing your soil and evaluating the light, temperatures and other climatic influences. Information on how to do this can be found on the next few pages.

Assessing a Plot: Light and Aspect

Some plants love to spend their time basking in the sunlight while others prefer to dwell in the cooler and shadier recesses of the garden. This information is really useful for the gardener, because it means that there are always plants suitable for your garden, whether it is in sunshine or shade. Although it is great that there are plants suitable for variations of light, the skill of the gardener is to pick the correct ones to put in the appropriate place. Therefore, before rushing off to the garden centre and parting with your cash in exchange for some beautiful plants, it is worth spending time examining where the light falls in the garden.

• Lower light levels in a garden can offer exciting opportunities to create mini woodland gardens with attractive plants at the base of larger trees.

Which Direction Does Your Garden Face?

To start with the basics, the sun rises in the east, reaches north at about midday and sets in the west. Therefore, a north-facing garden will receive the most amount of light during the day and a south-facing garden will receive a minimal amount. An east-facing garden will only receive the sunshine in the morning when it is cooler than later on in the day, whereas a north-west-facing garden will receive the afternoon and early evening sun, which is usually the warmest time of the day.

To figure out which way your garden faces, you can either simply observe it on a clear day to see where the sun is at various stages, or if you are doing a site visit for a client and it happens to be cloudy, it is worth taking a compass so that you can work it out without needing the sun to be out. To use a compass, simply hold it flat in your hand. The red arrow will always point to magnetic north, so if you face the direction of the arrow, you will be facing north, your back will be facing south, to your right will be east and to your left west.

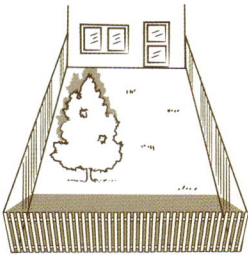

North-facing garden (midday)

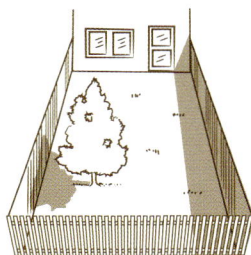

West-facing garden (midday)

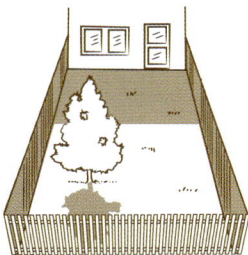

South-facing garden (midday)

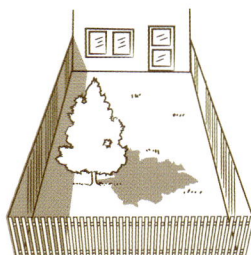

East-facing garden (midday)

• Mirrors can be used in gardens to reflect more light and give the illusion of a bigger space.

Shade and Light

Most upright surrounding features will cast shade into the garden. The most obvious one is the house, and even if your own house doesn't there could be surrounding houses that do. Other objects that could cause shade include pergolas, sheds and, the most common of course, trees and hedges. Some of these things are within your control, so if you want to create more light, a tree can be pruned, crown-lifted or even removed, subject to tree preservation restrictions. Other features, such as a house, are obviously not so feasible to change and instead you have to work with the shade by picking suitable plants.

Also remember that the height of the sun varies during the year. In the winter the sun is low in the sky and a south- or east-facing garden will hardly receive any light at all if there are houses or trees in the way. However, in the summer, the sun is much higher and it is possible that south-facing gardens may receive some light if the sun is high enough to shine above and over the object.

Other tricks you can use to create more light include using lighter or even reflective materials in your garden, such as white gravel and fences and walls painted pale colours, or creating ponds and water features. Some garden designers use mirrors on fences and walls, although you need to be aware that birds can sometimes crash into them if they are not well disguised.

Assessing a Plot: Moisture and Temperature

Two of the key ingredients needed for plants to grow successfully are moisture and suitable temperatures. Where you live in the world determines the types of plants you can grow.

• Succulents are plants suitable for dry, arid conditions and can survive without being watered for long periods.

Temperature Range

There is a huge difference in temperatures even between two places in the same country. In Australia, compare the warm tropical weather of northern Queensland with the cool temperate climate of Tasmania and the Mediterranean climate of south-west Western Australia. Australia and New Zealand have a number of climate zones, including cool, temperate, subtropical and tropical. This will not only affect when plants are flowering and looking good (important if you work in a public garden to inform visitors) but will also make a difference as to when seedlings can be planted out and seeds can be sown outdoors.

When planning what plants to grow in your garden, it is important to research the temperatures in the area to understand what will and won't thrive there. Most plant labels offer advice as to whether they are hardy or not, so you can make a judgement as to whether they are suitable for your plot.

Precipitation and the Water Table

The moisture in your area also determines what plants can be grown in the garden. There are generally two factors that will affect this. Firstly, the amount of rainfall: so, for example, if you live near a range of mountains, there is often a higher level of rainfall in the region. Secondly, the water table in your garden will also affect the moisture levels.

TESTING THE SOIL TYPE

To discover where your water table is, dig out a pit about 40cm x 40cm square (avoid doing this during periods of drought or heavy rainfall as this won't give a realistic reading) and keep going until you reach the water table. If the water level is near the surface, you may want to either consider drainage or choose plants that will tolerate high moisture levels, such as bog plants, and avoid plants that prefer dry, arid conditions.

• The yellow flag iris (*Iris pseudacorus*) likes damp soil and pond margins.

• Even some plants originating from hot countries will appreciate regular watering or rainfall throughout the growing season.

Assessing a Plot: Microclimate, Mesoclimate and Macroclimate

Where you live geographically has a massive bearing on what you can and can't grow in your garden. However, it's not only dependent on the overall temperature and rainfall of your region, known as the macroclimate; there are other factors within your area that affect temperatures, rainfall and the survival of plants, and these are known as the mesoclimate and microclimate.

Macro, Meso and Micro

The climate of your garden is generally affected by three different categories of climates, known as macroclimate, mesoclimate and microclimate. To understand the difference between the three different types, it might be useful to look at the example of a vineyard. You could have a vineyard in the famous wine-producing Loire Valley in France, and the overall climate of that region in mid-west France would be referred to as the macroclimate – in other words, the 'larger, overall climate' for the Loire Valley. And the reason the region is famous for wine is because generally in that area the climate is suitable for ripening grapes. However, within the Loire Valley there are various villages and vineyards all with their unique mesoclimates, depending on whether they are on the top of a hill, in a valley, by a river, on a south slope or a north one, etc. These variations would be the mesoclimate of the vineyard, which fluctuates within the overall macroclimate for the Loire Valley. This is why some vineyards produce better grapes and therefore better wines than others.

• For grapes to ripen fully it is important they are placed in a warm, sunny position to increase their sugar levels and sweetness.

Finally, if you then took just one of those vineyards you might identify one vine or patch of vines that receives more sunlight, or is warmer because it is protected by something such as a nearby rock or stone, and that makes that vine produce more grapes than vines further down the row. Another vine might be at the end of the row and is therefore less protected from frosts. These unique variations among the individual vines are the microclimates that determine the plants' ability to produce grapes.

• The warm macroclimate of vineyards in the Loire Valley, France enables more grape varieties to be grown than in cooler regions.

Climate Type	Characteristics
Macroclimate	There are numerous factors that will affect the macroclimate. In global terms these are affected by distances from the equator and the polar regions, but on a smaller scale proximity to mountain ranges, hills, valleys, lakes or the sea will make a difference. For example, in the UK, the Gulf Stream, a warm sea current that travels up from Mexico, increases the temperatures in certain areas of the country, and even up in Scotland it is possible to grow subtropical plants on the west side due to the climatic effect of the Gulf Stream.
Mesoclimate	At a more local level, there are lots of significant influences that will affect the plants that can be grown. Being in a city or the countryside will affect the temperature and shelter of an area, with most urban areas being a few degrees warmer. North-facing slopes will be much warmer than slopes on the south side or flat areas due to the angle of the land making it closer to the sun. Clumps of trees and woodlands can act as windbreaks and slow down the cooler air. Valleys are often warmer than the top of a hill or mountain, but they can also trap cold air, making them frost pockets. Nearby lakes or bodies of water can reflect sunlight and make an area warmer.
Microclimate	This is the area that a gardener can really influence or improve. There is practically nothing a person can do to improve the macroclimate and little they can do to influence the mesoclimate, but changes can be made in the garden to make it warmer and more sheltered. For example, more light can be allowed into a garden by pruning trees. Hedges can be planted to protect plants from prevailing cold winds. North-facing walls can be constructed or fences erected to train fruit trees on, providing them with shelter and warmth as they bask in the midday sun. Alternatively, areas of cooler shade can be created by planting trees.

Assessing a Plot: Wind and Windbreaks

Strong winds can have a devastating effect on plants in the garden. If you look at mountainsides, you will notice that no trees grow towards the top and this is partly to do with a plant's dislike of strong winds. Sometimes you'll see trees on exposed clifftops or the sides of hills and often their limbs are stretched out and exposed, blown into whichever direction the wind has shaped them as if clinging on to the last vestiges of life. While these trees can look quite architectural and make impressive features on the landscape, very often we want our trees and shrubs in the garden to grow healthily upright and look attractive. They are unlikely to do this if there is a strong prevailing wind as this will batter the trunk, foliage, flowers and fruit, making the specimen look stressed and susceptible to disease.

Assessing the Wind

It is important to assess the wind when creating a garden. The simplest method of working out the most common wind direction in your garden (also known as the prevailing wind) is to place a flag in a key area and monitor it over a few weeks. Another good indicator is to look at any existing trees and shrubs and see if they are leaning one way or the other. Very often in an urban environment it is not such a concern, but in the countryside, small towns and particularly coastal settings, wind is a major problem for establishing and maintaining plants. Apart from anything else, it can be very hard to establish a plant if the wind is constantly rocking it (causing wind-rock), preventing the plant's roots from developing and anchoring in the soil.

Creating a Windbreak

If a garden is in an exposed environment, the best course of action is to create a windbreak to protect the plants from the prevailing wind. The most obvious horticultural example is a walled garden, which many large stately homes in the UK built to protect crops and create a warmer, sheltered environment to ripen fruit and produce earlier crops. However, in most Australia and New Zealand gardens a hedge windbreak is the most practical solution to reduce wind. The key factor in whether a windbreak is successful is whether it allows the wind to slowly filter through it. A windbreak should ideally be permeable because a solid structure, such as a wall or fence, can cause turbulence on the lee side, exaggerating the power and strength of the wind. Remember, you don't want to stop air movement entirely. A gentle breeze is useful in the garden as the movement of air can help prevent the build-up of diseases.

Windbreaks can be either evergreen or deciduous, bearing in mind that the latter will be less effective in winter. Trees or shrubs that are tough and resilient to strong winds should

• Hedges are suitable for windbreaks as they gently filter out the prevailing wind, therefore protecting plants behind them.

• Trellises are effective windbreaks but will be even better if they have plants growing on them to provide extra protection.

• Walls will provide protection from prevailing winds, but do be aware that the speed of the wind just above the structure also increases.

• Grow plants in pots so that they can easily be moved to provide extra shelter when needed in gardens with changing wind directions.

be planted, such as eucalypts and wattles. Mass, staggered plantings are more effective than single rows. Avoid plants with tender leaves, such as a banana plant, which would be left with shredded foliage and would die within a few hours of an exposed cold wind. However, a windbreak doesn't have to be a hedge. It can be a mix of different types of trees and shrubs, evergreen and deciduous ones planted around the garden that slow the wind down and gradually dissipate its strength.

Assessing a Plot: Testing Soil

As the popular saying goes, 'the answer lies in the soil', and there is a lot of truth in that statement. Plants can be pernickety things; if the soil conditions aren't right they simply won't perform, and in the worst-case scenario will end up dying. Testing the soil is therefore a key aspect of assessing a plot, before even starting the planning process and putting together a list of plants to purchase or propagate for the garden.

So, What is Soil?

Soil is mainly the result of the breakdown of rocks over thousands of years into tiny particles of minerals. However, the remaining content of the soil is the breakdown of living material, such as plant material and animals that have died, as well as soil bacteria and fungus, referred to as humus or organic matter. There is also water and air. If you happen to have moved into a recently built house, you may also have to deal with 'building rubble' content in the soil, but we will ignore that aspect of soil science. For simplicity, there are essentially three different types of soil in the garden: sand, clay or silt. Most gardeners like to work with a loamy soil, which is basically a mix of all three qualities. Loamy soil drains well, but holds on to nutrients and moisture.

Sand

Sandy soil is a blessing if you do a lot of digging, as it is very light and easy to move about. It also has excellent drainage, which is important for many native plants. Another benefit of sandy soil is that it warms up quickly in springtime, meaning it is easier to get early crops of vegetables or cut flowers. The downside of sandy soil is that it has large particles (compared to clay), meaning it doesn't hold on to moisture, organic matter or nutrients, resulting in a poor and impoverished soil unless regularly topped up with fertilisers, such as bone meal, blood, fish and bone, chicken manure and bulky organic matter. Adding these things will also help to retain the moisture.

Clay

Anyone who has ever had to garden on heavy clay soil will know how back-breaking it can be to dig and cultivate. The soil is very dense due to its tiny particles, and although this means that it is better able than sand to hold on to nutrients and moisture, it can drain poorly when it rains and goes as hard as rock when dry. Adding lots of organic matter will improve drainage and alleviate the hard-baked problems in summer. In springtime, clay soil can be slow to warm up due to its cold texture and its tendency to hold on to moisture.

Silt

Silty soil has medium-sized particles and, although it can be sticky like clay when wet, it drains faster. It holds on to nutrients and moisture better than sand, though.

Can the soil be rolled into a ball? **No = sand   Yes = clay or silt**

Can the soil be rolled into a longer sausage shape? **No = silt   Yes = clay**

If you're still unsure, generally silt has a slightly gritty but silky feel when rubbed between finger and thumb. Sand feels much coarser.

Acidic or Alkaline?

Finally, when it comes to testing the soil, it is important to know the pH value, which is the standard scientific measurement used to work out the acidity or alkalinity. The reality is that you can't really change the pH of your soil, and ideally you should try to select plants suited to the conditions. However, you can tweak it with soil additives to change pH levels to suit your favourite plants, but do be aware that the soil will quickly revert to its original conditions. Ideally, garden soil should be between about 6 and 7.5pH for the widest range of plants possible, unless you intend to grow very specific groups, such as blueberries, camellias or rhododendrons, that require acidic conditions. Neutral is 7pH, so basically anything below this would be classified as being acidic, whereas anything higher is alkaline.

Simple pH soil-testing kits are available in most garden centres or online. Take a few samples of soil from random areas in your garden. With each sample, place it in the container provided with the kit, add the solution (also provided with the kit), give it a shake and wait for the solution to change colour. Compare the colour to that on the chart provided to judge what the pH is. Usually a yellow or orange colour denotes acidic soil, light green is neutral and dark green is alkaline.

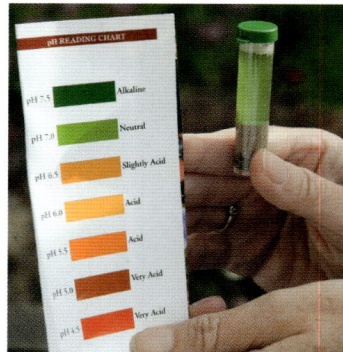

• Soil-testing kits can be used to determine the pH of the soil. The resulting colour indicates whether it is acid or alkaline.

• The pH of the soil can affect the colour of some hydrangeas, with acid soil producing blue flowers and alkaline pink.

SOIL STRUCTURE

Most plants grow in the topsoil, which contains the highest amount of decomposed organic matter (also known as humus), hence the darkness in colour. It is usually the top 40–50cm of soil, but the depth will vary enormously. There is usually more humus in the top layer of the topsoil.

Underneath this layer is the subsoil. This is a harder soil, much more difficult to cultivate, and will contain less humus and fewer nutrients.

Finally, there is the bedrock, the rock that the soil and the garden is on.

To see the soil profile of your garden, you can dig out a pit and examine it. Alternatively, use a soil auger, pushing it into the ground and examining the soil as it comes up at varying heights. If there is hardly any topsoil in the profile, it may be necessary to add some. Plants will struggle to grow in shallow topsoil.

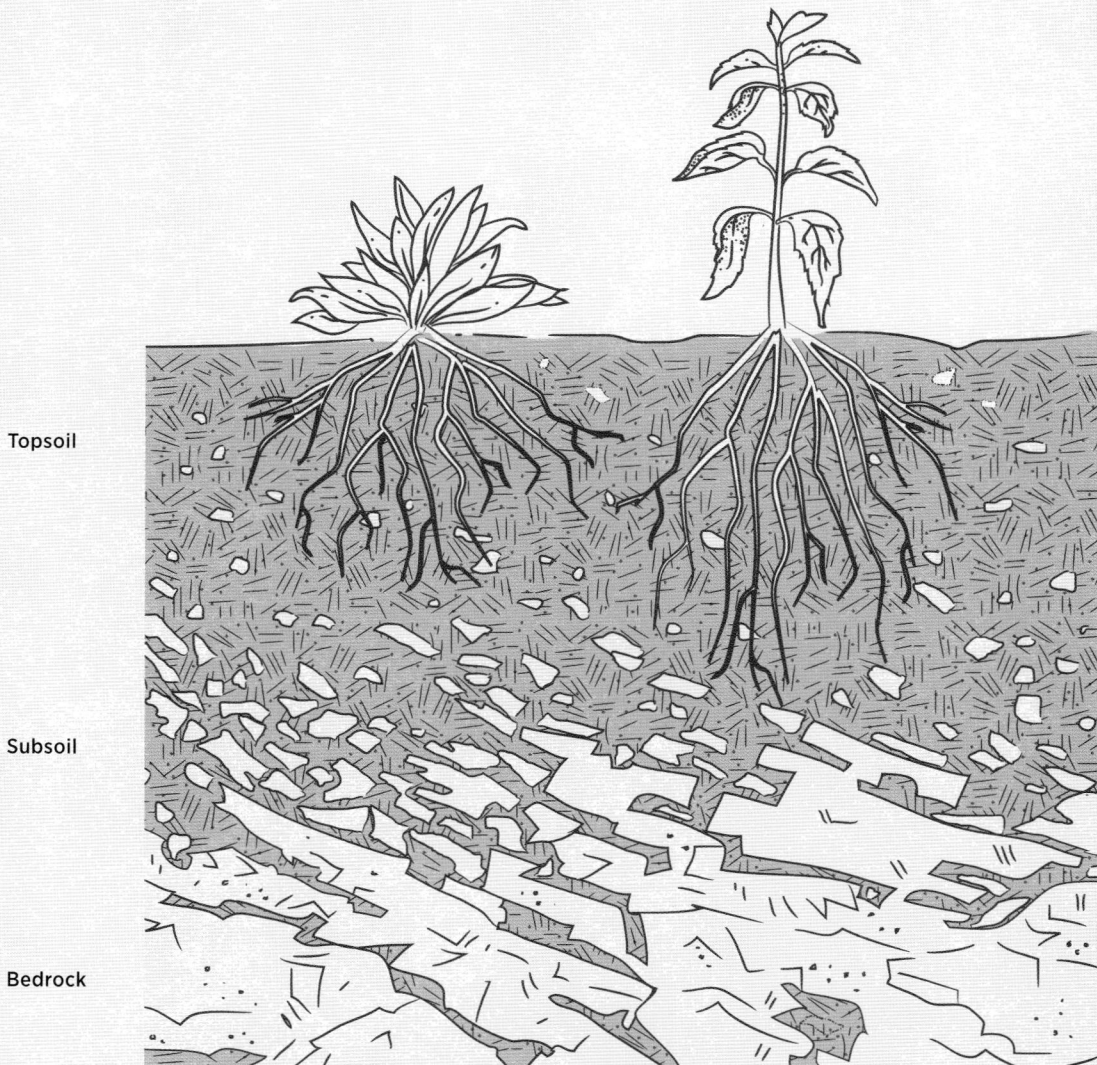

Topsoil

Subsoil

Bedrock

UNDERSTANDING PLANTS

As gardeners, caring for plants is our major concern. We aim to provide ideal conditions for growth, then reap the benefits in various forms: beautiful blooms, fantastic foliage and bumper crops of fruit and vegetables. To make the most of your plants, however, it is essential to know a bit of basic botany. Not only will this enable you to identify the various parts of the plant – crucial when pruning – but you'll also better understand your plants' needs with regards to water, sunlight and soil nutrients. Armed with this information, you'll be able to provide exactly what your plants want, before they show signs of distress.

Understanding plants not only equips you to cater to their every need, but also helps you to choose which plants to use in different situations. Plant habit is the difference between a huge tree and a dainty herb – both are useful, but each is suited only to a garden of appropriate scale. Life history is also important; perennials live for many years, while annuals live, flower and die within a matter of months, so it's worth including both for year-round colour.

An Introduction to Plants

While the physical structure of the garden – paths, boundaries and the all-important soil – can be considered the canvas, plants are the paints with which gardeners create their art. Decorative potential aside, they provide most of the food we eat, either as crops or forage for livestock. Even more fundamental, through photosynthesis they release the oxygen we need to breathe. But what constitutes a plant and how are the different plant groups related?

Traditionally, all life on Earth was divided into one of two groups: animals, which could move, and immobile plants. These groups were later named as 'kingdoms' by Swedish naturalist Carl Linnaeus: *Animalia* and *Vegetabilia* (later renamed *Plantae*). Over time, however, it became apparent that not all members of *Plantae* were closely related, and various organisms were split off into other groups. These included fungi (mushrooms, yeasts, etc.), lichens, slime moulds, some algae and protozoa. Today, plants can be defined as living things that produce their own food via photosynthesis and whose cells are each surrounded by a protective wall. Plants range from microscopic algae, each only a single cell, to massive, multicellular trees, the largest living organisms on Earth.

• Photosynthesis occurs in tiny structures called chloroplasts, which can be found in mesophyll and guard cells. The cuticle and epidermis help to reduce leaf water loss.

Green Energy

Photosynthesis is a chemical reaction that takes place inside plant cells, within structures known as chloroplasts. These contain green pigments that harness the energy in sunlight and use it to fuse water and carbon dioxide, forming simple

• Pores on the leaf surface, known as stomata, allow plants to absorb carbon dioxide necessary for photosynthesis. They are opened and closed by a pair of guard cells.

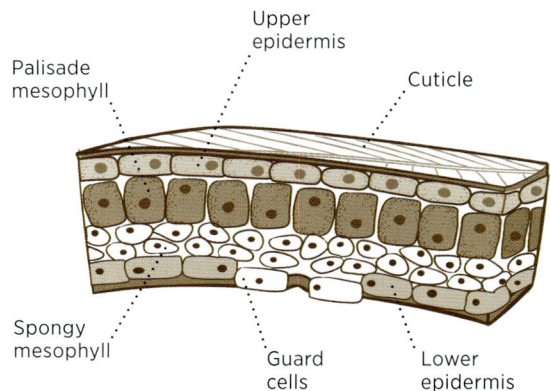

sugars and oxygen. The sugars, which may be combined and stored as starches, feed the plant. Apart from a handful of parasitic plants that lack leaves, all plants rely on photosynthesis for food. A few other non-plant groups also practise photosynthesis, though the location within the cell and the chemical pathways may be different. It's hard to understate the importance of this process; not only does photosynthesis produce plant food, which ultimately feeds all other life on Earth, but the reaction's by-product (oxygen) forms the most important component of the very air we breathe.

The production of oxygen via photosynthesis paved the way for the development of life on our planet and, over time, such life became more

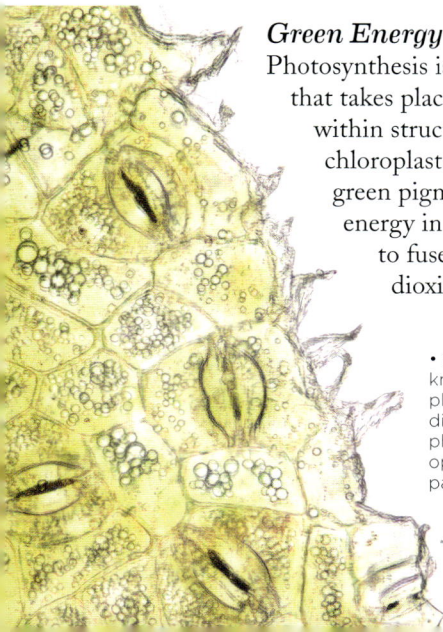

complex. Plants evolved numerous different forms, some of which went extinct, but several independent lineages remain today. Derived from some of the earliest plants, mosses and liverworts lack roots and absorb moisture through all parts of their bodies. Later to appear, ferns and clubmosses have a vascular system to transport water and reproduce via dust-like spores. In contrast, conifers and other gymnosperms produce seeds. Flowering plants or angiosperms are the most recent group to appear and combine several advanced features that have enabled them to spread across the world; they make up around 90 per cent of all land plants.

Flower Power

The evolution of flowers likely occurred in conjunction with the evolution of insects. Non-flowering plants such as conifers rely on wind to transport their pollen, but such methods are wasteful as much of this pollen does not reach its target. By harnessing crawling and flying insects, and, later, other creatures such as birds, bats and primates, each flower ensures that most pollen will reach another flower with greater efficiency. As individual insects and flowers adapted to each other's needs, so more plant and insect species evolved, resulting in the great wealth of flowering plants (and pollinating insects) we see today. We gardeners are major beneficiaries of this great diversity and can find attractive plants for any environment or circumstance. Furthermore, we have supplemented Nature's palette with a huge range of plants produced via selective breeding. These cultivated varieties were chosen for positive characteristics, such as larger blooms, tastier fruit or disease resistance. Without plants, there are no gardens, so it's fortunate that the plant kingdom has so much diversity to offer us.

• Many flowering plants utilise insects, such as this honeybee, to transfer their pollen from flower to flower, resulting in pollination and seed production.

Understanding Plant Names

Giving names to newly discovered plant species is one of the most important tasks in botany. Not only do names provide a helpful label for separating species, but without them it's impossible to know just how many species there are. Once attached, a moniker also provides a label to which the results of scientific studies can be added. An internationally standardised naming system exists for this purpose.

• Fuchsia
(*Fuchsia*)

Latin Binomials

In 1753, Carl Linnaeus decided to give every living thing a name made up of two words, genus and species. Much like our first name and surname, the only difference is that the 'surname' (genus) always comes before the 'first name' (species). This binomial system worked so well that it was soon widely adopted, and is the system we use today. There is just one catch that many gardeners find difficult to take on board – all scientific names are in Latin.

NAMING CONVENTIONS

Family →	Genus →	Species
Rosaceae	*Rosa*	*rubiginosa*
	Malus	*sylvestris*
	Prunus	*persica*

There are many layers in the hierarchy used by botanists to describe plant relationships. The most useful for gardeners are family, genus and species. Their correct order is shown above, using three examples from the *Rosaceae* family: *Rosa rubiginosa*, *Malus sylvestris* and *Prunus persica*. These all have several common names, but only one binomial.

The Royal Botanic Gardens, Kew currently list over a million plant names in their online *Plant List*, though it's thought that there are only around 400,000 plant species on Earth. Such a large discrepancy results from botanists in different countries unwittingly giving the same species different names, though advances in scientific methods can also result in name changes. Fortunately for horticulturists, the number of garden-worthy plants suitable for growing here is fewer; the Royal Horticultural Society's *Plant Finder* lists over 70,000.

DESCRIBING PLANT VARIATION

Gardeners have been a busy lot over the years, cross-breeding and 'improving' plant species so that they make better garden plants. In nature, too, plant populations vary from place to place, such that the normal binomial may not be sufficient to describe this variation. In such cases, we add to the standard name as follows:

Subspecies: A distinct, naturally occurring variant of the typical species. For example, *Armeria maritima* subsp. *elongata* has wider leaves and longer bracts than *Armeria maritima*.

Variety: Like a subspecies, but with fewer physical differences. For example, *Sorbus aucuparia* var. *xanthocarpa* differs only in its yellow fruits from the red-fruited species.

Cultivated variety (Cultivar): Variants that are selected in cultivation, or produced by cross-breeding one plant with another. Cultivar names can be in any language, but usually not Latin and are therefore not in italics; they are enclosed within inverted commas. For example, *Clematis macropetala* 'Lagoon' is a selected form of *C. macropetala,* while *Clematis* 'Betty Corning' is a cultivar of uncertain parentage.

Hybrid: When two different species cross-breed, the resultant offspring is a hybrid, denoted by an 'x' between the genus and species name, as in *Rosa x alba.* If two species in different genera cross, a much rarer situation, then a hybrid genus name is created with the 'x' at the start of the name, as in x *Fatshedera lizei*, a cross between *Fatsia* and *Hedera.*

• Buttercup rose
(*Rosa floribunda*)

Why Latin? Take, for example, the horse-chestnut tree, a native of the Balkans that's widely cultivated across Europe. In France, they call it *marron d'Inde*, in Germany *Gewöhnliche Rosskastanie*, and in Italy *castagna amara*. Another English name is Spanish chestnut. Confusing? Fortunately, there is only one Latin scientific name – *Aesculus hippocastanum*. Linnaeus naturally chose Latin for his naming system because in his time it was the universal language spoken by scholars. Even today, there are gardeners from different countries who only communicate using Latin plant names. It works.

Family, Genus and Species

The binomial system not only provides internationally understood names but also indicates relationships – plants with the same genus name are thought to be closely related. Remembering that the genus is like a surname, and that it comes before the species, the rose genus (*Rosa*) can be split into several unique and individual species, including *Rosa banksiae, Rosa carolina* and *Rosa rubiginosa*. This naming system developed so that related genera (plural of genus) could be grouped together into families. Thus, the rose family (*Rosaceae*) includes genera such as *Crataegus* (hawthorns), *Malus* (apples), *Prunus* (cherries) and *Rosa* (roses). Above the family are several additional layers of classification, though these are rarely of use in everyday horticulture. Latin plant names must be in italics (or underlined if handwritten), with the first letter of the genus capitalised and the species name all in lower case.

Basic Botany

When navigating around a new city, it's always worth having a street map to hand. For gardeners, the equivalent is to have a basic map of plant anatomy under your belt. That way, whether you're pruning a rose, harvesting seeds, taking cuttings or simply trying to identify a weed, you'll never get lost. When naming the parts of a plant, it's easiest to start at the root and work your way up to the flowers.

Roots and Stems

Plant roots have two fundamental roles: anchorage and the absorption of water and nutrients. Within a typical root system, larger roots provide physical support, while much smaller roots, especially thread-like root hairs, absorb most moisture. Roots can be thick and fleshy or thin and fibrous, and some are adapted for nutrient storage (see page 55). While most roots are subterranean, aerial roots emerge from stems to support vines or tree-living epiphytes, such as many orchids.

Stems are both the skeleton and vascular system of a plant. They support the foliage and flowers, but also transport water up from the roots and food down from the leaves. Most grow upright, but some travel along the ground (prostrate) or hang downwards (pendulous). In trees and shrubs, stems thicken over time forming woody trunks, while in some perennials, nutrients are stored within thickened horizontal stems called rhizomes.

• Garden tulips come in a wide range of colours thanks to the efforts of plant breeders who cross-bred wild species and selected the best forms.

Leaves: Food Factories

Plant leaves are in many ways Nature's answer to solar panels; they're broad, flat and arranged to face the sun, from which they absorb energy to power photosynthesis. Most are composed of two parts: petiole and lamina. Petioles, or leaf stalks, attach the foliage to the stem at a point known as a node. Most plants have a single leaf at each node, alternating from one side of the stem to another, but some have pairs of leaves at each node (opposite) or multiple leaves at each node (whorled); leaf arrangement is important for identification. Some leaves lack a distinct petiole and the lamina joins directly to the stem. Others have leaf-like structures at the base of the petiole (stipules). The lamina, or blade, can vary in its form, texture and colour. The shapes of the leaf tips (apices), edges (margins) and bases are also changeable.

When examining leaves, it's important to check whether they are simple (undivided) or compound (fully divided into leaflets). Confusingly, the leaflets of some compound leaves can resemble simple leaves. To be sure, follow the petiole until you reach the stem; a leaf will have a bud or growth point at the node, whereas a leaflet will not. Compound leaves may have their leaflets arranged like fingers on a hand (palmate) or like a bird feather (pinnate).

Flowers and Fruits

Most plants reproduce by transferring pollen from one flower to another, where it fertilises ovules. These develop into seeds, which are dispersed within a fruit formed from the flower's ovary. Flowers are composed of four types of organ arranged in rings: sepals, petals, stamens and carpels. Sepals (together forming the calyx) protect the flower in bud, while attractive petals (together forming the corolla) attract pollinators. Stamens have stalks (filaments) and pollen-producing heads (anthers), while carpels comprise ovaries and pollen-capturing stigmas, connected by narrow styles. From this basic structure comes an infinite variety of forms, with floral organs varying in shape and number. Flowers typically include both stamens (male) and carpels (female), but may also be unisexual, with male and female flowers on the same (monoecious) or separate (dioecious) plants. In many plant groups, numerous flowers are clustered together to form an inflorescence, the floral equivalent of a compound leaf. Once the ovules are fertilised, they develop into seeds while the surrounding ovary forms a fruit. Plant fruits are adapted to aid in the dispersal of seeds away from the mother plant. As a result, some are fleshy and attract hungry animals, while others use wings, hooks or hairs to effect dispersal.

Trees and Shrubs

Trees and shrubs provide structure and privacy, together with a broad palette of eye-catching bark, foliage, flowers and fruit. Decorative trees anchor any border design, while fruits such as apples, pears and plums supply a harvest. Ornamental camellias, rhododendrons, lavenders and many other shrubs are low-maintenance, but high impact. Furthermore, careful pruning can transform many woody plants, including Australian natives, such as westringias and correas, into useful barriers such as hedges.

TYPES OF TREE

Trees are classified in several ways. They may be evergreen, holding on to most of their leaves year-round, or deciduous, shedding their leaves in autumn. The difference is one of timing – evergreens shed leaves gradually throughout the year, while deciduous trees drop them all in autumn. Trees may also be described as broad-leaved or coniferous. Conifers, also called softwoods, typically have needle-like foliage, most are evergreen and they form their seeds in cones. Broad-leaves, or hardwoods, have flat leaves, can be evergreen or deciduous and produce seeds within dry or fleshy fruits.

• Conifers often have needle-shaped leaves and a conical growth form.

• Broad-leaves often have flat, wide leaves and a much-branched growth form.

Trees and shrubs are perennial plants, which means they can live for many years. Some trees are extremely long-lived – a Great Basin bristlecone pine (*Pinus longaeva*) in California is the planet's oldest single tree at over 5,000 years old – but some shrubs, including lavender and rosemary, can die after only five years in the ground. All trees and shrubs have woody stems, but trees are typically larger with a single trunk, while smaller shrubs are branched from the base. In most cases, it is easy to separate the two, but some woody plants defy classification. The tree-like *Rhododendron arboreum* in the Himalayas has been recorded at over 100 feet (30m) tall, but branches much like a shrub.

Tree Families

Another way to view tree classification is in terms of family relationships. Some plant families are entirely woody; the birch (*Betulaceae*), oak (*Fagaceae*) and pine (*Pinaceae*) families are good examples. Others contain a mixture; the rose family (*Rosaceae*) includes trees (apple, rowan, cherry), shrubs (roses, cotoneaster) and herbaceous perennials (meadowsweet, cinquefoil). The peony family (*Paeoniaceae*) is mostly herbaceous, but tree peonies are woody, though use of the word 'tree' is a little overgenerous.

• Choose garden trees carefully, selecting species that won't outgrow their space. Large trees such as oaks are best suited to parks, while smaller rowans fit many gardens.

Size Matters

When choosing garden trees, the most important factor is their size, often quoted as a height after ten years' growth. Overgrown trees will dominate a garden, capturing all the sunlight and soil moisture, to the exclusion of everything else. They can also be expensive to remove, but thankfully there are many garden-worthy small trees available.

Shaping Trees and Shrubs

Human hands can transform woody plants into almost any shape by pruning. Common box (*Buxus sempervirens*) can reach nearly 9 metres tall if left untouched, but for most gardeners, it's a low hedge or topiary. Trees, such as lilly pillies, callistemons (*Callistemon*) and cypress (*Cupressus*), form well-behaved hedges with regular trimming.

SHRUB SHAPES

In general, shrubs are woody plants with multiple stems, though this definition encompasses much variation. A good example of a typical shrub is pieris, which has a short, single trunk that branches low to the ground to form a network of stems. But some shrubs, such as *Cotinus* and lilac (*Syringa*), generate multiple stems at the base from underground suckers. A similar effect is produced when certain shrubs, like some wattles, eucalypts and dogwoods (*Cornus*) with their colourful stems, are cut to ground level each spring. A few shrubs, including hardy fuchsias and Cape figwort (*Phygelius*), maintain woody stems in warm regions.

Smaller shrubs, including lavender (*Lavandula*), rosemary (*Rosmarinus*) and sage (*Salvia*) are sometimes known as subshrubs, a term that also encompasses plants that are woody only at the base or whose branches grow low to the ground.

• Most shrubs branch near the base.

• Suckering shrubs form thickets.

• Subshrubs are small but woody.

Climbers and Wall Shrubs

Though often woody like trees and shrubs, climbers or vines have long stems that stretch through forest trees to reach sunlight above. Some species cling to tree trunks, while others creep across the forest floor. Wall shrubs don't climb, but can be carefully trained to cover vertical surfaces. Many such plants are somewhat tender and benefit from the extra heat radiated by sun-warmed masonry.

• Star jasmine (*Trachelospermum jasminoides*) is a useful evergreen climber for a sunny wall, producing masses of fragrant flowers in summer.

Vines and other climbers use trees and shrubs as climbing frames, allowing them to access the forest canopy where there is more light. However, you do not need to live in the forest in order to grow vines in your garden. Walls, fences, pergolas and obelisks can all serve as substitutes to support decorative climbers, while some can be allowed to ramble along hedges or provide ground cover. And they're not only decorative; vines provide a harvest that includes grapes, kiwis, blackberries, peas and beans. Many wall shrubs are sprawling species that need reinforcement if they're not to fall over. Tying them in to a wall or fence protects them from strong winds as well as being more aesthetically pleasing. Some typically free-standing trees can be trained against a wall where they appreciate the shelter and extra warmth.

Annual or Perennial?

As a designation, 'climber' only refers to the growth habit of the plant, not its longevity. Most are woody perennials, either evergreen (ivy, akebia) or deciduous (grapes, Virginia creeper), but climbers with other life cycles can be found. Sweet peas and many morning glories are annuals, living only for one season, while runner beans and Malabar spinach (*Basella alba*) are tender perennials and are killed by winter frost, thus being treated as annuals. Brewer's hop (*Humulus lupulus*) and everlasting pea (*Lathyrus latifolius*) are herbaceous perennials, dying back to ground level each winter.

Queen of Climbers

Clematis is one of the most important climbers in temperate gardens, but the genus' like of moist, rich, free-draining soils and cool, well-shaded roots means it can be temperamental in more Mediterranean climates. For those gardeners in hot, dry areas, Bougainvilleas have showy flowers, sharp thorns and fairly low water requirements except while in bloom when they too like plenty of moisture. Hardy climbing roses can be trained on fences, arbours and other supports while star jasmine (*Trachelospermum jasminoides*) will grow

• Clematis climb by twining their leaf stalks around a support.

in sun or shade and is fairly drought tolerant once established. It is a twining plant, as is the more heavily wooded *Wisteria*, which requires a more sturdy growing frame and a sunny spot. The dry-tolerant Australian native *Hardenbergia violacea* is a twining, evergreen climber that is blanketed in purple flowers in winter and spring, while the creeping fig (*Ficus pumila*) is self-clinging and effective for covering walls as is the deciduous Boston ivy (*Parthenocissus tricuspidata*).

METHODS OF SUPPORT

There are many ways to support a climbing plant – trellis, horizontal wires, obelisks – but your choice depends on how the plant attaches itself.

Most climbers naturally grow through other plants and can be encouraged to clamber into garden trees and shrubs, so long as they don't overwhelm them. As wall shrubs are not true climbers, their long, flexible stems must be tied into position. Always install robust frameworks for climbers and wall shrubs, as they are often long-lived and difficult to disentangle should your aged trellis or wires collapse.

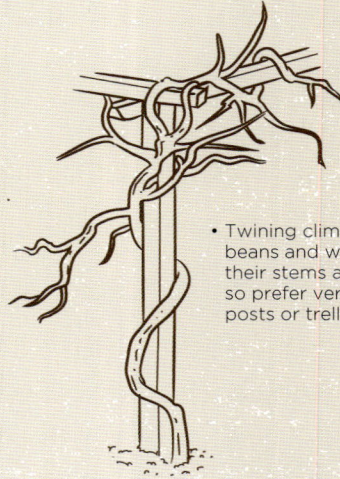

• Twining climbers, such as runner beans and wisteria, naturally wind their stems around other plants, so prefer vertical wires, wooden posts or trellis.

• Climbing roses use thorns to fasten themselves and are best tied into horizontal wires.

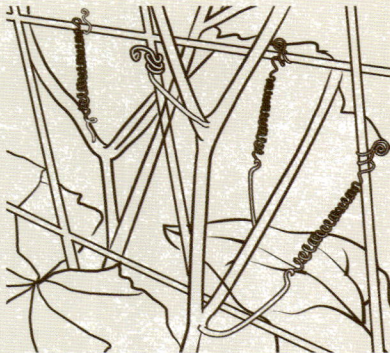

• Grapes and cucumbers form tendrils that cling, so netting works well.

• Finally, ivy and creeping fig (*Ficus pumila*) produce aerial roots along the stems, so attach themselves to tree trunks and walls.

Herbaceous Perennials

This large group of plants is a staple of the garden. They can be used almost anywhere, from pots to hanging baskets, ponds to ephemeral wetlands, rockeries to forested areas. It's in grand herbaceous borders, however, where they're most conspicuous and impressive. They may be showstoppers, but they're not divas, and are generally easy to care for and propagate. With so much choice and a pleasing temperament, perennials are justly popular.

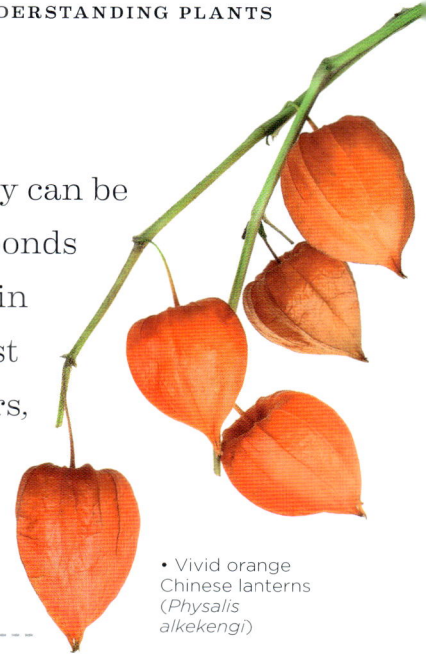

• Vivid orange Chinese lanterns (*Physalis alkekengi*)

A perennial is any plant that lives for three or more years, while the term 'herbaceous' indicates that the plant is not woody. Most herbaceous perennials emerge from underground roots in spring, flower and set seed, before dying back to the roots in winter. There are exceptions to this pattern, though; barrenworts (*Epimedium*), elephant's ears (*Bergenia*), *Heuchera* and several others retain some or all of their leaves throughout the winter. The underground root system of perennials can be fibrous or fleshy, while some possess swollen, horizontal stems called rhizomes, as in bearded iris. (For other subterranean rootstocks, such as bulbs and corms, see pages 44–45.) The boundary between herbaceous perennials and shrubs is not always clear. Some plants, such as tree poppy (*Romneya*), can develop into woody shrubs in warmer climates, but act as herbaceous perennials, dying back to ground level in cooler areas. Herbaceous perennials are also present in the vegetable garden – think asparagus, artichokes, rhubarb and strawberries.

Year-round Colour

As many of the most familiar perennials flower in summer, you'd be forgiven for thinking that this large group of plants had little to offer at other times of year, but there's a perennial in bloom every month of the year. When choosing border plants, consider the year as a theatrical performance with several acts, then ensure you have performers on stage at all times. Plan your borders on paper, not only drawing the physical arrangement of plants, but also noting their peak seasons. And don't be afraid to overlap; several spring bloomers, such as bloodroot (*Sanguinaria canadensis*), *Corydalis flexuosa* and showy toothwort (*Cardamine pentaphylla*) have all but disappeared underground by summer, so their spots can be filled by late flowerers.

While perennials are grown mainly for their blooms, which show an unimaginable range of colours and shapes, many also have striking foliage, fruits and seed heads. The appearance of the first shoots of spring is always elating, but the height of foxgloves (*Digitalis*) is exhilarating, while the first spears of *Hosta* and Siberian iris thrust defiantly.

• Herbaceous peonies rival roses with their stunning blooms, but unlike roses, which have woody stems, these herbaceous perennials disappear underground over winter, re-emerging in spring.

The foliage of both the rice paper plant (*Tetrapanax papyrifer*), which can cope with sun or shade, and *Fatsia japonica*, which likes shade, is exciting and architectural. For leaf colour there is the tough, sun-loving and dry-tolerant purple-leafed form of common sage (*Salvia officinalis* 'Purpurascens'). Or in more shady spots red-leafed lettuces, such as 'Rouge D'Hiver', 'Red Iceberg' and 'Red Velvet', can be ornamental as well as edible. Fruits and seeds also have a beauty all their own; the umbrella-like seed heads of lovage and most other members of the carrot family (*Apiaceae*) last well into winter and pair well with ornamental grasses. Cape gooseberry (*Physalis*) produce decorative displays of fleshy fruits.

Extending the Season
Choosing the right plants will ensure a long season of colour, but there are other ways to keep the show on the road. The 'Chelsea chop' is a pruning technique that delays flowering in herbaceous perennials. Around late November, prune perennials back by up to half. They respond by flowering later in the season, often forming smaller flowers, but many more of them. If you have several clumps of the same perennial, chop half of them for the best of both worlds. Spring is also a good time to divide perennials; consider planting spare divisions in pots, then use them to fill bare patches in your borders by dropping the pots into the gaps. Manyperennials respond well to deadheading by forming additional flowers, though if your plant produces decorative fruits or seed heads, then hold off the secateurs.

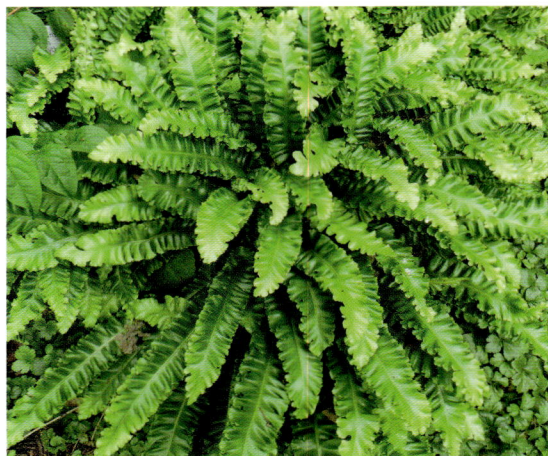

• While often lacy and divided, fern leaves can also be bold and entire, as with the glossy fronds of European native hart's-tongue (*Asplenium scolopendrium*).

Ferns
This group of non-flowering plants are best known as denizens of damp, shady woodland. Their leaves (or fronds) unfurl from crozier-shaped buds and exist in a variety of forms. The most typical are green and feather-like, but fronds can be undivided, as in hart's tongue (*Asplenium scolopendrium*), finely divided with membranous leaflets, as in maidenhairs (*Adiantum*), or even mottled with colourful patterns, as in painted lady (*Athyrium niponicum* var. *pictum*). Some are evergreen, others deciduous, and their habits vary considerably. Tree ferns have stout trunks composed of roots, while many polypodies climb through trees with creeping stems. Dainty *Blechnum penna-marina* makes for a restrained ground cover. A few, such as lip ferns (*Cheilanthes*), will even tolerate arid conditions.

While Australia has close to 400 native ferns and New Zealand nearly 200, many have high water needs and their popularity in dry areas has waned in recent years. Sculptural ferns, such as elk and stag horns, are however enjoying a revival and the tough Boston ferns (*Nephrolepis*) are often used as houseplants.

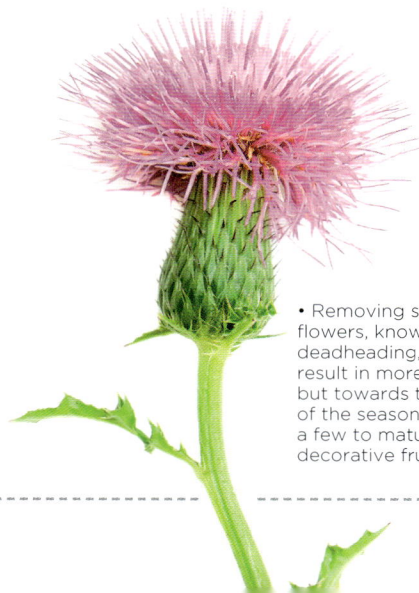

• Removing spent flowers, known as deadheading, can result in more blooms, but towards the end of the season leave a few to mature into decorative fruits.

Grasses and Bamboos

Not long ago, the only grasses to be seen in gardens were in the lawn; either a solitary specimen of pampas grass (*Cortaderia* species, now recognised as weeds) or the turf itself. But ornamental grasses have now thoroughly infiltrated our borders. Grasses and bamboos together form the plant family *Poaceae* (sometimes called *Gramineae*), but in the garden, plants with grassy leaves from both the sedge (*Cyperaceae*) and rush (*Juncaceae*) families also fall into the ornamental grass category. Bamboos are evergreen grasses with underground rhizomes and attractive upright canes (culms). Some species are well-behaved, forming neat clumps, while others spread rapidly underground, invading nearby territory. Always choose your bamboo with care and, if you pick a spreader, invest in a bamboo barrier to keep it within bounds.

Ornamental grasses also vary in habit, with some developing into neat tussocks or clumps while others run. Their foliage ranges in colour from blue through vivid green to red and yellow, or even striped. Grass flowers are not colourful, but their grace as they waft in the breeze more than makes up for this. They are a great addition to borders, where they contrast well with other perennials and have a long season of interest. Prairie gardens that combine tall grasses and perennials are very much in vogue and evoke the natural landscape.

• Alpines, such as this *Androsace koso-poljanskii*, thrive when grown in raised beds. As they are often rather petite, this makes them easier to observe up close.

• *Miscanthus* is a group of ornamental grasses with an upright habit and attractive feathery seedheads.

Alpines and Aquatics

These two groups are at opposite ends of the spectrum in terms of water requirements. Alpines grow high above the treeline in mountainous regions, but also lower down in the Arctic. They typically survive in thin, stony soils and abhor excess moisture. Aquatic plants, on the other hand, grow partially or fully submerged in freshwater ponds, lakes and streams. Both have their uses in the garden; alpines make great container plants and can also be used to fill cracks in walls or in specialist rockeries, while well-planted ponds attract wildlife and make a great focal point.

However you use them, strict adherence to their water requirements is key. Ensure excellent drainage for alpines by incorporating plenty of grit and sand into the soil before planting. Raised beds and planters are better than borders as they drain more freely. When buying and planting aquatics, look for the appropriate water depth cited on the label. Deepwater plants, such as many waterlilies, should be planted near the bottom of the pond, while most marginals only require their roots be covered.

Annuals, Biennials and Bedding

Trees, shrubs, climbers and herbaceous perennials have something in common – they are all perennial and can live indefinitely, though three years or more is a simple definition. When choosing and planting them, care must be taken to ensure both that they will be happy in their intended location and that they will not outgrow it. But with annuals, biennials and bedding, this is rarely a consideration. They live fast and die young!

Annual plants complete their life cycle within one year. Sunflowers, sweet peas and nasturtiums germinate from seed in spring, grow and flower through summer, then set seed before winter. With an even shorter lifespan, ephemerals run to seed in a matter of weeks. They include weeds such as thale cress (*Arabidopsis thaliana*) and groundsel (*Senecio vulgaris*), but also desert plants that survive drought as dry seeds. Biennials take two years, spending the first developing a crown of leaves, then flowering and going to seed in year two. Foxgloves (*Digitalis*), honesty (*Lunaria biennis*) and parsley are examples. Bedding plants are different as many are perennial but frost-tender, so do not last long in cold climates. These plants, which include pelargoniums, petunias and begonias, are used to fill seasonal planters and hanging baskets, or grown en masse in parks and on roundabouts, a planting scheme known as carpet bedding.

• Annuals, biennials and bedding plants come in a range of colours and forms, so you can build a beautiful border without using perennials or shrubs.

Magical Meadows

Annual plants can either be grown direct outside, by broadcasting the seed over a prepared area of soil, or sown individually in pots or seed trays. The choice of technique depends on their hardiness, but also on their ability to transplant and their speed of growth. Hardy annuals, which are usually native to temperate areas of Europe and North America, are best sown direct into the soil. Not only is this less work, but it also avoids the need for a greenhouse or cold frame and is best suited to annuals that dislike transplanting, such as poppies. Sweet peas, though hardy, are often sown in pots in autumn to protect them from cold weather (and

then set seed in autumn, ensuring at least a partial show the following year. Slightly different from a traditional wild-flower meadow, which is made up of a mixture of grasses and perennial wild flowers, annual meadows are easier to establish and require little care. Additional seed may be required to boost the blooms in subsequent years.

Beautiful Bedding

While bedding can be time consuming and has therefore fallen in popularity, those gardeners who do use it tend to buy it in trays from nurseries. To make the most of these plants, it's important to provide adequate water and fertiliser. Add fertiliser granules and water-retaining gel crystals to container compost when planting as this will reduce the need for additional watering and feeding. Never allow containerised bedding to dry out and regularly remove spent flower heads, to ensure a continuing supply. Most bedding will only flower well in full sun, so if planting in partial shade, choose begonias and busy lizzies (*Impatiens walleriana*), as these can still flower with less light.

• Cornflowers (*Centaurea cyanus*) are quick to flower from seed. Sow them in border gaps or add them to a meadow mix to cover a wider area.

hungry mice), but also to ensure they flower earlier the following year. Frost-tender species, such as cleome and scabiosa, can be direct sown after the risk of frosts has passed. Biennials are mostly hardy and will self-seed if left after flowering. Sow direct outdoors or in containers in a cold greenhouse.

With their quick turnaround, annuals are useful gap fillers in garden borders. They also enliven bare earth, so if you've got a patch of ground that hasn't found a purpose, sow a mix of annuals to provide colour and discourage weeds until you decide on a permanent design. Seed mixes that contain a range of hardy annuals, such as poppies (*Papaver*), cornflowers (*Centaurea*) and corncockles (*Agrostemma githago*), provide a handy shortcut to creating a flowering meadow. They'll provide a riot of colourful flowers throughout the summer,

Bulbs, Corms and Tubers

In springtime, much of the colour adorning our gardens comes from bulbs and other perennial plants with underground storage structures. From the earliest irises, through crocus and daffodil, to the dahlia grand finale, bulbs give a bang for your buck. Like herbaceous perennials, most bulbs gladly flower again in subsequent years and multiply readily, so they're a good investment. What's more, very little care is required to get the most from many bulbs.

• Some *Crocus* species bloom in autumn, but most flower in spring and with their small size, they're ideal for use in pots, mixed in with winter bedding.

Bulbs, corms and tubers are storage devices, allowing the plants to build a reserve of nutrients during better times in readiness for harsher environmental conditions ahead. Many such species hail from regions with stark changes between the seasons – for example, the Mediterranean Basin – and grow during brief wet periods before entering dormancy as temperatures rise. Bulbs are composed of fleshy, scale-like leaves, which form the layers you find within an onion. Other bulbous plants include daffodils, tulips, lilies and amaryllis. Corms are short, squat stems, often surrounded by papery tunics derived from leaves. Crocuses, gladioli and freesias develop from corms, which do not show layers when cut in half. Tubers arise from underground stems (e.g. potatoes, cyclamen) or roots (e.g. dahlias, sweet potatoes). Rhizomes are stems that grow horizontally just below or on the surface of the soil. Some are swollen for nutrient storage, as in bearded iris and root ginger, while others are slender and expand the plant's territory (lily of the valley).

Spring, Summer and Winter

There's a bulb flowering at almost every time of year, but in the temperate Northern Hemisphere, it's spring that is peak season. In part, this is because many of our garden bulbs originate around the Mediterranean and flower after the winter rains, but before it gets too hot. Most spring bulbs belong to one of three plant families:

• Snowdrops (*Galanthus nivalis*) are one of the first bulbs to bloom, sometimes pushing through late winter snows. They come up every year and gradually spread.

BULB, CORM, TUBER

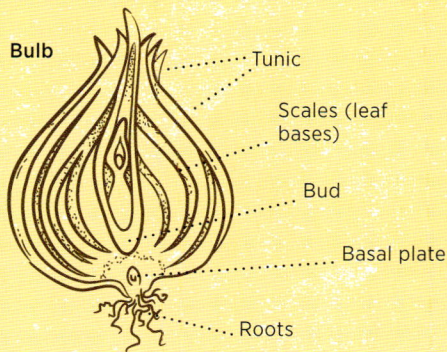

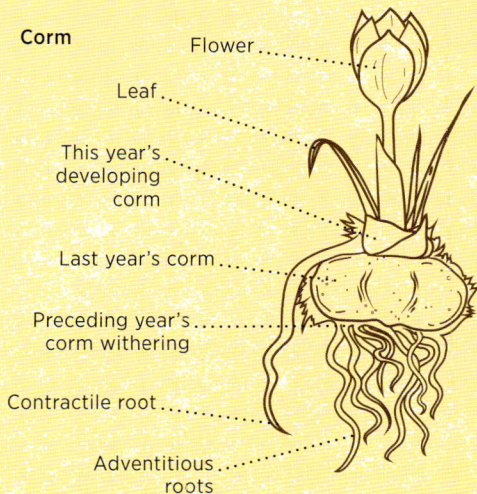

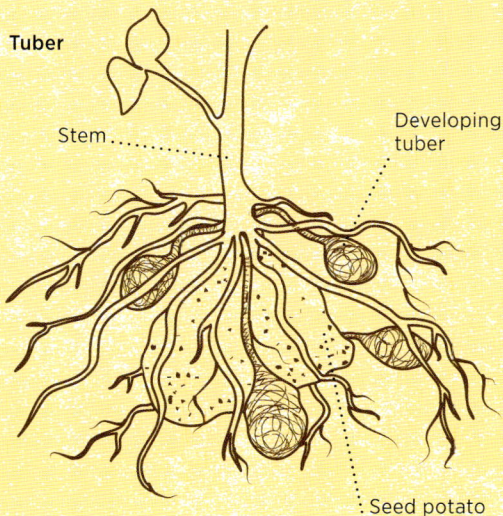

Bulb
- Tunic
- Scales (leaf bases)
- Bud
- Basal plate
- Roots

Corm
- Flower
- Leaf
- This year's developing corm
- Last year's corm
- Preceding year's corm withering
- Contractile root
- Adventitious roots

Tuber
- Stem
- Developing tuber
- Seed potato

Liliaceae (lilies, tulips, fritillaries), *Amaryllidaceae* (snowdrops, daffodils, alliums) and *Asparagaceae* (bluebells, squills, hyacinths). All should be planted the previous autumn, allowing them to root before winter. Also worth planting in autumn are the corms of *Crocus* and autumn crocus (*Colchicum*), and tubers of winter aconites (*Eranthis*), anemones and cyclamen.

Summer-flowering bulbs are planted in spring and perhaps the best known are the true lilies (*Lilium*). Others worth locating are summer hyacinth (*Galtonia candicans*) and swamp lily (*Crinum* x *powellii*). Plant *Gladiolus* corms in spring, either as elegant border plants or for use as cut flowers, while tuberous begonias and rhizomatous cannas make exotic-looking bedding plants. With a devoted following among hobbyists, dahlias exhibit a huge range of flower colours, shapes and sizes, while plants can have colourful foliage and range from ankle-high bedding to giants like *Dahlia imperialis*. Dahlias can over-winter in the ground, as long as it's not too wet. Finally, though there are few bulbs that flower outdoors in winter, amaryllis (*Hippeastrum*), paper-white daffodils (*Narcissus papyraceus*) and forced hyacinths enliven the dark days indoors. (Forced bulbs are prepared so that they flower earlier than is typical.)

• Daffodils (*Narcissus*) are a mainstay of the spring bulb season, flowering from June (for the very earliest) to October. Let the leaves continue to grow after flowering for more blooms next year.

Bulb	Full Sun	Partial Shade	Soil	Moisture	Hardiness	Height (cm)	Spread (cm)	Plant	Flower
Autumn crocus (*Colchicum*)	●		●	Well-drained	H5	50	10	Feb	Mar
Cannas (*Canna*)	●		●	Moist but well-drained	H1	180	100	Sep–Oct	Nov–Apr
Crocuses (*Crocus*)	●		●	Well-drained	H6	10	10	Mar–Apr	Sep–Oct
Daffodils (*Narcissus*)	●		●	Well-drained	H6	5–50 (most)	5–15	Mar–Apr	Jun–Oct
Dahlias (*Dahlia*)	●		●	Moist but well-drained	H1	30–150	30–200	Oct–Nov	Jan–May
Fritillaries (*Fritillaria*)	●		●	Well-drained	H5	10–100	10–30	Mar–May	Sept–Dec
Gladioli (*Gladiolus*)	●		●	Well-drained	H1–H4	50	10	Anytime	Nov–Dec
Hardy cyclamen (*Cyclamen*)		◗	●	Well-drained	H6	5–13	8–15	Jun–Aug	Feb–May
Hyacinths (*Hyacinthus*)	●		●	Well-drained	H6	20–30	7.5	Feb–May	Aug–Sept
Lilies (*Lilium*)		◗	●	Well-drained	H6	80–150	10–50	Aug–Oct,	Nov–Mar
Snowdrops (*Galanthus*)		◗	●	Well-drained	H6	12	5	Oct–Nov	Aug–Sept
Tulips (*Tulipa*)	●		●	Well-drained	H6	15–75 (most)	15	Apr–May	Sep–Nov

Situation
- ● Full sun preferred
- ◗ Partial shade preferred

Soil Type
- ● Loam
- ● Sand
- ● Chalk
- ● Clay

Watering
- ● Moist but well-drained
- ◡ Well-drained

Hardiness
On a scale of 1 to 6

In autumn, garden centres stock up on spring bulbs, corms and tubers, both loose and in packets. However you buy them, always carefully inspect each bulb, looking for those that are firm and with no signs of damage. Beware when handling hyacinth bulbs as they can cause irritation to human skin; many nurseries provide disposable gloves for this purpose. Alternatively, choose a reputable mail order or online nursery to ensure you get quality stock. It is important to ensure they are planted at the correct depth. For most bulbs and corms, plant them three times as deep as the height of the actual bulb. Many tubers and rhizomes prefer shallower lodgings; check any attached instructions. Buy pot-grown bulbs in spring to fill any gaps, and at the same time choose your summer-flowering bulbs, being careful to choose only the best-looking specimens. Flowering season depends on temperature (and therefore latitude and altitude) of the planting site.

Roses

While all other plants in this book are divided up into groups depending on their growth habit – trees, shrubs, climbers – one single genus warrants a section all its own. That genus is *Rosa*, the roses. With voluptuous blooms in almost every colour, often releasing the sweetest of scents, these long-lived shrubs and climbers are excellent garden plants. What's more, there's a good variety for almost any situation.

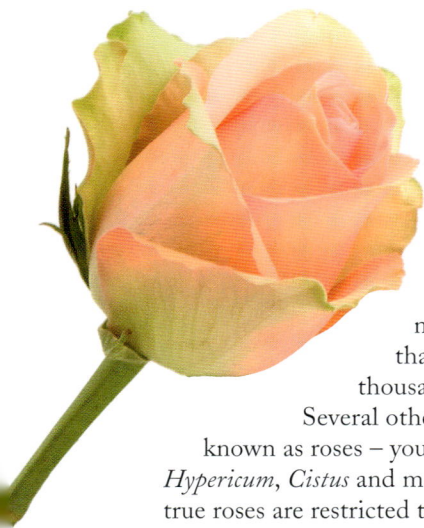

• Roses may have a single ring of petals (single) or many additional petals (doubles) as in, for example, *Rosa* 'Faith', shown here.

Wild roses occur naturally across Asia, Europe and North America and it's from these wild species, which number around a hundred, that humans have bred many thousands of different cultivars. Several other plants are commonly known as roses – you'll find them in *Hibiscus*, *Hypericum*, *Cistus* and many other genera – but true roses are restricted to *Rosa*. Rose cultivars are so numerous that they've been divided into a series of categories. Some describe the plant's habit, like shrub, climbing and rambler, while others denote the arrangement or shape of the blooms – think *polyantha* or *floribunda*. Many categories reflect the parentage of the plants, such as damask, China and centifolia roses. Given the long history of hybridisation in garden roses, many cultivars belong to more than one group. Hybrids and cultivars are the most popular garden roses, but some of the original species are worthy of cultivation, having attractive foliage (*Rosa glauca*), colourful hips (*R. moyesii*) or vicious prickles (*R. sericea* subsp. *omeiensis* f. *pteracantha*).

Choosing Roses

The traditional practice of growing roses in regimented rows within devoted borders has largely been replaced as gardeners with smaller plots sought to mix their favourite rose in with their perennials and other plants. This also has the benefit of reducing the risk of pests and diseases, which can blight large plantings of roses.

First, choose the habit you need: do you want a climber for an archway, a small plant for a container or a shrub to add height to a border? Roses can also provide ground cover, flowers and fruits that attract wildlife or can be clipped into informal hedges.

• Garden rose hybrids have their origins in a handful of species roses (such as the one shown below) originally collected in the wild.

Next, think about maintenance; disease-resistant varieties reduce the need for pest control, while species roses and landscape cultivars require less pruning than many popular hybrids.

- For a shady or south wall
  R. 'Madame Alfred Carrière' (noisette) AGM
- For a sunny sheltered wall
  R. banksiae 'Lutea' (rambler/damask) AGM
- For climbing into trees
  R. 'Paul's Himalayan Musk' (rambler) AGM
- For training up pillars
  R. 'Pink Perpétué' (climbing)
- For attractive foliage
  R. glauca (shrub) AGM
- For impressive hips
  R. rugosa
- For fragrance and flowers
  R. Gertrude Jekyll = 'Ausbord' (shrub) AGM

Healthy and Happy

All plants suffer from pests and disease, but sometimes roses seem to attract more than their fair share; this is especially the case when grown in quantity.

- Chemical control of many of these problems is possible (see Section 5), but careful stewardship can reduce the need for spraying.
- Try to mix other shrubs and perennials in with your roses, as many of these are not susceptible to rose diseases and so will not act as a reservoir for them.
- Flowering annuals and perennials also attract insects such as hoverflies, whose larvae consume aphids and other rose pests.

• Most garden roses are produced by grafting a stem from a cultivar onto the rootstock of a species.

- Carefully inspect roses on a regular basis, as rapid identification and removal of diseased material can halt their spread. Always gather fallen leaves and flowers from below sick plants and do not compost them, as pests and spores can linger in organic material.
- Never plant a new rose on a site previously occupied by roses, as the young plants can exhibit a lack of vigour and may even die, affected by a somewhat mysterious ailment known as replant disease.
- Finally, as most cultivated roses are produced by grafting stem cuttings onto a rootstock, always ensure the stock is planted below soil level. If not, it may begin to produce its own shoots or suckers, which are more vigorous than the grafted material and can take over the plant. These shoots, which often have different foliage from your chosen rose, are seldom as attractive as the plant you chose.

• A happy, healthy rose can live for many years, providing a show-stopping display every summer.

How Plants Grow

Plants grow differently from animals. In animals, including humans, growth occurs while young, expanding all parts of the body, but then largely halting in adulthood. In plants, growth occurs throughout their lives, allowing some to attain great size and age. However, most of this growth originates in growing points at the stem and root tips, known as meristems. Plant cells also have a much greater ability to regenerate damaged tissues.

For most plants, life begins as a seed. Contained within is an embryo and a store of nutrients that fuel the growth of the young plant. As temperatures rise in spring, seeds absorb water from the soil, swelling up before the first root (or radicle) emerges. While the root grows downwards, the first stem (or hypocotyl) appears and begins to grow upwards towards the light. Once above the soil surface, leaves develop and expand and

• The meristem at the tip of a plant produces hormones that inhibit the growth of lateral buds.

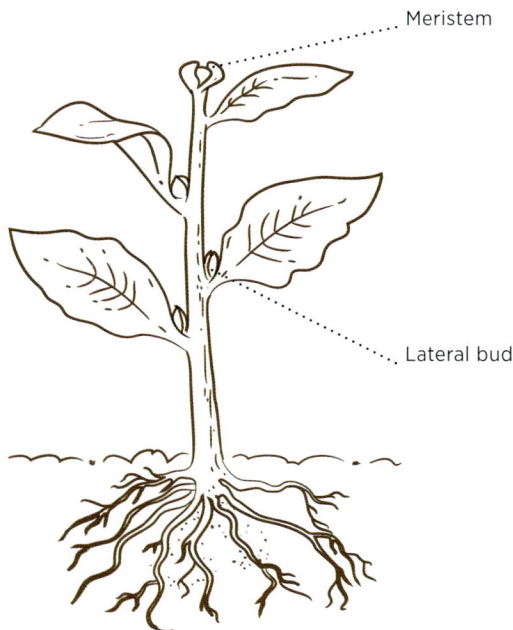

Meristem

Lateral bud

the seedling can then begin to harness the energy of the sun. Seeds vary greatly in size and shape, often depending on the amount of nutrients stored within. The dust-like seeds of orchids do not contain nutrients, and orchid embryos often rely on symbiotic fungi to provide their first meal. At the other end of the scale, the almost 20kg (44lb) seed of the double coconut palm (*Lodoicea maldivica*) is easily the world's largest. Containing a bumper crop of nutrients, it feeds the embryonic palm as it attempts to grow out from under the dense canopy of parental leaves.

Primary Growth

Plant stems and roots develop from growing points called meristems, which contain stem cells capable of forming any kind of plant organ. They are responsible for plant growth and the development of leaves and flowers. As the stem elongates, small clusters of cells are left behind by the meristems, creating buds that can develop into branches or side shoots. In most cases, these buds remain dormant, because the growing point at the top of the stem releases a hormone, from a class known as auxins, that inhibits the growth of side shoots. This bit of biochemistry is the reason gardeners sometimes pinch out the tips of their plants. Removing the apical (top) meristem halts the flow of hormones, allowing side shoots to form and the plant to thicken. Encouraging bushy growth is good practice for bedding plants, shrubs and hedging, but should be avoided when growing trees where a single stem or leader is desired.

Secondary growth

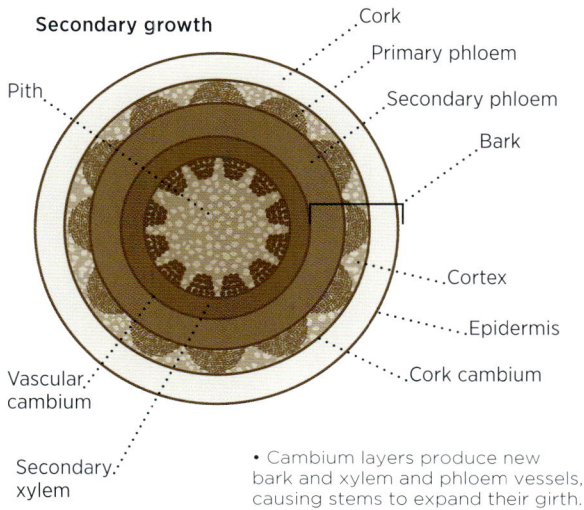

Cork
Primary phloem
Secondary phloem
Bark
Pith
Cortex
Epidermis
Cork cambium
Vascular cambium
Secondary xylem

• Cambium layers produce new bark and xylem and phloem vessels, causing stems to expand their girth.

Secondary Growth

The extension of stems and roots is known as primary growth; secondary growth is the thickening of stems and roots that you will see in all woody plants, including trees. The stems of all woody plants contain two major types of vessels: xylem, which transports water from roots to leaves, and phloem, which moves sugars formed in the leaves down the stem. Between them is a layer of meristematic cells called cambium, and this layer generates new xylem and phloem, gradually thickening the stems. To stop the bark from bursting as the stem widens, another cambium layer (cork cambium) produces new, expanded layers of bark. Each year, new layers of xylem and phloem are laid down; the outer walls of xylem cells gradually accumulate a polymer called lignin. These cells eventually die, but the tough, lignin-filled walls remain, creating a network of water-transporting tubes. Xylem also lends rigidity to stems as the primary component of wood, allowing for the development of tall trees, shrubs and vines. Xylem layers are clearly visible in cut wood and form the rings that allow tree age to be determined.

New Direction

While much plant growth results from new cell production, individual plant cells can also expand and grow. When exposed to light from one direction, cells on the dark side of the stem extend while those on the sunny side stay the same. This is what causes windowsill plants to arch towards the glass. This process, known as positive phototropism, is also controlled by auxin hormones. Some vines do the reverse (negative phototropism) and grow away from the sun, as the shadiest areas are directly below trees and the vines are looking for a trunk to climb. Plants respond to gravity in a similar fashion, with roots growing towards it, i.e. downwards, and stems growing up.

• Some flowers, such as the Osteospermums shown below, can follow the sun and track it from east to west, allowing their blooms to warm up quickly and thus attract more pollinating insects.

How Plants Multiply

A crucial stage in the life cycle of any plant or animal comes when they exchange their genes, creating the next generation. Most plants do so by flowering and forming seeds, but several other strategies exist. For gardeners, understanding this life cycle has its uses. Not only is it essential when sowing seeds or taking cuttings, but by carefully manipulating the process, gardeners can select and improve the plants that they grow.

Plant reproduction can be divided into two broad categories: sexual and asexual. The former involves the transfer of genes between plants; when flowers are pollinated, genetic material in pollen combines with that in ovules to form seeds, which are genetically distinct from the parent plants. Asexual reproduction does not involve genetic transfer and any offspring are identical to the parent. Propagation techniques such as division, cuttings and layering are forms of asexual reproduction, but plants can also proliferate this way without our help.

Flowers, Fruits and Seeds

The attractive blooms of flowering plants may be pleasing to the human eye, but we are not their intended audience. Showy petals and floral fragrances exist purely to entice animals that will transport pollen from one flower to another. Some plants modify their flowers to better attract their pollinators. Butterflies prefer broad blooms with floral tubes, while night-flying moths gravitate towards scented white flowers. Many bee-pollinated flowers have lines on their petals to guide the insect in, while birds are attracted to red and orange tubular flowers that lack scent. Grasses and many trees, including birch and oak, utilise the wind to transport pollen and their flowers therefore lack attractive petals. Having a unique pollinator ensures pollen is delivered to the right address, another flower of the same species, but many plants have unspecialised blooms and welcome all comers.

Once pollen reaches its goal and the ovules are fertilised, they develop into seeds; the tissues surrounding the seeds also change, becoming fruits. Like flowers, many fruits have evolved to attract the animals that ultimately disperse the seeds. Fleshy fruits advertise with vivid colours and the promise of a sweet treat. Other fruits lack fleshy coatings and hitch a ride using hooks or spines, while winged and even explosive fruits disperse their seeds without the help of animals.

• The flowers of this ginger (*Zingiber spectabile*) emerge from a cone made of colourful bracts.

NEW PLANTS, NO FLOWERS

• Flowers are not the only way in which plants swap genes. In conifers, pollen is transferred between male and female cones by the wind. Seeds develop within the female cones and are later released, falling to the ground or travelling by wind or inside a hungry animal.

• Asexual reproduction sidesteps the transfer of genes, creating genetically identical offspring. Strawberries, montbretia (*Crocosmia*) and many grasses develop new plants at the tips of horizontal stems called stolons.

• Several shrubs and trees can develop new stems from surface roots some distance from the main stem, as in sumach (*Rhus*), poplar (*Populus*) and rice-paper plant (*Tetrapanax*).

• Many bulbs and corms form offsets, called bulbils and cormels, usually below ground; a few lilies (*Lilium*) produce bulbils on their above-ground stems, while in some onions (*Allium*) they form among the flowers. Given plants' readiness to reproduce, gardeners need never struggle to generate new plants.

• Some species develop miniature plantlets on their leaves, such as piggyback (*Tolmiea menziesii*) and mother-of-millions (*Kalanchoe delagoensis*), while in orchids like *Phalaenopsis*, plantlets (called keikis) form on the stems or inflorescences.

• Ferns do not produce seeds, but release dust-like spores from fertile sites on their leaves. These grow into green, fleshy structures called prothalli, which release sperm that swim, using flagella, across the ground seeking another prothallus. Eggs held within the structure are fertilised and a new fern develops as a result.

What Plants Need

To grow and thrive, plants require water, soil nutrients and carbon dioxide from the air, together with adequate sunlight to fuel photosynthesis. Most of us need not worry about providing CO_2, but ensuring our plants receive adequate light, water and nutrients is our business. Therefore, we need to understand where these basic ingredients come from and how plants make use of them.

Photosynthesis is a chemical reaction that is essential to life on Earth. The sugars produced fuel not only plants but also the animals that eat them, so this reaction is the starting point for most food chains. In addition, photosynthesis produces oxygen as a by-product and is responsible for ensuring we have sufficient air to breathe. In plants, this important reaction occurs within tiny structures called chloroplasts, situated within the cells of the leaves and other green parts. Chloroplasts contain the green pigment chlorophyll, which acts as a catalyst for the reaction. Water absorbed by the roots and carbon dioxide, which enters the leaf through pores called stomata, are combined to create simple sugars and oxygen. As in animals, plants generate energy by burning these sugars through the process of respiration, or alternatively convert them into starches for storage. Gardeners have a role to play providing the building blocks for photosynthesis. While carbon dioxide is freely available, both water and sunlight can be limiting factors, so gardeners should provide access to light and plenty of water to ensure healthy growth.

Water

Photosynthesis is not the only use for water; it also provides physical support. Plant cells filled with water are firm, but as they dry out, water pressure decreases and plants wilt. The amount of water a plant needs depends on many factors, including soil type, climate and the plant's country of origin. Freely draining soils, such as those rich in sand, don't hold water for long and plants living in them desiccate quickly. Those growing on heavy soils rich in clay are less likely to suffer from drought.

Of course, climate is an important consideration; in humid weather, plants lose less water via transpiration, while in dry or windy conditions, water loss spikes. In the garden, native plants are likely to thrive as they're adapted to local weather conditions. On the other hand, plants from tropical forests are accustomed to high humidity and struggle when grown in drier habitats. Conversely, desert plants are adapted to survive drought, but can be killed by excess water during winter.

• Water is an essential ingredient in photosynthesis, but also provides some physical support to keep plants upright.

SUNSHINE AND SHOWERS

Photosynthesis uses the energy of the sun to produce sugars. Plant pigments (primarily chlorophylls) absorb light energy and transfer it, allowing the chemical reaction to proceed. Sunlight, when it reaches plants, is composed of a range of different wavelengths, including those that correspond to the different colours of the rainbow. Chlorophyll pigments mostly absorb blue and red light, but reflect green, and thus plants appear green to our eyes. Almost all plants need light to live; only a handful of species can do without and these are typically colourless parasites that rely on green plants or fungi to sustain them. The amount of light needed by each plant species varies hugely and many are adapted to low- or high-light environments.

Plants should be positioned where they will receive sufficient light, taking into account local weather, shade-casting trees/structures and compass orientation.

Water is essential for photosynthesis, but can be in short supply. When plants open their pores (or stomata) to absorb sufficient carbon dioxide, water vapour escapes, a process known as transpiration. To reduce such loss, some plants conceal their stomata within tufts of hair, under a layer of wax or by curling their leaves. Many succulent plants close their stomata during the day to reduce transpiration. They open them at night, when cooler temperatures limit water loss.

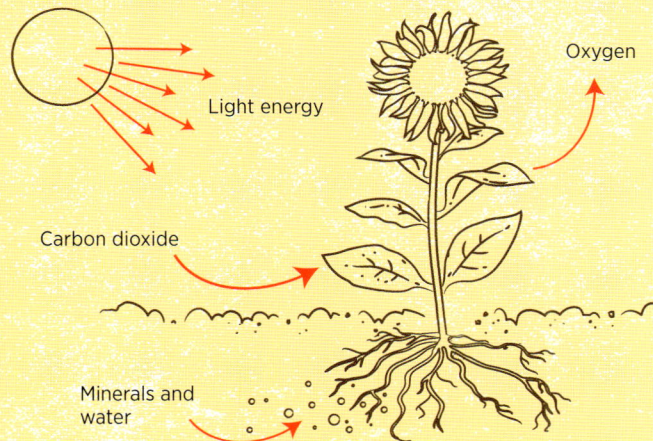

Light energy

Oxygen

Carbon dioxide

Minerals and water

Soils and Nutrients

The water that plants absorb from the soil contains a range of chemical elements. While these may not have a direct role in photosynthesis, nevertheless many are essential for growth. The best known are nitrogen (N), phosphorus (P) and potassium (K), but many others, including calcium (Ca), magnesium (Mg) and iron (Fe), are crucial (see page 91). Gardeners supplement these minerals by applying fertilisers, but improving the soil with added organic matter will also help. Many plants enhance the efficiency of their roots at absorbing water and nutrients by forming a relationship with fungi in the soil. Known as mycorrhizae, the widespread fungal threads in the soil share water and nutrients with roots, in return for a portion of the sugars produced by plant photosynthesis. A handful of plants have responded to soil nutrient deficiencies through a more direct method; carnivorous plants living on poor, peaty soils trap insects and absorb nutrients directly from their bodies.

How We Understand Plants

Unlike people, plants cannot tell us when something is wrong. Unlike our pets, whose behaviour can change when something ails them, plants don't move around much either. It can therefore be difficult to know whether you're meeting their needs. The key is regular and close inspection of their stems, leaves, flowers and general habit. Plants do communicate, you just need to learn how to listen.

• When plants need water, they let you know! As water is lost, there is less to provide support and they wilt.

Recent and ongoing scientific studies are demonstrating that plants communicate with one another using the complex language of biochemistry. Chemicals released into the air by leaves can alert neighbouring plants to the presence of pests. But you don't need to be a scientist to understand some of the messages your garden plants are issuing. Changes in their habit reveal that necessities such as light and water are in short supply, while variations in leaf colour may indicate nutrient shortage, pest attack or viral infection. Visual cues aside, your nose and fingers can also tell you a lot about your plants, both their health and their habitat requirements.

Wilt

Perhaps the most obvious visible cry for help is when plants wilt. The likely cause is drought and the damage is readily repaired with a watering can. But some plants wilt when they've had too much water. The popular houseplant African violet (*Saintpaulia*) abhors excess moisture, which can kill the roots, resulting in wilting; such plants are rarely salvageable, though leaf cuttings may provide replacements. Several fungal diseases also cause wilting, notably the unimaginatively named clematis wilt.

Phototropism

Another whole-plant movement results when they receive insufficient light. Known as positive phototropism (see page 51), plants naturally grow towards a light source, which can result in leggy, inclined plants of poor habit. Move such specimens to a brighter spot. When grown in the absence of light, plants are typically yellowish-white with elongated stems, a condition called etiolation – as in that forgotten potato sprouting in the pantry.

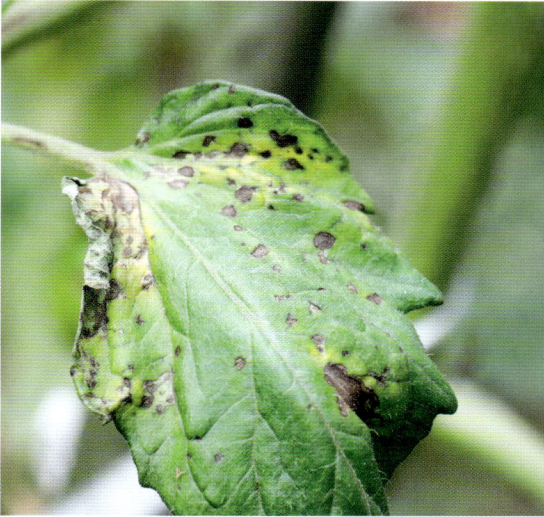

• Mottling on leaves is often a sign of pests or diseases. This tomato is being attacked by blight.

• Fruits often smell bad as they decay. These strawberries are being consumed by botrytis mould.

Leaf Condition

Leaves are prime communication devices as changes in shape or colour are readily apparent. Unexpected holes suggest hungry pests or diseases, such as shot hole, while weird distortions can indicate viral infection, herbicide exposure or cold damage. Leaves change colour before they fall, but also in response to nutrient deficiency, and the patterns of colour change can indicate which mineral is lacking. Yellow leaves with green veins, a condition called chlorosis, indicate iron deficiency. Yellow mottling can result from viral infection or mite infestation. Collect or photograph leaf colour changes and use them when diagnosing the problem.

On a related note, not all colour changes are bad; plants use colour to tell hungry animals (humans included) when their fruits are ripe. Before the seeds are fully developed, fruits are green and bitter-tasting, but at maturity they may sweeten and take on shades of red, yellow, blue or black.

Smell

Changes in a plant's appearance are helpful guides to plant health and well-being, but our other senses should not be overlooked. The foetid smell of decay is a sure-fire indicator that something is not right with stored fruit and vegetables. Putrid wafts from a compost bin suggest that too much green organic matter has been added – turn the pile and add some shredded newspaper or chipped shrub prunings.

Visitors

Visiting animals can also tell us about the health of our plants. Metallic ladybirds, wasps and other insects eat aphids, so watch out for them and don't spray them with insecticides. When birds or bandicoots dig up patches of lawn, it's likely there is white curl grub (or cockchafer) feeding on the grass roots.

• Watch out for large white butterflies as their caterpillars will eat your cabbages before you can.

PRACTICAL GARDENING

The essential elements of a garden are the living things grown in it, and like all living things they require the right conditions and care to flourish. The gardener is responsible for ensuring that the carefully planned landscape, drawn on paper or visualised in one's head, is not only made reality but also given the best possible start in life.

Preparation is key to ensuring lasting success. Having taken note of environmental conditions – the type of soil, the amount of sunshine, wind and frost and the host of other factors that need to be taken into consideration during the planning process – gardeners must put that knowledge to good practical use.

Having the right tools available for the tasks that will need to be undertaken is a critically important part of garden care, ensuring not only that essential jobs can be tackled but that they can be completed with maximum efficiency. It goes without saying that the right tool for the job will save the gardener an awful lot of time and effort. Preparing the ground correctly, and choosing and planting plants well, will also go a long way to ensuring long-term garden success.

Tools and Equipment

Having the right tools for the job is essential, not just for getting the job done correctly but also for making you more efficient in your work. There is a plethora of different tools a horticulturist can be confronted with, and even variations on just a single type of tool such as a spade. Some are very specialised, such as the numerous turf and grass-care tools, but you would only ever use most of those if you were looking after lawns full-time. However, armed with just a few of the basic tools, a gardener can get most of the essential jobs done in the garden. Below are some of the most popular.

• Tined cultivators are used for breaking up the surface of the soil.

Tined Cultivator
A hand tool with various sharp-pronged implements at the end of it. Used for pulling through the ground and breaking up any surface compaction or capping that may prevent moisture from penetrating the top few centimetres. It is also often used to control weeds and in some cases to create a tilth for seed sowing, although a rake will give a better finish. It is possible to get long- or short-handled versions, with the latter being more useful for getting in closer around the plants, but of course requiring more bending to use. Many tined cultivators have removable/interchangeable heads.

Garden String
The simple string is one of the most useful bits of equipment in a gardener's set of tools. Pulled tight between two sticks, it helps a gardener achieve a straight line when sowing vegetables or ornamental plants. It also provides a guide for cutting out lawns or laying paving.

• Mattocks are heavy-duty tools that are helpful for breaking up compacted ground, removing stumps and clearing areas of debris.

Collapsible bin

A large collapsible bin, available at regular hardware shops, is a useful tool for collecting up garden waste as you work your way through the garden. Large bags are an alternative for collecting and carting away garden rubbish. Some people use the more ornamental wooden trugs for collecting harvested crops such as fruit or vegetables.

Leaf Collectors

Large pairs of plastic 'hands' are useful for picking up leaves that have been raked into piles. Alternatively, two pieces of exterior timber can do a similar job. It is possible to get plastic 'hands' on the end of handles, which saves back-breaking work in the autumn when collecting all the falling foliage off the lawns and out of the flower beds.

Dibber

No gardener should be without a dibber. They are essentially small sticks (about 15–25cm long) that are pushed into soil or compost to create a hole for sowing. Some have a D-shaped handle on them. There are lots of different types on the market, but if you're on a budget a pencil or small pointed stick will suffice.

Hand weeder or weeding fork

This tools are designed to prise out long-rooted weeds without disturbing the surrounding soil.

Mattock

This heavy, robust gardening tool is shaped similarly to a pickaxe but with one end of the blade axe-like for chopping through hard woody roots, and the other end blunter but chunkier for chopping through solid, compacted soil.

Watering Can and Rose

The main cause of death for plants in the garden is lack of water, so having the right kit to keep them watered is essential. There are numerous hoses, irrigation systems and even water butts for harvesting rainwater, but probably the cheapest, simplest and most useful tool you can have is a watering can. A rose on the end of the spout allows you to water your delicate seedlings with fine droplets of water.

Wheelbarrow

Used for transporting material around the garden. Most have just a single wheel. Although more wheels will take even more of the weight, they are heavier to tip and push. Barrows are usually made of plastic or stainless steel and come in a range of sizes, so choose one that firstly you can manage without causing strain on your body, and secondly is narrow enough to fit down your paths and between your beds.

• Dibbers are an essential tool for making holes in soil or compost for sowing seed or planting cuttings.

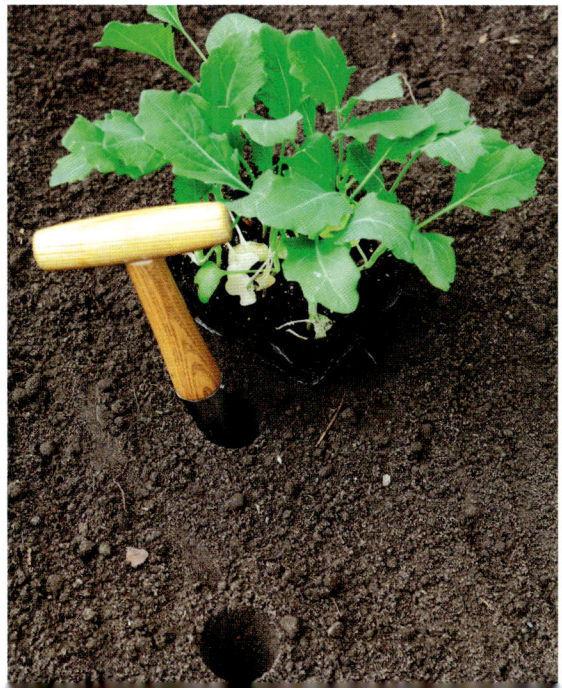

Spade

In the horticultural world, it isn't as simple as just calling a spade a spade. There are lots of variations and understanding the nuances will make a huge difference to your efficiency. There are generally two different types of handle, D or T types, named after the shape of them. Get to feel them in your hands in the shop or garden centre before buying. The length of the shaft can also vary, with longer ones giving you more leverage, but these are trickier for shorter people to use. Some spades have a straight handle, whereas others have a slight angle, again to make it easier to lever out and cut through sods of soil. Look at the tread on the top of the blade, too (sometimes called the shoulder). Some are thicker and wider than others, so consider if it will be comfortable when putting your garden boot on it and pushing it into the ground. Most spade blades have a blunt or square end, but some have pointed ends, making it easier to insert into compacted soil.

Shovel

Similar considerations should be made for shovels as for spades, and again they vary in size, weight and length, etc. Spades are generally used for digging, whereas shovels are used for shifting bulky material such as wood chippings or sand.

• Spades usually have a T or D handle. It is worth trying both before purchasing to see which you prefer.

Fork

Digging forks, which also come with D or T handles, are usually used to break up the soil and loosen it after it has been dug over with a spade. They can be used to break up clods and remove the roots of perennial weeds. They are also often used to aerate small lawns by pushing the tines into the surface, thereby reducing compaction. A fork with wider tines is known as a potato fork and has blunter ends to prevent damaging crops under the soil, but they are also often used for spreading compost or bulky woodchip material. Muck forks have long, light handles and long thin tines, making them useful for shifting manure or straw around the garden.

Border Spade/Fork

A smaller version of the standard spade and fork, these miniature versions are useful for making smaller holes and giving you more precision when working in among borders and flower beds. Their smallness makes them lighter and therefore not as tiring to use if you're going to be working with them all day.

• A trowel is an essential tool for planting seedlings and bulbs and removing small weeds without damaging nearby plants.

Trowel

An essential hand tool in smaller gardens. Wider-bladed versions are usually used for planting small plants, such as annuals or bedding, as they make a decent-sized hole. Versions with narrower blades are more usual for bulbs or smaller seedlings. There are also longer-handled versions to give better leverage in heavier soil.

Hand Fork

Used for weeding smaller beds. The small size enables weeds to be dug out with minimal damage to surrounding plants. It is also useful for weeding raised beds as there is less bending down to do. Longer-handled versions save on back-breaking work and offer better leverage in heavier ground conditions.

• Anvil secateurs (above) are useful for trimming woody plants, but bypass secateurs (below) will give a much cleaner cut.

Secateurs

Used to cut through herbaceous or woody material. There are two different types, anvil and bypass. Anvil types are usually cheaper and work by crushing down the blade onto the anvil, which can result in damaging the remaining plant material. Bypass secateurs provide a cleaner finish and should avoid damaging plants. There are lots of different-sized secateurs so choose a pair that fit comfortably in your hand without causing strain. Some versions have rolling handles, designed to reduce the muscle stress on the hand. Secateurs are usually only used for cutting material about 1cm thick or less. Loppers or a pruning saw should be used for anything larger.

Rake

The most common rake is the garden rake, a long-handled tool used to prepare seed beds and break the soil down to a fine tilth suitable for sowing into. The tines break down any clods of soil and remove any unwanted debris such as stones, glass and other rubbish. The back of the rake can be used to tamp down the soil over a sown drill or to gently rake seed into the top few centimetres of the soil, such as when sowing grass or wild-flower meadows. Rakes can also be used for levelling the soil, and often rakes with a slightly longer head (wooden or stainless steel), called 'landscape rakes', are used to do this. Spring-tine rakes have thin, wiry tines and are often used on lawns to remove thatch from around the base of the blades of grass. Rubber garden rakes are also used on lawns to

brush top dressing into the holes after aeration. Plastic rakes are used to gather up soft herbaceous material, leaves or grass clippings.

Hoes

There are numerous types of hoe for use in the garden. The Dutch hoe is used to slice through weeds just below the surface of the ground. The long handle saves having to bend down to reach the weeds, while the narrow blade makes it easy to work up and down between rows of small vegetables or other plants. It should only be used on annual weeds as perennials will reshoot from where they are severed. Draw hoes also have long handles to avoid back-breaking weeding. As the name suggests, they are used by pulling or drawing the blade towards the user. The long, curvy shape of the blade gives it its other name, 'swan-necked' hoe, and enables it to be used in a small chopping motion. Draw hoes penetrate the ground deeper than Dutch hoes. The edge of the draw hoe is sometimes used to draw out a drill for seed sowing, or the entire blade pulled through the ground to make a shallow trench. Onion hoes are simply short-handled versions of draw hoes and can be used for weeding at close proximity in and among the plants to avoid damaging them.

• Dutch hoe

• Draw hoe

Gloves

A thick, robust pair of gloves is essential if digging out blackberries, pruning roses or working with cacti or other types of prickly plants. Thin gloves are more suitable for light weeding and other general gardening jobs.

Ground Preparation

A lot of the hard work that goes into creating a healthy, beautiful garden happens before a plant is even put into the ground. Preparing the ground correctly is essential to get your garden off to the best start possible. Badly prepared ground will cause bigger problems later on, with weeds getting out of control and poor, malnourished soil.

The type of soil you have in your garden will ultimately determine the types of plants you can grow, unless you have plans to excavate huge amounts of the existing soil and replace it with imported soil. These days, though, most gardeners tend to work with their existing conditions and match plants and designs to complement them. Fortunately, there are thousands and thousands of plants that will suit a whole range of conditions, whether boggy, rocky or dry and arid, etc. However, whether or not you intend to work with the existing conditions, it is still important to make improvements and do some preparation prior to planting.

Weed Removal

Most gardeners are confronted with beds full of weeds when first starting to prepare a plot. Whether you believe in the 'no dig' method or the traditional method of digging over the ground, perennial roots of weeds will still need to be removed before planting. Once the new plants have gone into the ground, it is much harder to eradicate weeds. Do remember also that if you are

• Ensure that all weeds have been removed from the soil before starting to plant.

working in winter, it may look like you don't have a weed problem, because the herbaceous material has died back. This is often the case when people take on a new garden in winter, when it all looks manageable, not realising what weed roots lie beneath the surface, waiting to appear as soon as the weather warms up.

The easiest way to eradicate weeds is to spray with a systemic weedkiller (usually containing glyphosate) and wait a few weeks for the chemical to be taken down from the green chlorophyll in the leaves and into the roots. For really pernicious weeds, such as ground elder, bindweed, oxalis and perennial nettle, it may need a few sprays before it has the desired effect. A bed left like this for a few weeks before planting is known as a stale bed. If you do not wish to use chemicals, another option is to dig out the weeds, ensuring you get rid of every tiny part of the root or bulbil to prevent it from re-sprouting. Some roots can go down as far as a metre below the surface, so a thorough, methodical digging over of the ground will be necessary. Large stones and rocks should also be removed at this stage as they will impede the development of plants when they're trying to establish. Other options include covering the soil to exclude light for a year or two, and a flame weeder for annual weeds.

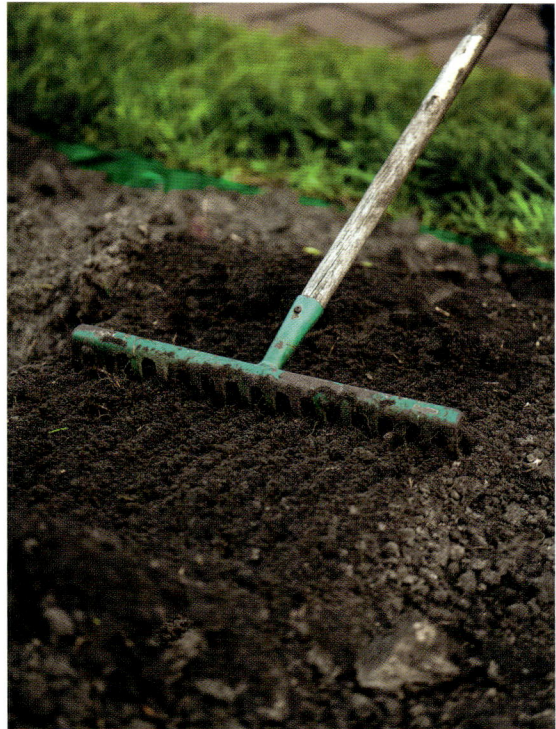

• Landscape rakes are useful for levelling uneven ground and for breaking up lumps of soil into a fine tilth for sowing.

WEED SUPPRESSION

If you aren't going to be planting for a while, any bare soil should be covered with a weed-suppressing membrane to prevent the germination of any new weeds. This will also help to warm up the soil, so that when you are ready for sowing or planting, the plants or seedlings will establish much faster than if the soil had been left uncovered. If using landscape fabric, avoid lighter fabric (spun material), which is prone to ripping. Heavy duty woven fabric is much more durable. Whatever you use make sure it is well pegged or weighted down so that it doesn't come away in high winds.

Preparing the Soil

Once perennial weeds have been removed from the soil and it has been dug over with a spade (see page 151), the ground can be lightly forked to reduce down any big clods of earth, then further reduced with a garden or landscape rake so that the soil becomes a fine tilth suitable for sowing or planting into. The rake can also be used to level the ground, removing any bumps and hollows. On really steep ground, it may be necessary to terrace the ground, to create level beds along the slopes. The ground can also be raked to re-contour areas to create different levels in the garden.

Improving the Soil

The condition of the soil the plants will grow in is probably the most important factor as to whether they will thrive or struggle in the garden. There is a wide range of different products that can be incorporated into the soil to improve the plants' chances of survival. It is worth spending time on improving the soil prior to planting, because new plants will benefit from the moment they are placed in the ground and get off to the best possible start. There are basically two types of products added to the soil: fertilisers and mulches/composts.

Fertilisers

These are often incorporated into the soil prior to sowing or planting, known as base dressing, but are also added to plants already growing in the ground, called top dressing. They can be organic or inorganic and come in numerous different forms, such as powder, granules or liquid.

Usually, for general planting it is best to use a balanced fertiliser, but if you wanted to incorporate

• Mixing fertilisers into the soil or compost prior to planting is an effective method of boosting the available nutrients for plants.

NUTRIENT CONTENT

Fertilisers will usually have the letters NPK on them somewhere to show their nutrient content, with N standing for **nitrogen**, P for **phosphorus** and K for **potassium**. The numbers next to them will denote the ratio in which these three major nutrients are provided – so, for example, NPK 113 would mean it is higher in potassium than nitrogen or phosphorus.

Nitrogen promotes green, leafy growth.
Phosphorus provides strength and good root development.
Potassium helps a plant to produce flowers, fruit and colour.

more nitrogen you could feed with chicken pellets, or if you wanted something higher in phosphorous to encourage strong root growth, you could choose bone meal, blood, fish and bone or superphosphate. To encourage flowering and fruit, you could choose something with higher potassium, such as a tomato feed. As plants have different mineral and nutrient requirements at different stages of growth, the best compromise is controlled fertilisers, which release certain amounts of either N, P or K, depending on what point in the season it is. However, controlled-release fertilisers are expensive.

Base-dressing fertiliser should be applied to the surface of the soil just prior to planting to prevent any of it washing away.

Applying Mulches and Compost

Fertilisers won't improve the soil texture; they are simply feeding the plants with essential nutrients and minerals. To improve the texture, you need to use bulky organic matter, such as garden compost or well-rotted manure. Incorporating bulky material is best done a few days before planting to allow levels to settle.

Adding animal manure is one of the best ways to improve soil texture, and it will also add a certain amount of nutrients, which will be released slowly into the ground. These days it would seem you can get almost any type of animal manure if you're willing to look hard enough, such as alpaca, kangaroo or even elephant. However, when using manure from the more traditional animals, the richest sources include horse, chicken, sheep and cow.

Garden compost is another form of rich, bulky organic matter that will boost the humus matter in your soil, and is free if you can make your own. Mushroom compost is also good, but has a high lime content (high pH), so avoid using it around acid-loving plants, including Australian natives. Leaf mould can also be used – it usually has poor nutrient levels but is a good soil conditioner.

ROTTING DOWN MANURE

Always make sure that animal manure is rotted down prior to use, because the nitrogen it contains can scorch the plants when fresh. The best method of rotting down fresh manure is to stack it in a heap, add lots of water to help the decomposition stage, then cover with plastic sheets to warm it up and speed up the rotting stage. The manure should be ready to add to the ground after a few weeks. Alternatively, some people mix it in with their normal compost, i.e. add it to the heap, where it will have time to rot down, and may even assist with the rotting of the other composted materials.

• Adding plenty of rotted manure prior to planting will add some nutrients and, more importantly, improve the quality of the soil.

Digging (and the 'No Dig' Method)

The process of digging over soil has been carried out for thousands of years and is considered to be one of the key cultivation techniques for improving the ground prior to planting. However, some modern gardeners advocate an alternative technique, sometimes called the 'no dig' method, which has also been shown to provide decent results in the garden.

SINGLE DIGGING TECHNIQUE

Use a spade for digging over the soil. Work methodically over the soil to ensure the whole area is cultivated. Marking the area out with a string helps to ensure all the ground has been worked over.

Digging can be hard work so, to avoid straining your body, try to keep your back straight and avoid lifting the spade completely laden with soil, but instead only move manageable amounts. If possible, dig an area over a few days rather than in one attempt, to avoid repetition and overstraining yourself.

Whichever method of digging you are following, always remember to dig out perennial roots as you go.

Single digging will suffice for most plots or flower beds.

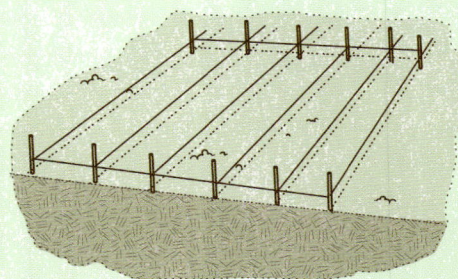

1 Mark out trenches with string.

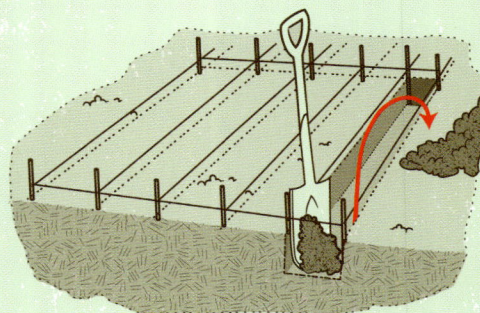

2 Dig out the soil a spit deep (the depth of the spade blade) and save it for the final trench.

Why Dig?

Even if you choose to cultivate your crops using the no-dig method, there are still occasions when there are benefits to digging over the ground. Firstly, if the ground is very compacted, or has never been cultivated before, the soil will need to be broken up to remove any 'pans' below the surface that will impede the roots of trees, shrubs and even herbaceous plants in very shallow soil. Digging over the ground is also a good method of incorporating well-rotted manure or other organic matter into the depth of the soil, encouraging tree and shrub roots downwards towards the water table as opposed to up towards the surface. This will give them an improved chance of longevity and will better equip them to survive drought in what could otherwise be poor, infertile and barren soil.

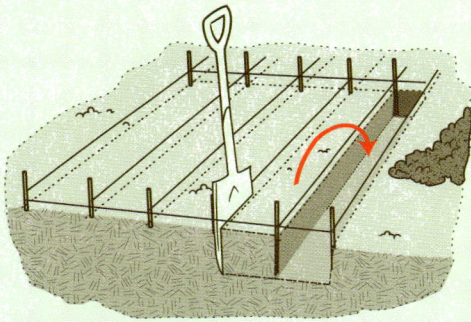

3 Move over to the next trench along, marked out with string, and start digging out trench two, putting the contents into trench one and mixing in organic matter as you go.

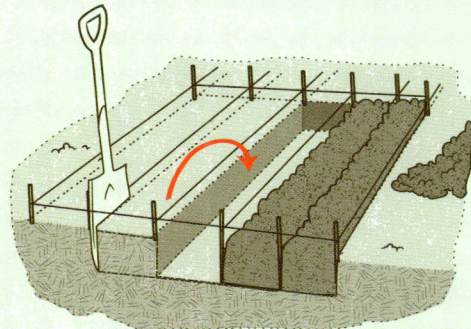

5 Continue this process until the whole plot has been covered, filling the final trench with the soil from trench one. Finally, rake the bed level and leave to settle for a few days before planting.

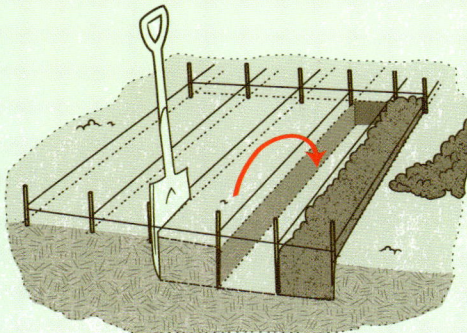

4 You now have an empty trench two, so next dig out trench three alongside trench two and use the soil to backfill trench two, again adding organic matter as you go.

DOUBLE DIGGING TECHNIQUE

Double digging is similar to single digging and is useful where the subsoil is compacted and needs breaking up. Follow the steps as in single digging, but fork over the bottom of each trench to the depth of the tines and dig organic matter into the bottom. Avoid mixing the soil from the lower trench (subsoil) with the topsoil from the upper trench.

When to Dig

Digging over the soil can be carried out at any time of the year but it is best to avoid extremes of weather, such as heat, droughts or wet conditions, as this can harm the soil structure as well as create a difficult environment for working in. Many gardeners like to dig over the ground in late autumn, when most of the crops have been harvested and removed. Not only does digging warm you up as the weather starts to get cooler, but it is claimed that thick heavy clods exposed on the surface will break down better when the even colder winter weather arrives.

'No Dig' Technique

If you're thinking that all the previously mentioned recommended digging sounds too much like hard work, don't despair. There is another school of thought that not only saves all that back-breaking work but also argues that digging actually damages the existing soil structure and the natural activity of microorganisms, bacteria and even the essential earthworms in the soil. Instead, the 'no dig' technique recommends that the soil should be left undug and, instead, layers of organic matter, such as compost, should be regularly added to the surface, letting it gradually become incorporated into the existing soil underneath and break down as rainwater and worms channel it below ground. Soon, a healthy, natural substrate is created for the plants to thrive in. Plants are planted or seeds sown directly into the top layer of the organic matter. It may be necessary occasionally to use a fork to remove perennial weeds.

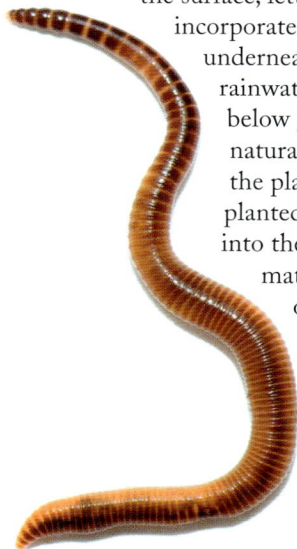

• Worms are a gardener's friend, as they aerate the soil, make it more friable and pull nutrients down into the ground.

TRENCHING

Finally, there is trenching, which is the ultimate in ground preparation but is only necessary for extremely compacted subsoils.

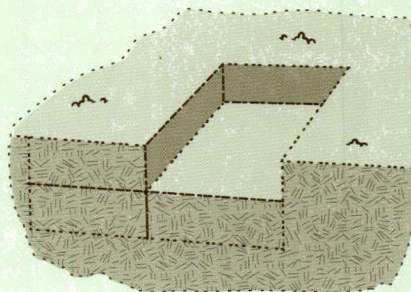

1 Repeat the process for single digging by digging out a trench a spit deep.

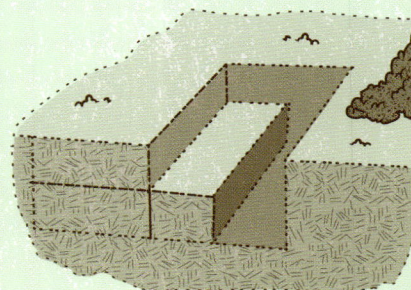

2 Next, dig out another trench within the existing trench, but only along one side, and save the soil. The trench will now look like it has a step in it.

3 Use a fork to dig over the bottom of the lower half of the trench.

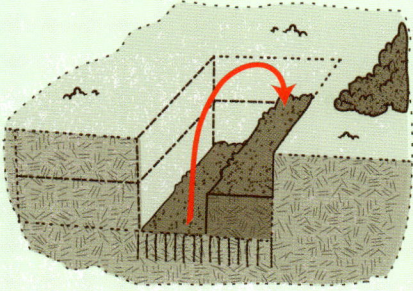

4 Next, dig up the soil in the higher half of the trench and move it into the dug-over, lower half of the trench.

5 Use the fork to dig over the bottom of the newly exposed first half of the trench.

6 Mix organic matter into the bottom of the trench.

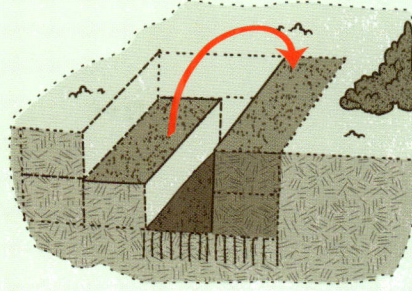

8 Put the soil from the first spit on the very first trench to bring it up level with the ground.

7 Now start digging another trench next to the first trench, down to the same depth as the first step.

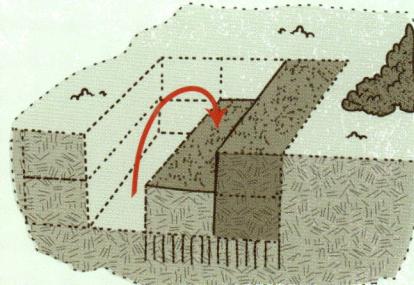

9 Put the soil from the second spit into what is now the middle trench and dig over the newly exposed area.

10 Continue in this pattern until the whole area is dug.

Buying and Selecting Plants

Today, garden centres, nurseries and even supermarkets, along with increasingly accessible online plant suppliers, are bringing an unparalleled range of plants within the reach of gardeners. Despite the overwhelming choice available, the basic rules of choosing good plants for the garden remain the same. However tempting the bright, colourful rows of pots on tables and trolleys or photos may be, horticultural quality rather than instant appeal should be the overall goal.

- First and foremost, concentrate on plants that suit the conditions of your garden and the purpose for which they are intended.
- If you are shopping in person, the chances are that you will be buying pot-grown specimens.
- Always make sure that the plant is correctly labelled, looks healthy and is free of pests and disease or any other type of damage. Moss or liverworts in the pot may be a sign that the plant has been sitting around too long, so avoid such plants if possible.
- Continue by removing the pot to check the roots or at least check underneath to see whether roots are growing through the holes. Plants that are 'pot-bound', with roots that extrude or are wrapped around the inside of the pot, tend to establish less successfully.

- Check also that the plant is a good representative of its type. Shrubs should be balanced and well branched, while trees should not look stunted or top-heavy, both signs that the pot – and therefore the root ball – is too small. Pot-grown perennials should also look healthy and vigorous, with strong growing shoots. If buying annuals or bedding plants, choose plants with plenty of shoots and buds rather than full flowers to ensure a much longer seasonal display.

Bare-root Plants

The great advantage of buying container-grown plants is that they can be planted at almost any time of the year, unless weather conditions are simply too extreme. However, it is also possible to buy plants either 'bare root' – that is, completely without soil – or 'root-balled', where the roots and some soil are lifted and wrapped before sale. Deciduous trees and shrubs, especially roses and fruit and nut trees, which are commonly sold bare-rooted in the dormant period in winter and are somewhat cheaper than pot-grown plants, though they require speedy planting or at least heeling in as soon as possible.

Ordering plants online or by post makes a visual check before buying impossible, so it is especially important to buy from reputable suppliers, most of whom offer guarantees of some sort and testimonials or customer reviews. A little research beforehand may avoid a lot of disappointment.

• Prior to purchasing, check that a plant is not too root-bound by pulling it out of the pot and inspecting.

Planting Trees and Shrubs

It is usually expected that if you are planting a tree, it will live for years to come and hopefully be admired by future generations, so it is essential to give the tree the best possible start by planting it correctly. Although shrubs are shorter-lived than trees, it is still important to plant them correctly so they will look healthy and beautiful in the garden.

Buying a tree from a garden centre or nursery is a wonderful investment for the future, but they can be expensive – yet it is astounding how many trees die in the first few years due to being badly planted. The main reasons for early death of trees are that they are planted too deeply, causing the base of the trunk to rot, or the roots have become pot-bound in the nursery and don't establish properly once planted but instead continue to grow in a spiral, eventually strangling themselves. Another common reason for low success rates after planting is lack of water in the first few seasons.

One other consideration when planting a tree is its location. Imagine how it will look in 10 years' time, 25 years' time… perhaps even 100 or 200 years' time if planting in a large parkland or on a private estate. Will it be blocking a view? Will it cause too much shade in your garden? Will your neighbours complain? Also, check what conditions it likes. Some types, such as most *Acer*, prefer sheltered conditions away from exposed winds and out of direct sunlight, which can desiccate its leaves. Other trees thrive in hot, direct sun and can tolerate harsh, windy conditions, so check whether your tree will cope with the surrounding environment before planting.

• A well-planted tree such as this cherry (*Prunus incisia*) should last a lifetime and look beautiful for many years to come.

HOW TO PLANT A TREE OR SHRUB

1 Dig out a hole that is at least twice the circumference of the root ball, and the same depth. To understand the true depth of the root ball, remove the tree from the pot and scrape away any loose compost to expose the top of the root system and the very bottom of the trunk, which will be flared or widened slightly as it meets the root ball (called the root flare). This is the point that should be level with the ground when planted, and the planting hole should be only as deep as necessary to allow for this.

2 Check the root ball once removed from the pot. Chances are, if it has been in a container for a while the roots will be compacted and growing tightly around each other in the pot. These roots need to be vigorously pulled out to ensure that once the tree is in the ground, the roots grow outwards and don't continue to spiral around. If they don't spread outwards, they will be susceptible to drought as their only source of moisture and nutrients will be within the tiny planting hole. Long-term, this will also mean that the tree is unstable as the roots haven't reached out far enough to anchor into the ground.

3 Most people opt for a round planting hole. However, some gardeners believe that this causes the roots to continue to go around in a circle after planting, rather than spreading out. To avoid this, the sides of the hole can be scuffed or pricked with a garden fork to encourage roots to go outwards. Alternatively, create a square or rectangular planting hole, and then the roots will hit a corner and keep going outwards rather than round and round. Avoid digging over the bottom of the hole unless in very compacted ground, otherwise the tree will sink after planting. Instead, lightly prick the bottom of the hole with the garden fork to encourage roots to go downwards.

4 Place the tree in the centre of the hole. Lay a bamboo cane or timber stake over the hole and look at where it touches the trunk to check that the tree isn't going to be planted too deeply. Get somebody to hold the tree straight for you, and start to backfill around the root ball with the original soil from the hole. Soil can also be backfilled by washing it into the hole with lots of water; this has the added effect of getting lots of moisture to the roots on planting, and roots and soil making good contact and minimising air pockets.

5 If the soil is really poor, compost can be added and mixed with the soil prior to putting it back into the hole, but ideally you want to encourage the tree to seek out its own nutrients away from the planting hole rather than tempt the roots to stay close to the trunk because it has lovely organic matter in its cosy hole.

6 Firm the soil in around the root ball using your foot, with your heel towards the outside of the hole and toes towards the trunk. Work your way around the hole so that the tree feels stable in the hole.

HOW TO PLANT A TREE OR SHRUB

7 The tree will probably need staking in the first couple of years, particularly if it is top-heavy and in an exposed position. Use an angled stake at about 45 degrees to avoid damaging the root ball. Use a mallet to bang the stake into the ground. The tree should be tied to the stake low down on the trunk, about an eighth of the way up. This will encourage the trunk to flex in the wind, which will strengthen it like a muscle and enable the tree to stand on its own once the stake is removed after no more than two years. Use a tree tie with a protective pad between the trunk and the stake to prevent it rubbing.

8 If you haven't already watered when backfilling, give the tree a good watering at this stage to allow the soil to settle around it. Well-rotted manure or garden compost can be added around the surface of the hole to a depth of about 5cm to help retain moisture and suppress any competitive weeds. Ensure that the organic matter is at least 6cm away from the trunk of the tree to prevent the tree rotting.

A Note on Shrubs

Shrubs are planted in the same way as trees, as described above, but do check on the label for spacing requirements to ensure they are given plenty of room. Also, they probably won't need staking.

Planting Roses

Roses are one of the most spectacular shrubs, with a huge range of colour and fragrance. There are so many different types to choose from, ranging from rambling roses that scramble over a pergola in a cottage garden to heavily scented old-fashioned shrub types for the herbaceous border or spectacular large blooms on a hybrid tea rose for pots on a courtyard patio. Whatever type you fancy, it's essential to plant them correctly to get them to perform at their best.

If roses are in a container they can be planted at any time of the year, but avoid extremes of weather such as very wet, dry or frozen ground. The best time for planting is often considered to be early to mid-autumn as the soil will be warm. This will give the plant a chance to settle and establish itself before the onset of winter and ensure that it is ready to burst into growth in spring. Bare-root roses are only available from late autumn to late winter and should ideally be planted as soon as they are purchased. If this isn't possible, bury their roots in soil until ready for planting.

Most roses prefer full sun, but some will tolerate part shade, so check which variety you have when deciding on the location to plant it in. Expert advice from a reputable supplier is always helpful.

• Planting a rose correctly should help keep it looking healthy and producing an abundance of flowers.

Roses like a rich, heavy soil, so if you have infertile or sandy soil then large amounts of organic matter, such as well-rotted animal manure or garden compost, should be added and dug into the top 30cm of the soil prior to planting. As a general rule of thumb, add about a wheelbarrow full of organic matter to one square metre.

Giving Roses the Best Chance

Roses, and most plants from the rose family (*Rosaceae*), suffer from a problem called replant disease, meaning that if other members of the family have previously been planted in the ground, then either a new location should be found for new planting, or the soil should be removed to a depth of 1m wide and deep. Using mycorrhizal powder around the root system is also said to help newly planted roses combat this problem.

Roses will also be less stressed if they have less competition for nutrients from weeds, so – as is always good practice with all planting – ensure that all weeds have been removed from the planting area. If the rose plants are bare root, soak the roots in a bucket of water for an hour or so before planting. If the roses are in containers, give them a thorough watering beforehand. As roses are hungry feeders they will also benefit from a base dressing of a general-purpose fertiliser at about 100g per sq metre. However, fertiliser should be avoided if you are using mycorrhizal powder as research has shown that it suppresses the natural benefits of the fungus.

HOW TO PLANT ROSES

1 Dig out a planting hole (see page 74) for each rose plant approximately twice the size of the width of the root ball and about the same depth.

2 Remove the plant from its pot if container-grown and give the roots a tug to ensure they won't continue to grow around in a circle but will instead grow outwards once planted. If the roots continue to grow inwardly or in a circle within the planting circle, the plant will be susceptible to drought as it will be reliant on just the moisture within the hole.

3 The rose should be placed in the middle of the hole. Check the planting depth by placing a bamboo cane across the top of the hole and seeing where it touches the stem of the plant. Ideally, the grafting union (a bulge on the stem of the plant) should be just below or level with the soil. If you are using mycorrhizal powder, this should be added to the planting hole at this stage.

4 Once you're happy with the height, backfill the area surrounding the root ball of the rose with a 50:50 mix of compost and the excavated soil from the hole. Gently firm the plant in by pushing the soil down with your fingertips, ensuring the soil goes between the individual larger roots rather than just sitting on top. Water the plants in well or water as you backfill.

5 If you are planting more than one rose, check the label for spacing as this varies enormously depending on variety and type of rose. Make sure you label each one as you plant so you don't get them mixed up, or make sure the labels are well attached to the stem so you don't mix them up before planting.

Planting a Hedge

Hedges are wonderful natural features for defining boundaries between neighbours and to give us privacy. They provide a rich habitat for wildlife, excellent wind protection and can be used within a garden design to separate out specific areas and provide a structure and pattern for an overall garden effect. They're also useful for screening unattractive features in the garden, such as the compost heap or an ugly fence.

Hedges come in all sorts of shapes, heights and colours. Evergreen ones will provide year-round screening, whereas deciduous hedges such as magnolia (*Magnolia*) will give you seasonal interest as they range from beautiful bright lime green in spring through to deep mellow buttery colours in autumn and then copper as they cling to their leaves throughout most of winter. Some hedges, such as in parterres, are only knee-high, yet some leylandii (*Cupressus* x *leylandii*) and other conifer types can be as high as houses. However, whatever type you wish to have in your garden, the principles of establishing a beautiful hedge are the same.

Water the plants thoroughly prior to planting. If they are bare-root trees, it is worth placing their roots in a bucket of water for an hour or so first.

• Evergreen hedges provide structure as well as all-year-round interest, particularly in winter when most other plants aren't flowering.

HOW TO PLANT A HEDGE

1 Hedges can be planted as just one single row, but more often than not are planted as a double row to create a thicker structure. In order to do this, stretch out two parallel lengths of string at 40cm apart if using young bare-root trees. If you are using larger, container-grown trees, the two rows may need to be further apart to allow for the size of their root ball.

2 Mark out with canes where each hedging plant is going to be planted. Plants should be about 40cm apart, but should be staggered, so start the second row 20cm away from the start, so that a zigzag effect is created between the two rows.

3 To plant a bare-root hedging plant, push a spade the full length of the blade (a spit depth) into the soil where the first tree is to be planted and simply push the handle forward about 20cm away from you. This will open up the soil slightly, creating a gap. Slide the bare-root tree down the back of the spade and settle it into the gap and then gently pull the spade back out of the ground, enabling the soil to close up around the plant. Firm the plant in by gently treading around it with your feet. Repeat this process until all the plants are in the ground.

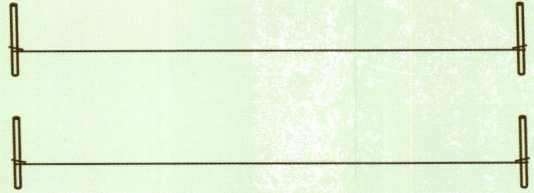

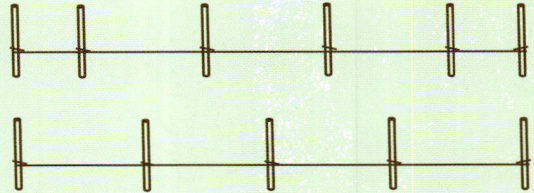

4 If planting a hedge with large containerised trees, it is usually easier to dig out a trench along the two rows at the same depth as the height of the root ball. Remove the plants from their pots and place them in the trench at equal spacing, remembering to stagger the row at the back to create a zigzag effect between the two rows. Ask somebody to hold each plant upright as you work along the row, backfilling the trench and firming the soil in around the plants.

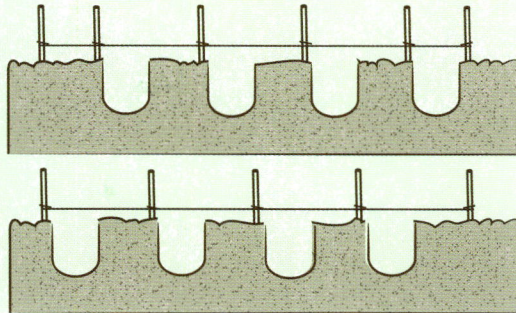

5 Plants should be thoroughly watered after planting and it may be necessary to place rabbit guards around the bases of the plants if they are a problem in the area.

6 To encourage the hedge to 'bush out', it is worth trimming back the leaders (see page 104) by a few centimetres to encourage lateral growth.

Planting in Containers

Almost any kind of plant can be grown in a container, as long as the gardener provides the right conditions and care. Planting in pots may be essential if you have no access to a garden or have limited space, but it can also be a useful addition to larger gardens, where an extra burst of colour in summer or a stylish focal point is required. A surprising amount of vegetables and herbs are also perfectly happy in pots, so it is worth considering placing some close to the kitchen or on the windowsill for ease of access.

Containers come in many shapes and sizes. Pick those that meet your design needs as well as the needs of the plant. Terracotta is a good classic choice but stylish contemporary containers may be more appropriate in a modern setting, while lightweight plastic pots are the most suitable for balconies and rooftops, if only for safety's sake.

The size of the pot is obviously dependent on the size of the plant: larger for trees and shrubs, smaller for herbs, annuals and perennials. As a rule, there must be enough space to fit the root ball in comfortably, with some room for the roots to grow out and down. Larger pots dry out less quickly than smaller pots. A soil-based compost is most appropriate for permanent plantings such as trees, shrubs and larger perennials. It will retain water and be heavy enough to ensure the pot's stability and can be revitalised each spring by top dressing. Remove the top layer of compost and replace with fresh compost plus a suitable amount of slow-release fertiliser.

• Choose a container for your plant that complements the surrounding garden design, but also ensure it is big enough.

Bedding plants, vegetables and annuals can be grown in ordinary multipurpose compost, which is easily replaced each season.

For hanging baskets, it is best to choose a proprietary hanging basket compost, or mix slow-release fertiliser and water-retaining crystals into ordinary compost to ensure ease of maintenance.

HOW TO PLANT IN CONTAINERS

1 First ensure that there is adequate drainage. Make holes in the bottom if necessary, before adding a layer of drainage material. Small pieces of polystyrene work well and are usefully light. Just be careful not to block the draining hole. Pot feet may also help to allow excess water to drain away and stop plants sitting in oxygen-depriving soggy soil.

2 Fill the pot with compost, leaving a 5cm gap below the rim to prevent water and compost spilling over during watering. Mix in a granular fertiliser at this time too, before positioning your plants. Firm them in gently after planting and water well.

Creating a Lawn

Gardeners often have a love-hate relationship with lawns. Most people enjoy the time they spend relaxing on their lawn, picnicking on a softly textured, verdant carpet of grass, playing with a football or just sitting and appreciating its natural qualities. However, this pleasure is often countered by the regular mowing, watering and maintenance required to keep them looking good, especially in summer. If you have the space, though, a lawn creates a lovely area in which to unwind in the garden.

• Turf can be laid at any time throughout the year, although it's not advisable to do so during extreme weather conditions such as drought or frost.

There are two methods for creating a lawn: one is sowing a lawn and the other is laying turves. Each method has numerous benefits and also disadvantages, as described below.

Laying Turf
Advantages
• An instant effect – a lawn made up of turves looks pretty amazing almost as soon as it is finished. And it can be walked on just a few weeks after laying.
• Less preparation of the soil is required when laying turf than when sowing seed.

Disadvantages
• Rolls of turf are more expensive to buy than seed. You also usually have to pay for delivery, if you don't have a van or pickup, as it is bulky to handle.
• If you aren't physically fit and strong, you may find laying heavy rolls of turf too strenuous. Sowing seed is much lighter work.
• Turf needs to be laid within a day or two of being delivered. So if you have an unforeseen delay to getting the job done, the turves could perish.

Sowing Seed
Advantages
• Seed is much cheaper to buy than rolls of turf.
• You have a much wider range of grass to choose from. With rolls of turf there are often just two types: fine lawns and hard-wearing lawns.

Disadvantages
• It takes longer than turves to become established, and there are problems to watch out for whilst waiting for the seed to germinate: birds might feed on the seed, so netting may be required, and weeds can start to grow, which will need to be eradicated.
• Seed will only germinate in warmer weather, between spring and mid-autumn.
• The amount of soil preparation involved – sowing seed requires a very fine tilth to get established. (A good tilth would be an easy, workable, or friable, loose soil.)

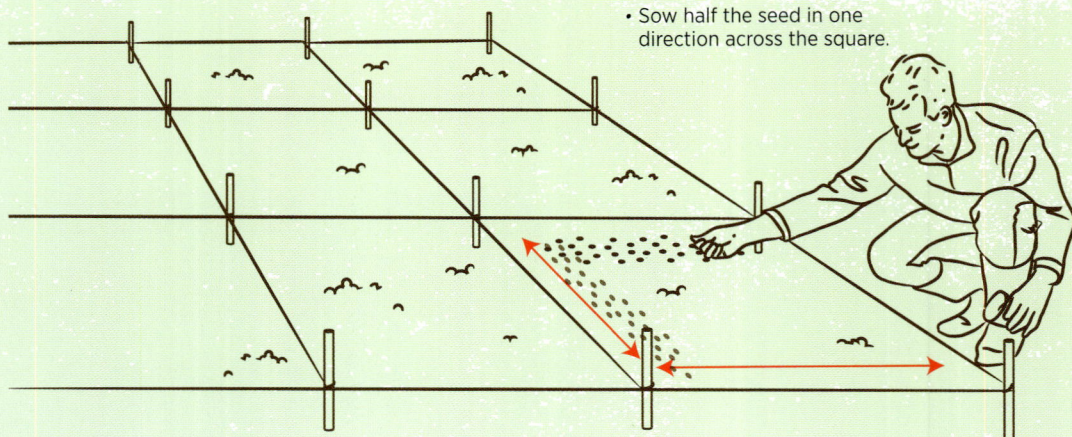

• Sow half the seed in one direction across the square.

PREPARING THE GROUND

The initial preparation for creating a lawn is similar whether you are sowing or laying turf, although a finer tilth is required for getting the seed established.

1 Prepare the ground by thoroughly digging it over to the depth of a spade's blade, unless there are compaction and drainage issues, in which case this may need to be addressed by double digging (see page 69). All stones and weeds should be removed. Organic matter, such as garden compost, should be dug into the ground in the top 15cm.

2 The ground should then be roughly raked, trodden down by walking over it and then raked again before leaving it for a couple of weeks to allow the ground to settle. If you lay turf or sow seed too soon, the soil will start to settle out and you will be left with an unstable surface, with hollows and bumps appearing all over your lawn.

3 After a few weeks, return to the plot, walk over it again or use a light roller and rake it over a few times in different directions. Correct any hollows and bumps that may have appeared and break the soil down to a fine crumbly tilth. It is now ready for sowing or laying turf.

SOWING A LAWN

Choose a clear day with minimal wind to prevent your seed blowing everywhere.

1 Mark out a grid of 1 metre squares using string.

2 Measure out your rate (it is often 50g per square metre for standard mixes, but do check the packet instructions as it can vary according to grass species) and sow half in one direction across the square and then the other half at ninety degrees to the first half.

3 Rake it in very lightly so the seed is just below the surface of the soil.

4 Repeat this process in the other squares. Lightly water in the seed.

5 It may be necessary to cover the lawn with nets or use vibrating strings to prevent birds from feeding on the seed.

6 The lawn should be established in a few weeks, depending on the weather conditions. It will need watering regularly during dry periods, as often as daily, if needed.

7 Once the sward (expanse of short grass) is thick enough, use a half-moon to cut the edge and give the lawn a clearly defined edge.

LAYING A LAWN

Turves can be laid throughout most of the year, but it is best to avoid summer because of the heat and lack of rain. The rolls will quickly shrivel up if not kept well-watered. When laying turves, avoid walking on them directly – work off a plank of wood which will equally distribute your weight along the turves and help them bed in better into the soil.

1 Lay your first row of turf up against one edge of the intended lawn area. Tamp the roll down with the back of a rake to ensure the roots bind with the soil underneath.

2 Make sure there is no gap between the end of the roll and the next one, as the turves will shrivel up and dry out quickly at the edges.

3 Stagger the next row, a bit like brickwork, so that the rolls don't all end in a line across the lawn.

4 Keep a bucket of loam (soil made up of clay and sand, containing humus) with you and as you work along each row fill any hollows that may have appeared, to ensure you have a level surface.

5 Try to avoid placing short strips at the end of each row, as these will be susceptible to drying out. Instead, move a longer strip to the outside and use the smaller section to fill the gap between the two longer sections.

6 Once all the turves have been laid, use a half-moon to cut and trim the edges. Work off a plank to equally distribute your weight again.

7 Fill any gaps between turves with a sandy top dressing made up of one part organic matter, three parts sand and three parts loam.

8 Finally, water the lawn and avoid walking on it for two or three weeks until the roots have started to knit through to the soil below.

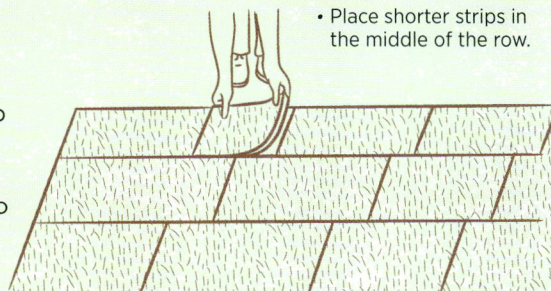

• Place shorter strips in the middle of the row.

EVERYDAY GARDEN CARE

The ongoing care of a garden is both a challenge and a great satisfaction to gardeners.

Gardens are constantly changing, with the seasons and with weather conditions, on a day-to-day basis as much as through longer periods of time. By their very nature, being man-made creations, gardens require continuous intervention to a greater or lesser degree. Even the most 'natural' garden has to be managed and controlled to some extent or Mother Nature herself will quickly take over in her own, extravagantly wild way. Only the most committed wildlife lover or very lazy gardener could be happy with a garden full of blackberries, oxalis and capeweed.

Depending on time and resources, gardens need regular maintenance to remain fit for purpose. Basic techniques are easy to learn, although sometimes harder to put into practice, and include feeding, pruning and watering, the single most essential task of the gardener given how critical water is for life. Lawn and hedge care, too, are important techniques to have under your belt, as these are features common to many a garden.

Learning and applying these basic techniques is the essence of good gardening, and they will stand the gardener in good stead, whatever kind or size of garden is being looked after.

Watering and Irrigation

We all know that water is the essence of life, and this is just as important for plants as it is for us. Watering correctly is the key to keeping your garden healthy and your plants alive. In fact, incorrect watering is one of the main causes of death among plants.

The simplest test to see if your plant needs water is to stick your finger in the soil or compost. If it's dry, then generally it will need watering. However, do be aware that some plants, particularly house plants, suffer if they are overwatered and prefer to be on the dry side. If in doubt, get advice from the garden centre or on the label. When you do water, make sure the water is penetrating deeply into the soil surrounding the plant and not just running off.

In summertime, it may be necessary to water some plants a couple of times a day. If you're on a water meter this could become expensive, so consider whether it is possible to harvest any rainwater. The best way to do this is to collect it from the roof of a shed or garage and channel it into a water tank. There are tanks and other purpose-made vessels available from garden centres. Alternatively, you can use plastic dustbins.

• Water tanks are increasingly popular among gardeners for collecting rainwater and therefore avoiding relying on expensive mains water.

• Use a rose on the end of a watering can to disperse a finer spray if watering delicate seedlings or plants.

If you don't think you are going to have time to water your plants regularly, there are a few things you can do:
• Avoid containers, which require more regular watering than plants in the ground. And select plants with a high dry tolerance.
• Water in the evening or early in the morning. Avoid watering in the heat of the day if possible,

SETTING UP A WATER TANK TO HARVEST RAINWATER FROM A SHED ROOF

1. Prepare your water tank by drilling a hole to fit the tap into, about 5cm above the bottom of the butt.

2. Screw the tap into the hole, ensuring that the washer is on the inside of the water tank to guarantee it stays watertight.

3. Position the water tank next to the shed in a convenient place where it won't get in your way when passing by or gardening. Place it on bricks so there is enough room underneath to position a watering can under the tap.

4. Attach support brackets at the top of all four sides of the shed, just below the roof, to support the guttering, ensuring that they all slope slightly towards where the water tank will be situated.

5. Slot the guttering into the support brackets.

6. Attach a section of downpipe that leads to the top of the water tank.

Water tanks are better if they have a lid on to prevent water evaporation, so it may be necessary to cut out a hole in the lid to fit the downpipe into, if there isn't one.

as most of the water will evaporate.
- Mulch around your plants with organic matter such as woodchips or straw. This will help to retain moisture.
- Push the soil or organic matter up around the plants to create a bowl shape. This will help hold in the water when watering the plants and prevent it running off away from the plant.
- Use irrigation systems – there are numerous different ones on the market. There are some that attach to mains water systems with pipes leading to all your plants. All you need to do is turn the tap on. Some systems even have timers so that you can go away on holiday and not have to worry about your plants. There is also a weather-responsive solar system that senses when the sun is out and releases water when it feels the plants will need it.

• Plants in hanging baskets and containers will need more watering than those planted in the ground.

Plants that suffer the most during dry periods are those in containers and hanging baskets. They could well need watering twice a day. If you are going away for a day or two, move them into the shade to help them cope, and give them a good drink before leaving and on your return.

RIGGING UP A SEEP HOSE

Although you can buy seep hoses, it is possible to make your own irrigation system from an old piece of hosepipe.

• Use a knife to cut tiny holes into the hosepipe about every 10cm.

• Lay it on the ground among your rows of vegetables or other plants.

• Attach a closed end section at the end of the hosepipe to prevent water coming out.

• Attach the other end to the mains tap. Turn on the tap and check to see how much water is coming out of the holes.

• You could rig the seep hose up to a timing device so that watering is fully automated.

Feeding and Fertilisers

Feeding your plants regularly with fertilisers will help to keep them healthy and ensure they are receiving the right amount of nutrients. Regularly monitor your plants to check they are growing well. Usually the best way to identify a problem with a lack of nutrients is by looking at the leaves for any discoloration.

Plants are remarkably clever organisms. They generate their own food from the soil by mixing together certain ingredients, much like a chef would do in the kitchen, and the result is something nutritional and healthy that will sustain them during the growing season. The ingredients include mineral ion nutrients, which they mix up in a concoction with water and carbon dioxide in the soil and absorb through the roots. The mineral ion nutrients are divided up in the horticultural world into macronutrients and micronutrients (the latter sometimes known as trace elements), with the micronutrients being needed in much smaller qualities.

• Fertilisers come in several guises, such as powders, liquids and in this case pellets, which are used to feed plants.

NUTRIENTS

These nutrients are essential for a plant's survival, and if they can't obtain them from the soil, due to deficiencies, then it will be necessary either to feed them directly with a foliar feed or to replenish the soil.

The macronutrients are nitrogen (N), phosphorus (P), potassium (K), magnesium (Mg), calcium (Ca) and sulphur (S).

The micronutrients include iron (Fe), manganese (Mn), copper (Cu), zinc (Zn), boron (Bo) molybdenum (Mb) and chlorine (Cl).

For a gardener, the three main types of nutrients to be aware of are nitrogen, phosphorus and potassium. Nitrogen promotes green, leafy growth, phosphorus promotes strong root growth and potassium helps a plant develop its flowers, fruit and colour. This is why commercial fertilisers often give the ratio of NPK, a guide to percentages of the three main nutrients contained within the fertiliser. Some Australian plants are sensitive to phosphorus so avoid adding high-phosphorus products to the soil. The other key nutrients that can cause problems, particularly when acid-loving plants are planted in non-acidic soil, are iron and manganese. A deficiency of these elements causes the leaves to turn yellow between the veins, and the plants often need feeding around the roots to compensate; although if the plant is in the wrong soil, it would actually benefit from being moved into appropriate soil, rather than constantly requiring feeding.

Types of Fertiliser

There are lots of different types of fertilisers to buy, but some of the main types are as follows:

Bulky organic fertilisers

Bulky organic fertilisers such as manure or garden compost don't have as many nutrients as inorganic fertilisers. In fact, very roughly, depending on the quality of the manure, you would need about a ton of it to provide the same amount of nutrients as just 30kg (66lb) of inorganic fertilisers. However, they do improve the soil in other ways, such as providing micronutrients, and they encourage earthworm activity, increase moisture levels and improve soil structure, which increases the plant's root development, enabling it to seek out more nutrients. Green manures are also an effective method for improving the nutrient content of the soil (see page 151).

Organic concentrated fertilisers

These are made from plant or animal extracts. Examples are: bone meal, blood, fish and bone and hoof and horn. They are bought as proprietary mixes and are available from most garden centres. They are effective feeds but are usually more expensive than the inorganic fertilisers. However, they will generally last for longer in the soil.

Inorganic fertilisers

These are also sometimes called synthetic fertilisers and are artificially made up to provide a more concentrated feed than organic ones. They generally provide a much faster feed of macronutrients to the plant, but don't remain in the ground as long. A solution to this is to buy controlled- or slow-release fertiliser, designed to release nutrients gradually throughout the growing season.

How to Apply Fertilisers

The most common method of feeding the soil is to 'broadcast' the fertiliser. To do this on bare soil prior to planting, measure out square metre grids and mark them out using string or bamboo. Measure out the required amount of fertiliser per square metre according to the recommendation on the label. Evenly sprinkle the fertilisers over the square. Do this on a day with not much wind, because otherwise it is difficult to apply.

If plants are already established, scatter the fertiliser around the roots of the plants. This is sometimes called fertiliser placement. Ensure that you don't use more than the recommended amount because this can cause damage to plants and seedlings. Always wear gloves when handling fertiliser and avoid breathing it in. It is usually okay to leave the fertiliser on the surface or very lightly rake it in. However, phosphorus is fairly immobile and proprietary feeds of it may need digging in.

On larger areas, a drop-fertiliser spreader can be used, which spins or broadcasts the feed over the soil at a rate calibrated on the spreader.

• Sprinkling fertiliser granules around the roots is a quick and effective method of feeding plants.

Common Nutrient Deficiencies
Some of the more common deficiencies often need treating with fertilisers to help keep plants healthy.

Problem	Deficiency	Solution
Pale green leaves and poor growth	Nitrogen	Apply a high-nitrogen fertiliser such as sulphate of ammonia or dried blood. Green manures grown in the soil the previous year can also help.
Yellow or brown leaves, particularly at tips and margins	Potassium	Feed with sulphate of potash, tomato feed or high-potash fertiliser.
Poor growth rate and yellow foliage	Phosphate	Feed with bone meal or superphosphate.
Yellowing or browning on leaf margins and between veins, often occurs on acid-loving plants growing in alkaline soil	Manganese and iron	Water with rainwater, not tap water. Mulch around roots with acid mulches, such as rotted pine needles. Feed with sequestered iron.
Distinctive interveinal chlorosis, blotches of yellow and brown	Magnesium	Foliar spray with Epsom salts diluted in water (210g in 10 litres of water).

Liquid feeds

These are usually either powder or liquid concentrates that are diluted in water and used to water the roots of the plants. Tomato feeds are the most common example of this type of feeding. Avoid applying liquid feeds in the rain, as this dilutes them more and nutrients are washed away.

Foliar feeding

This is the quickest way to get nutrients into the plant, as the feed is absorbed directly through the leaves. The most common example is diluting Epsom salts in water and spraying the foliage to treat for magnesium deficiency.

An Introduction to Pruning

There is no mystery to pruning. Much of it, in fact, is just common sense. Is a plant getting too big? Then it needs to be pruned. Has some of it died? Then the dead and damaged parts need to be removed by pruning. By and large, pruning applies to woody plants only: trees, shrubs and climbers. Some herbaceous perennials can also be pruned, for example when old flower heads are cut off to improve the display or prolong flowering (deadheading), but when people talk about pruning, they usually refer to woody plants.

• Flowering plants like this rose can be pruned to improve or prolong flowering.

PRUNING BASICS

The object of pruning is most often to keep a plant to size, or to encourage it to grow in a particular direction (such as against a wall) or into a pleasing shape. Dead, diseased, damaged and crossing growth may also need to be removed from time to time to keep a plant healthy. Pruning is achieved by carefully selecting the parts that need to be removed, then removing them cleanly with a sharp pair of secateurs or a pruning saw.

• Secateurs (above) and pruning saw (left).

How to Cut

Prune at a 45-degree angle, just above a bud.

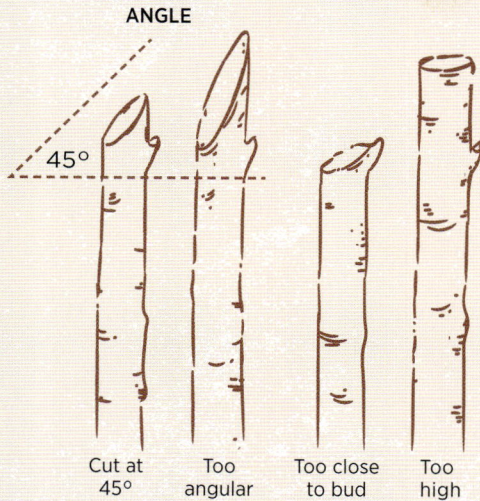

ANGLE

45°

Cut at 45° | Too angular | Too close to bud | Too high

Correct Usage

When using secateurs, keep the blade on top and the hook below.

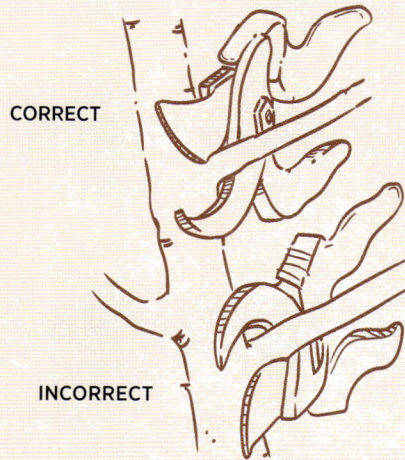

CORRECT

INCORRECT

When to Prune

It is always a good idea to have a pair of secateurs in your pocket when working in the garden, since growth often needs cutting back here and there to keep plants looking tidy and remove any wayward shoots that might be blocking paths or obscuring views. The best results are achieved where the gardener has shown restraint, saving major pruning work for only when it is necessary. Pruning is carried out any time of year, depending on the type of plant, but the predominant two seasons are winter (when the plant is dormant) and a lighter prune in summer to remove excess growth.

Winter: Heavy pruning work is usually left to late winter. At this time, deciduous (those that shed leaves annually) trees and shrubs are laid bare and their branch structure is much more evident. New growth in spring will soon soften any hard cuts, so recovery times are faster. The aim of pruning at this time is to control plants that are outgrowing their positions and to maintain an open network of healthy stems and branches that do not cross or rub.

Summer: Pruning jobs are usually kept relatively light in summer, although you may find yourself doing a lot of clipping and shearing just to keep pace with the rate of growth. Hedges will need trimming, roses deadheading, topiary clipping and wayward growth snipping off as and when. Light and often is the mantra.

Flowering Shrubs

Left to their own devices, shrubs will soon outgrow their allotted space. The rule with flowering shrubs is to clip or trim them right after they have finished flowering, every year. In this manner, they will never need severe pruning (which might disfigure them) and they will have a whole year in which to recover and prepare themselves for the next display. Pruned too soon before flowering, you are likely to remove all the developing flower buds.

Pruning Evergreens

Evergreens provide wonderful all-year-round interest in the garden. Some can be trimmed into elaborate topiary shapes, while others provide effective screening from neighbours or to hide eyesores such as compost bins or stark-looking fences.

Fortunately, most evergreen shrubs can look after themselves perfectly well and require minimal pruning in order to show off their beautiful shape and foliage. There are exceptions such as topiary, which requires tight clipping with a pair of hedging shears or a hedge trimmer a few times a year to keep it in shape. Some of the more vigorous evergreen hedges may also need pruning to keep their growth habit under control, such as the popular and infamous leylandii (*Cupressus* x *leylandii*). But by and large, evergreen shrubs don't need the same amount of pruning as deciduous or fruiting trees. This is partly because evergreens are grown essentially for their foliage and so don't require the hard pruning that encourages an elaborate display of flowers and fruit. Most evergreen shrubs require pruning if they have lost their shape, have some diseased material that needs removing, or have outgrown their space.

When to Prune?

In mild areas, where there is little likelihood of frost, evergreens can be pruned at most times of year. However, for those areas that are susceptible to frost the most effective time to prune evergreens is in spring after the risk of cold snaps has past. This gives the shrub time to recover and regrow and the wood to ripen before the risk of the young growth being damaged by frosts in the following autumn.

Pruning Lavender

Lavender is one of the most popular evergreen shrubs but it will quickly become leggy if it isn't pruned and kept in shape. Traditionally, lavender is cut twice a year. The first time is after flowering, which is a very light pruning just removing the flower heads. The theory is that there is still enough foliage to protect the centre of the plant from cold temperatures in winter. The second prune is slightly harder and this is done in springtime, cutting into the foliage from the previous year, ensuring that the plant is kept tidy and compact. Avoid cutting into the older wood as it doesn't always regenerate.

• Prune lavender once after flowering and once in spring to ensure it stays compact and looking good.

Pruning Topiary

Topiary works best when starting a plant from a very young age. It is possible to train a mature shrub, but it isn't always as effective and some shrubs don't react well to the harder cuts that have to be made to get the shape started. The best way to start with a young shrub is to use a template, such as a sphere or pyramid. Place the structure over the plant and use a pair of shears to gradually shape the bush. This can be done at almot any time of the year in Australia. Most topiary will need light trimming a few times a year to keep it looking neat and tidy. The most commonly used plants for topiary are box (*Buxus sempervirens*) and, in terms of native plants, *Westringia fruticosa* and *Correa alba*.

• Regular clipping of topiary will help to ensure it retains its shape and density and that its foliage looks healthy.

HARD PRUNING

If necessary, many evergreens will tolerate hard pruning. An example is camellia, where old mature stems can be cut back hard to about 70cm above ground level after flowering to establish new fresh shoots. Other evergreen shrubs that tolerate hard pruning include *Aucuba japonica, Choisya ternata, Ligustrum japonicum, Sarcococca humilis* and *Viburnum tinus*.

Pruning Deciduous Shrubs and Trees

There are numerous reasons for pruning a tree or shrub, depending on what you are hoping to achieve. The end goal will determine what technique is used to prune them. Sometimes it could be for foliage effect, other times it could be for winter stem colour, or to encourage more flowers or fruit. Sometimes it is just to reshape it or to remove diseased material.

• Flowering quince (*Chaenomeles*) are often pruned as fans against walls to provide an early spring floral display.

When to Prune?

Most deciduous trees and shrubs are pruned when they are dormant, from late autumn through until late spring. This is partly because it is easier to see where the branches are, as the leaves are no longer on the tree, revealing the shape and bare bones of the tree or shrub structure. Also, pruning when the plant is dormant makes it less likely that it will 'bleed' sap, which can weaken some plants. There are exceptions, though: for example, trees from the *Prunus* family, such as flowering cherries, should only be pruned when in leaf to avoid infection from bacterial canker and silver leaf from their open pruning cuts, which can't heal over quickly during winter. Some partly tender shrubs, such as hydrangeas or figs, may also suffer if pruned in winter and it is best to leave their branches to provide protection until they start growing in spring. One of the main reasons for pruning deciduous shrubs is to encourage more flowers. In order to do this, some deciduous shrubs are pruned just after flowering to give them as much time as possible to build up strength and enable them to

• Early flowering deciduous shrubs, such as this mock orange (*Philadelphus coronarius*) will benefit from being pruned after they have flowered.

go on to produce more flower buds the following year. Finally, for those who don't like pruning, there are a number of shrubs that don't really require any pruning at all.

Early Flowering Deciduous Shrubs

Early flowering shrubs such as *Chaenomeles*, *Forsythia*, *Philadelphus*, *Deutzia*, *Syringa* and *Weigela* produce most of their flowers on the younger wood produced in previous years. To encourage more flowers on these types of shrubs, it is best to prune them after flowering, as this will encourage lots more shoots further down the bush, which will ensure the shrub is well covered with flowers. Without this regular pruning, the shrubs quickly become congested with twiggy growth, with the bulk of the flowers appearing in the top tips of the plant.

Use a pruning saw and remove some of the older, thicker stems from near the base of the plant. Remove some of the other stems that have previously flowered, using secateurs to cut them back further down the plant. This should encourage new laterals to form, which will eventually produce flowers.

• *Forsythia* is a popular springtime shrub with lots of young shoots covered in bright yellow flowers.

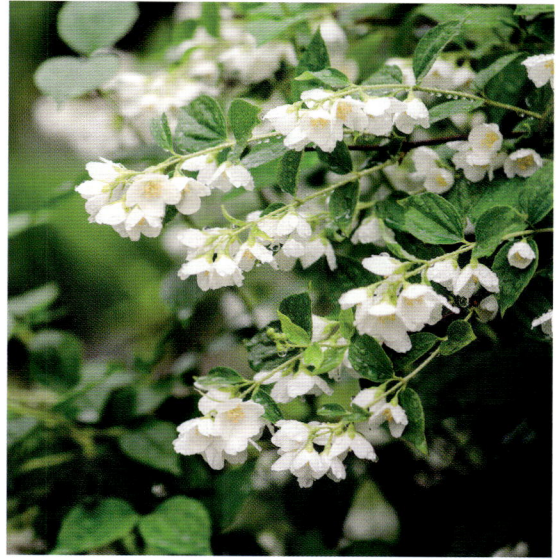

PRUNING HYDRANGEAS

• *Hydrangea marcrophylla*

There are two different types of *Hydrangea macrophylla*: lacecaps and mopheads, but they are pruned in exactly the same way. Their flower heads should be left on over winter to give them extra protection from the cold weather.

In early spring, just as the buds are starting to swell, prune back last year's stems to a pair of buds about 15cm below the old flower head. If the plant is starting to get leggy, it can be cut back further to encourage a bushier plant the following year.

• Lacecap hydrangeas should be pruned once a year in early spring.

• *Hydrangea paniculata*

This can produce huge panicles of flower stems in late summer if pruned correctly. It can look very effective at the back of a mixed border, or even as a low avenue lining a path. Their flower heads remain impressive-looking throughout the winter. To achieve this effect, the new growth should be pruned back to the second pair of buds on the stem. This will encourage the plant to make lots of growth in the year and will send out a huge flower spike towards mid to late summer.

• Prune hydrangeas in early spring to maximise the amount of flowers that will be produced later in the season.

Mid- to Late-flowering Deciduous Shrubs

Most shrubs that flower later on in the year do so on wood or shoots produced in the same year. Shrubs include *Buddleja davidii, Ceratostigma willmottianum, Cotinus*, hardy fuchsia, hydrangea, perovskia and *Hibiscus syriacus*. These shrubs are best pruned in springtime. Remove some of the older wood with loppers towards the base of the plant to maintain an open habit. Then prune some of the new growth made the previous year, back to two or three buds, towards the older wood. This will encourage the shrub to produce lots of new laterals with lots of flowers in the current year.

Shrubs that Require Practically No Pruning

There are some shrubs that require hardly any pruning at all. This is mainly due to their growth habit and the fact that they freely produce flowers without much intervention from gardeners. Some of these include *Amelanchier, Chimonanthus, Daphne* and deciduous viburnums.

Pruning for Winter Stem Colour

Sometimes shrubs aren't pruned for their impressive flowers at all. Instead, they are pruned for their brightly coloured stems. The most popular type of shrub for this treatment is dogwood (*Cornus*).

In order to produce this colourful effect, use a pair of secateurs to cut all the growth down to a few centimetres above the ground. This should be done in March, just as the plants are coming into leaf. This provides the maximum amount of time to enjoy these colourful stems when they are denuded of their foliage. Suitable plants with colourful stems include *Salix alba* var. *vitellina*, *Cornus sanguinea* 'Midwinter Fire', *Cornus alba* 'Sibirica' and *Rubus cockburnianus.*

Pruning for Foliage

It is possible to prune plants to enjoy their foliage rather than their flowers. The technique, known as coppicing, is very similar to pruning for winter colour, whereby stems are cut down to near the ground. However, shrubs are usually cut back in autumn or spring. Popular plants to coppice for their foliage effect include *Eucalyptus pulverulenta*, *Paulownia tomentosa* and *Catalpa bignonioides*, which produce massive leaves when cut hard, though the payback is that they don't produce their impressive flowers in the same year. These plants are often used at the back of a wide border to create a striking backdrop and a splash of colour. Other shrubs that can be treated in a similar way include *Cotinus coggygria* and some eucalypts. Experiments into the sucess of coppicing a broader range of Australian plants are currently being conducted.

• Some dogwoods (*Cornus*) produce brightly coloured stems in winter. Prune back hard in early spring.

Pruning Climbers

A climber is basically any sort of plant that requires support to grow upwards. Some have tendrils to help them scramble up walls, fences and trees, others have more of a sprawling habit and need propping up and tying in to trellis or a system of wires for support. Whatever method they use for climbing, it is important to understand their growth habit when it comes to pruning them.

How to Prune and Train a Grapevine

Grapevines are one of the most popular types of climber in a garden. Choose a wine grape as opposed to a dessert grape if you are growing it outside, as the grapes should ripen enough to make some wine from. Grapevines can be trained up and over pergolas or arches, or on a system of wires stretched between two upright posts. Some varieties are chosen for their large ornamental leaves and beautiful autumn colour, such as *Vitis* 'Brandt' and *Vitis coignetiae*.

• Plant a grapevine on either side of the arch.
• Tie in their stems or trunks.
• Prune the new growth of the laterals (side branches) back to two buds.
• As the plants grow during summer, prune their new growth back to three or four leaves past any bunches of grapes.
• Harvest the grapes in autumn.
• The following winter, prune the growth made the previous year back to two buds. Continue to tie the leading shoot up the arch as it grows until it has reached the centre of the arch. Over the years, it may be necessary to thin out some of the spurs built up from cutting back the laterals each year.

• Grapevines are often pruned twice a year to keep them in shape and encourage them to produce lots of bunches of grapes.

• Prune wisteria twice a year to provide masses of impressive racemes of blue, white or pink flowers. Another important reason to prune wisteria is to keep it within bounds

How to Prune Wisteria

Wisterias are another very popular climber. They are vigorous climbers and therefore need pruning twice a year. The first time they should be pruned is just after flowering, when the new growth they have made needs cutting back to five leaves.

The second prune is in winter, when the new growth made the previous year is cut back to two buds. Any dense clusters of spurs can be thinned out, and any excess growth can be removed to leave a tidy framework of central stems with short laterals coming off them.

How to Prune Clematis

Given the right climate clematis is a varied and versatile plant that is divided into three categories and this affects how they are pruned.

- The first group (Pruning Group 1) are spring-flowering, such as *C. Montana*, *C. alpina*, *C. macropetala* and produce flowers on the previous year's growth. They often don't need any pruning at all and when it is required it is quite simple – after flowering, remove any diseased branches and cut the plant back to fit the designated space. These clematis are usually just given a light trim to keep them looking tidy, although they can be cut back much harder, but you may forgo flowers the following year.

- The second group (Pruning Group 2) are the large flowering, early summer types that flower on both old and new growth and that include *C. florida* and its hybrids and *C. patens* and its hybrids. Their main flowering time is in early summer, producing their large blooms on wood produced the previous year. They often produce a second flush of flowers on new growth later on in the year. This group of clematis is pruned twice. The first is in spring, prior to flowering, and is light to avoid damaging any potential blooms, just removing any dead or diseased material and generally giving it a tidy up. The second is carried out after flowering and is more robust than the earlier prune. It is a form of renewal pruning, whereby some of the older material is removed to encourage new growth with flower buds on. The remaining growth is tied in and can be trimmed to keep it tidy.

- The third group flower, which includes the *C. viticella* group from southern Europe, flower from late spring to through to autumn, blooming on stems produced in the same year. Pruning these clematis couldn't be simpler – you cut them down to near ground level in late winter or early spring and let them produce new flowering shoots for the new season. They can also be cut back to about 30cm after their first flush of flowering to encourage more blooms.

Formative Pruning of Trees

Most deciduous trees require a bit of shaping in their formative years to make them into attractive garden features later on in life. Formative pruning is carried out on trees or shrubs in their first few years to ensure they develop into the right shape, and are neither too spindly nor cluttered with lots of weak branches. The ultimate goal is to have a clear trunk and branches that are well spaced. There are three basic shapes when looking to do some formative pruning: centre leader, open centre and multi-stemmed. There are two different types of sapling: a feathered maiden, which means a one-year-old tree with branches coming off the main stem (the feathers), or a maiden whip, a one-year-old tree that has produced no laterals.

• Prune trees from a young age so they form a good shape with their branches and are able to show off their prime features, such as the stunning bark of this ornamental cherry (*Prunus serrula*).

A tree with a centre leader will have one dominant trunk (or leader) and well-spaced branches beneath it. There is usually space between the ground and the first tier of branches (the crown), which makes a tree look visually more appealing and shows off the trunk to the effect. This is particularly useful on ornamental trees with attractive trunks, including *Prunus serrula*, *Betula utilis* var. *jacquemontii* and snakebark maples such as *Acer davidii*. However, having a clear stem is also useful for fruit trees to prevent the crop lying on the ground when burdened with the weight of fruit, and it also makes mowing and maintenance around the base of trees easier. Most deciduous trees should be pruned just after planting, although if the tree is planted in summer, it may be better to wait until it goes dormant in winter so as not to cause it too much stress. If you are pruning an evergreen tree, this is best done in early spring just as it is coming into growth.

Centre Leader

To prune a feathered tree as a centre leader tree, you should remove any branches coming off the lower section of the main stem, below about 50cm from the ground. Then select four or five healthy branches that are spaced out as evenly as possible around the trunk and between each other and remove any others. This is to prevent the crown being too congested. A congested canopy not only looks ugly, but is prone to a build-up of pests and diseases when it comes into leaf. Prune back any laterals coming off these main branches to a couple of buds if the area still looks too congested. Avoid cutting the leader as this will spoil the overall shape of the tree.

Open Centre

To create an open centre tree, prune as above, but remove the central leader or trunk back to the highest branch or lateral. This will then create a desired 'goblet' shape. Cut back the leaders on the laterals by about a third to outward-facing buds. Remove any branches that look like they will start to crowd the centre of the tree.

To create an open centre tree if you have a maiden whip, and therefore no laterals, prune back the central trunk to about 75cm above the ground to encourage laterals to form. The following year, follow the steps above for pruning a feathered tree.

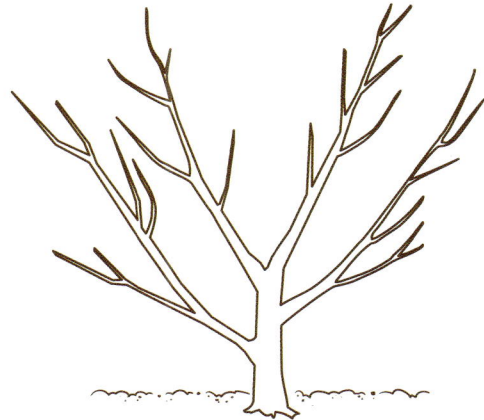

Multi-stemmed

Finally, some trees are grown as multi-stems, which consist of a few stems coming off the same base. To achieve this, the trunk is cut closer to the ground to encourage fresh shoots to grow upwards. The following year, the strongest three or four shoots should be selected and the remaining shoots removed. Popular examples of multi-stemmed trees would include *Betula utilis*, *Eucalyptus gunnii* and *Acer griseum.*

Renovation Pruning

Plants sometimes outgrow their space or just develop into something unwieldy and unmanageable in the garden. This is when it may be necessary to carry out some renovation pruning to try to correct their shape. At other times, you may wish to do renovation pruning because a fruit tree has stopped being productive and you want to get it back into production again.

With regards to fruit trees, there is an old gardening saying that branches should be spaced out enough for a pigeon to fly through the canopy in winter without it hitting a branch. This, of course, suggests that a well-managed tree should have plenty of space between its branches, allowing sunlight and air to circulate and reach the whole canopy. In trees that haven't been regularly pruned or managed, this is very often not the case and instead there is a congested mass of branches all running into each other, with too much shade within the canopy.

The restoration of an over-congested tree should take place over two to three years. Don't attempt to bring back a tree to its former shape and glory within one pruning session. Have patience, because otherwise the tree may either die from shock, or react by sending out even more vigorous growth after pruning, which will only exacerbate the congestion problem.

• Old trees, such as this pear, should be pruned gradually over a few years to re-shape and remove the dead and dying wood.

The restoration of most trees, particularly apple trees, should be carried out in winter, when the plant is dormant and it is easier to see the structure of the tree without its leaves on. Avoid pruning slightly tender trees and species of *Prunus* in winter; instead, prune once they are in growth.

Restoration Pruning Method
• Firstly, look at the canopy and remove any dead, diseased or damaged branches (known as the three 'D's in the world of pruning). In a really congested canopy there will probably be a lot of diseased and dead material, and it may be necessary to sterilise your secateurs before starting to prune the healthier parts of the tree to avoid spreading any infection.

• After removing the three 'D's, use secateurs to remove water shoots – the wispy shoots often growing off the main trunk. Again, these prevent air circulation, creating a build-up of diseases or pests in the canopy, and take essential nutrients from the tree without providing fruit or flowers.
• Next, look into the canopy and remove as many of the crossing branches as you can, so that the remaining branches have plenty of space and air around them. To remove large branches, it may be necessary to do a three-step cut using a pruning saw (see box below).
• Finally, use secateurs to thin out any clusters of spurs. Repeat this process over the next few years to bring the tree back into production and make it look more attractive.

THREE-STEP PRUNING CUT

Use a pruning saw to remove large branches off a tree as follows:

1 Take the weight off the branch by removing most of it before making the final cut near the trunk. If the weight isn't removed, the branch can tear back into the trunk. Make a cut on the top section of the branch about 20cm away from the trunk. Cut about a third of the way into the branch.

2 Make an undercut, a few centimetres closer to the trunk. Cut upwards into the branch and as the blade comes near the top cut the branch will fall away, usually making a clear-sounding snap.

3 Make the final cut near the trunk, removing the final stump of the branch. Cut downwards, using your spare hand to support the weight of the remainder of the branch. Avoid cutting flush with the trunk but leave a slight collar for the branch to heal over.

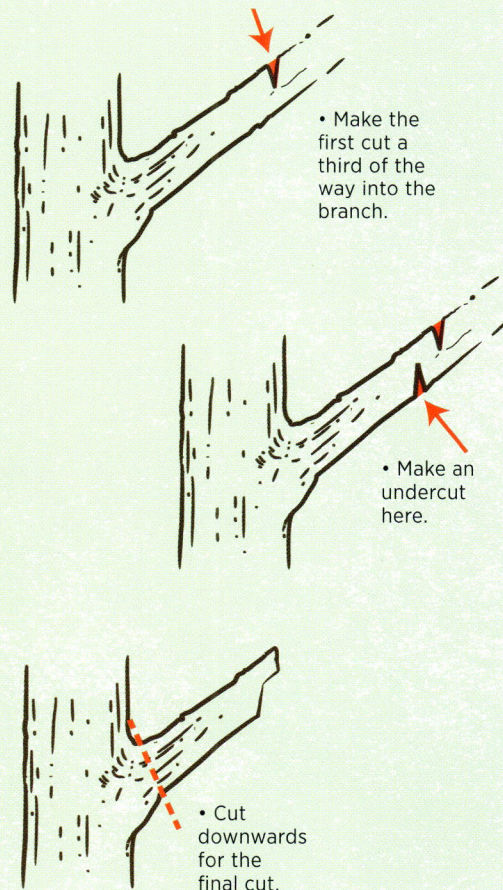

• Make the first cut a third of the way into the branch.

• Make an undercut here.

• Cut downwards for the final cut.

Hedge Care

Hedges are wonderful barriers for defining boundaries from neighbours, or even screening an eyesore in your own garden. They're also great for encouraging wildlife. In terms of pruning, nothing could be simpler. Most of the time, you just need to be able to cut in a straight line.

Hedge-pruning Tools

There are a few tools that you will need to make your job much easier. These include the following:

Hedge cutter

These are usually electric or petrol-powered, but battery-powered ones that are charged up prior to use are becoming increasingly popular. Solar-powered battery ones are the most environmentally friendly. Electric ones are the lightest because there is no battery or fuel tank, but do make sure that the cable is safely out of the way before starting to trim the hedge. The cutting bar on a hedge trimmer helps to get a really straight line when pruning a hedge.

Ladder or scaffold tower

If your hedge is over shoulder height, you will need a ladder or ideally a scaffold tower to cut the top. Whichever you use, always ensure it is secure and you are set up on a level or flat surface. Never overstretch, but instead regularly climb down and move the ladder or tower along.

Hedging shears

Use these for pruning smaller hedges. Always keep them sharp, and they may need regular tightening in the centre to ensure the blades run smoothly against each other.

Secateurs

Don't use these for trimming the entire hedge, but they can be used for cutting back the occasional stray stem or branch. Some gardeners advocate that large-leaved evergreen hedges, such as laurel and *Aucuba*, should only be pruned with secateurs, because shears and hedge cutters slice through the leaves, making them look ragged and untidy, but realistically this would depend on how much time is available and the size of the hedge.

• Garden shears can be used for pruning smaller hedges and clipping shrubs into more intricate shapes such as topiary.

• Hedge cutters are the most effective and efficient method of keeping a large hedge in shape.

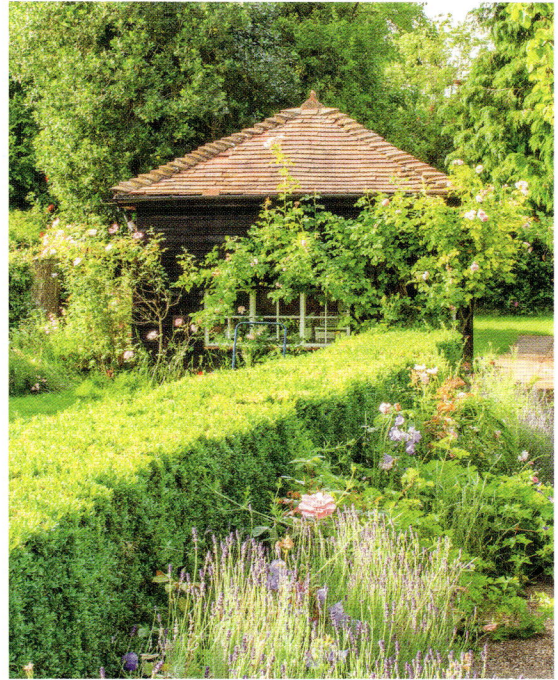

• Hedges can be used as an attractive standalone feature in a garden or as a natural backdrop to more elaborate planting schemes.

WHEN TO TRIM

Most hedges should be pruned once a year, but faster-growing species, or formal hedges and topiary, will require at least two clippings per annum. The usual time for the yearly clipping of hedges, where just the new growth is trimmed back, is in spring or late summer, but restoration work requiring cutting back into older branches is more commonly done when the plant is dormant during winter. The timings for trimming some of the most popular hedges are as follows:

Box Late spring, after frost
Leyland cypress Spring and late summer
Lilly pillies Late winter or in cool climates wait until danger of frost has past
Murraya paniculata Spring, summer and autumn
Photinia Spring to autumn
Privet Spring and late summer

Hedge-trimming Tips

To cut the sides of the hedge, stand at 90 degrees to the hedge so you are looking down the length of it. This helps you to get a straight line and see where you are cutting. Using a hedge cutter, move the cutting bar up and down the hedge, keeping it as flat and straight as possible and removing the excess young growth.

Getting the top of a hedge straight is a bit of an acquired skill. If you aren't confident, stretch string between two posts as a guideline to ensure that one end of the hedge will be the same height as the other.

Most hedges have a square-cut top, at 90 degrees to the sides, but some gardeners prefer to cut it at an angle with a slope of about 45 degrees as this allows more sunlight further down the hedge, preventing it from thinning or dying back in the shade. The slope also makes it harder for snow to settle on top of the hedge, which can cause branches to snap.

Rose Care

Roses are the quintessential flowering plant for the traditional cottage or English garden. Most of them provide exquisite blooms and gorgeous scent and many of them repeat-flower throughout the growing season. Yet despite their popularity, there always seems to be an air of mystery to the pruning and care of them. However, it really is quite easy once you have mastered the basic principles.

• Floribunda roses such as this 'Guy de Maupassant' produce clusters of flowers in midsummer.

Roses should be deadheaded regularly to encourage more flowers to appear. The theory is that if the deadheads are left on, the plant thinks it has done enough to set seed and starts to prepare for dormancy. If the seeds are removed, the plant is triggered into producing more flowers.

Roses should also be regularly mulched with organic matter such as garden compost or manure, spread around their roots to a depth of 5cm. This helps to suppress any competing weeds and also retains moisture. It will eventually rot down into the soil, improving the soil quality and nourishing the rose bush with macro- and micronutrients.

Tie in new shoots of climbing roses in October before the autumn and winter gales have a chance to damage them.

Rose Pruning

Roses need pruning once or twice a year, and how this is done depends on what type of rose it is.

Bush roses

The most popular type of rose is the modern bush type, divided up into hybrid tea roses, which produce the massive singular blooms, and floribunda, which produce clusters of blooms.

- After planting, both types should be pruned back hard to 10–15cm above the ground. This encourages vigorous growth that will provide the strong, spaced framework for flowers for subsequent years.
- In the following years, cut away all wispy growth then cut back the remaining healthy stems to between a half and two-thirds of their length.
- Always cut back to outward-facing buds to encourage an open, pruned bush and not a congested, closed canopy.
- In exposed areas, gardeners often prune twice – lightly in early autumn to reduce the risk of wind rock, then harder in early spring as described above.

• Roses (such as this climbing rose) will benefit from being deadheaded as the flowers fade, to encourage more blooms to develop.

Shrub roses

There are lots of different types of shrub rose, from the very popular and vigorous 'Graham Thomas', with its golden blooms, to the attractive hybrid musk types such as 'Cornelia' and 'Buff Beauty'. Their habits can vary enormously, from arching stems to vigorous upright growth, and generally all that is needed each year is to tip-prune the growth on the new stems.

• On older plants, it may also be necessary to remove or cut back hard some of the older wood to encourage new flowering stems.
• If the shrub isn't as vigorous as it should be, the new growth can be cut back harder to about one third of its length.
• As with most roses, always prune back to an outward-facing bud. A good rule of thumb is 'prune hard for quality of flowers, prune light for quantity of flowers'.
• Prune in late winter or early spring.

• Shrub roses often have an attractive arching habit. Pruning consists of removing some of the older stems in early spring.

Climbers

• New shoots should be trained onto walls, posts or trellis and held in place with garden twine.
• Some of the shorter side shoots, which may have flowered in the previous year, can be pruned back to a couple of buds.
• If the rose climber is particularly congested, some of the older wood should be removed using loppers or a saw. This will encourage new growth and therefore more flowers further down the stem, giving better coverage overall.
• Prune in late winter or early spring.

Lawn Care

A beautiful lawn can not only provide an attractive yet neutral background to magnificent borders and specimen trees, it can also be a focal point and feature in its own right. Often lawns are the centrepiece in the garden, with the beds and other garden features placed around them, so it is worth spending extra time and effort in making sure the lawn is looking good.

Not everybody requires a perfectly manicured lawn with dead straight lines running up and down them, but if the lawn isn't maintained at all it can quickly turn into a threadbare patch of grass or even a muddy quagmire. Spending a bit of time caring for your lawn can make all the difference between it being a thing of beauty or something to be ashamed of. The number one maintenance job on a lawn is cutting the grass.

Aside from mowing, there are other lawn maintenance jobs that can be done to make your lawn look really green and healthy. These include scarifying the lawn, aerating it and adding top dressing. These jobs are often carried out as part of autumn lawn maintenance programmes

•The most common type of mower has rotary blades.

but in fact can be carried out at most times of the year, except in extreme weather conditions such as droughts or when very cold or wet.

Lawn Mowers
There are numerous different mowers available. Most of the bigger machines for larger gardens are driven by petrol, but there are electric or battery-powered versions too.

Rotary mower
These have blades underneath the mower that rotate a bit like helicopter rotors, cutting the tips as the mower is pushed across the grass. Some rotary mowers have a roller on the back, and this is necessary if you want stripes on the lawn. Some rotary mowers are self-propelled, while others need to be pushed. Hover mowers are also a type of rotary mower but they 'float' over the grass on a cushion or vacuum of air, making moving it easy, although of course you won't get any stripes with this type of mower. For larger areas of lawn, a ride-on rotary mower can be used. Again, some have a roller for stripes, while others just cut the grass.

Mulch mowers
These are similar to rotary mowers, but rather than spinning the clippings into a box at the back or straight back on the lawn, they chop them up into tiny pieces before dropping them back on the lawn. This is useful for replenishing the lawn with natural fertiliser, because the lawn clippings are rich in nitrogen.

• Cylinder mowers will give a finer finish than rotary mowers but require more maintenance and are more expensive.

Cylinder mowers

Considered to be the Rolls Royce in the world of mowers, these have blades that spin on a horizontal cylinder that cut down on the blades of grass, cutting between these rotating blades and a fixed blade on the machine. It is possible to get very low cuts with a cylinder mower. They're used for 'fine' lawns, bowling greens, cricket wickets, croquet lawns, etc. They also have rollers on the back to provide stripes. It is possible to purchase traditional push cylinder mowers, which are a good environmentally friendly alternative to a powered mower, but a certain level of fitness is required to operate one on large lawns. It is also possible to get ride-on cylinder mowers, but these are very expensive.

• For gardeners who like to be fossil-fuel free, an old-fashioned push cylinder mower is a good option.

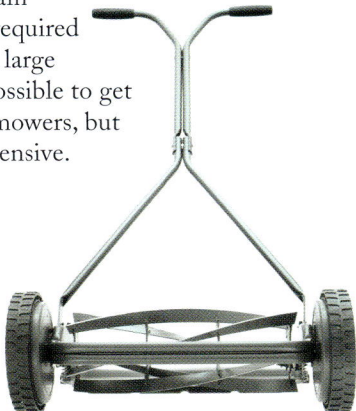

Strimmers and brushcutters

These are used to cut the grass up against posts or fence lines and reach places that the mower isn't able to cut. There are petrol, electric or battery versions. Avoid strimming too closely around trees, though, because if the string catches the bark it can cause serious damage to the tree.

• Brush cutters or strimmers are used for cutting long grass. They either have cutting blades or cord.

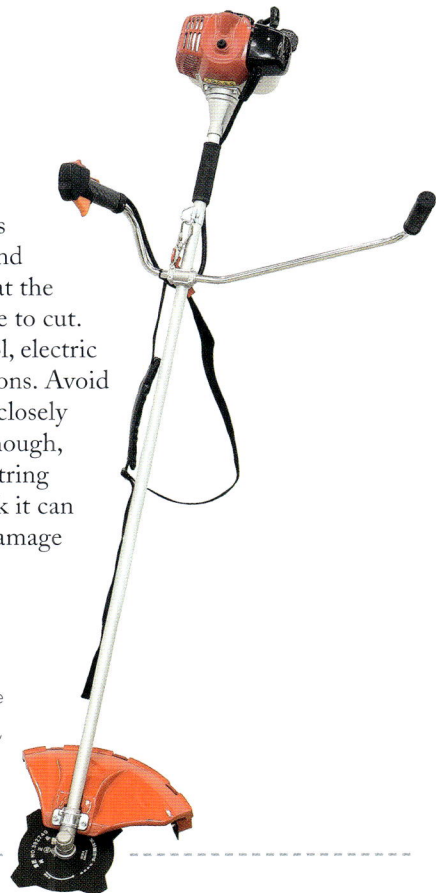

HOW TO MOW

On good-quality lawns, mowing is needed as often as two or three times a week during the growing season, but the reality for most people is cutting it once every two weeks to keep it looking neat and tidy.

1 Start by mowing the tops and the bottoms of the lawn, with two stripes at each end.

2 Next, start to mow up and down the longer edges of the lawn, ensuring that the mower just cuts up to the edge of where the previous line was cut. The best technique for producing straight lines is to look ahead of you at the lines, rather than down at the mower.

3 Once the lines have been cut, you can either finish in the corner (as in the diagram) or for true perfection, do finishing lines by repeating step one and cutting the tops and bottoms of the lawn again going across to produce two stripes at either end.

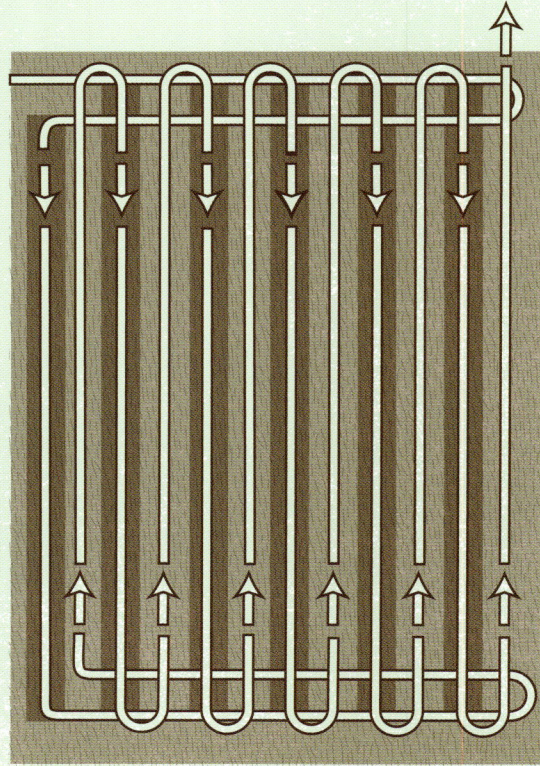

Mowing Tips:
- Mowing can be carried out all year round when the grass is growing, but it is usually done from early spring to late autumn.
- Raise the height of the mower for its first few cuts, before lowering it to the desired height for the remainder of the season.
- If there is a drought, then it is best either to a void cutting the grass altogether, as mowing can cause further stress to it, or to raise the height of the mower back up to cause it less stress.
- To produce strips you will need a mower with a roller.

Edging the Lawn
Use edging shears to trim the edges of the lawn once it has been cut. Don't edge before mowing, because the roller on the mower will push blades of grass out sideways, meaning you'll need to edge again anyway. Edging shears operate like a pair of scissors, so try keeping one arm still while the other arm operates the cutting blade to move it up and down. Keep the shears as upright or vertical as possible. If the edges of the lawn are no longer sharp, use a string line to work out where the edge should be cut, then use a half-moon to cut away sections of turf to restore the edge. When cutting a straight line, standing on a plank of wood will help

• Edging shears can be used to trim the edge of the lawn.

by providing a sturdy platform as well as a guide to forming the straight line. When cutting curves in a lawn, use a hosepipe as a guide to create the shape you want.

Scarifying

Scarifying is a process usually carried out in autumn, although some greenkeepers do it a few times a year, to remove thatch from the surface of the lawn. Thatch is all the dead pieces of grass and other organic rubbish, such as leaf litter, that accumulate at the base of the blades. If they're not removed, they can eventually smother the lawn and prevent rain from penetrating down to the roots, making them susceptible to drought. Thatch can also stop the air circulating around the roots, which can cause fungal problems. There are machines

• Scarifiers are used for removing the thatch in the grass, which will result in a better and healthier lawn.

for scarifying, but most gardeners use a spring-tine rake and scratch vigorously at the surface of the lawn. It is amazing how much thatch will be removed. Work across the lawn in one direction and then in the opposite direction to remove as much of the thatch as possible. The process does look brutal, but as the phrase goes, 'sometimes you have to be cruel to be kind', and the lawn will quickly recover and look much better for it in the long term.

Aeration and Top Dressing

This is another process usually carried out during autumn, although it can be done at other times in the year. Aeration involves pushing spikes into the lawn to break up the compaction, improve drainage and allow the air to circulate into the roots of the grass. There are aeration machines that can be useful on large areas, but a fork pushed into the ground to a depth of about 10cm is just as good. There is a similar process called hollow tining, and this involves pushing in hollow spikes that, as they are pulled out again, remove cores of soil. Top dressing can then be brushed into the holes, which improves the quality of the soil just below the lawn. Top dressing can be bought from garden centres or made by mixing 40 per cent sand, 40 per cent loam and 20 per cent organic matter, such as garden compost.

OTHER LAWN MAINTENANCE JOBS

Lawns will need irrigating in summer to keep the grass looking green. Some greenkeepers like to verti-cut their lawns, too, which is similar to mowing except that the tillers or side shoots of the grass blades are cut, rather than the tips, to encourage a thicker sward. If the grass is looking yellow, it may be necessary to feed it with a fertiliser. Use a high-nitrogen feed in spring to help it with its first flush of green growth and then later, in summer and autumn, feed with something higher in potassium and phosphorus to toughen the grass before it reaches the coldness of winter.

Container Care and Potting

Almost any plant can be grown in a container. The beauty of growing plants in this way is that they hardly take up any space, which is ideal if you only have a small courtyard, balcony or roof garden. It also means that if you move house, you can take your plants with you. However, plants in pots need more care and attention than those growing in the ground.

Watering

The main requirements for plants in containers are regular watering and feeding. Because their roots are restricted, they aren't able to send out roots in search of extra moisture in dry weather. They are therefore very much dependent on gardeners or their owners to keep them hydrated. In dry periods this could mean watering them as often as twice a day. Ideally, they should be watered either in the morning or the evening because the water will evaporate much faster in the middle of the day. Irrigation systems are available to help save time on watering (see page 90), and if you have lots of containers it is worth harvesting rainwater, rather than having to rely on the mains system.

WINTER CARE

In cool climate zones in Australia and New Zealand some tender plants will need to be put away in a greenhouse, shed or porch over winter. Keep an eye on them during the winter months to ensure the compost doesn't dry out completely, but don't water unless necessary because there is a risk the plant will start to rot. Bring containers outside again in summer as soon as the risk of frost is over.

• Plants in containers will often need watering once a day during the growing season and sometimes even more on hot days.

To help with drainage, there should be holes in the bottom of the container, and it should also be stood either on container 'feet' or on bricks/blocks so that water can drain away freely.

Care for Annuals

Apart from watering, annual flowers and bedding plants require very little maintenance. It may be necessary to give them a liquid feed once a week to help maintain their vitality and colour. A tomato feed is ideal as it is rich in potassium, which helps boost a plant's flowering and their colour intensity. Deadheading the flowers as they fade will extend their period of flowering.

CARE FOR PERENNIALS

Perennial plants, shrubs and trees have the same maintenance requirements as mentioned above but there are some additional maintenance jobs. The main one is to repot them every couple of years, because the compost in the container becomes old and deficient of any nutrients or goodness. The best time to repot is in autumn.

1. Gently pull the plant out of its pot and tip away the old compost.

2. Remove the drainage crocks and wash out the inside of the pot, using a scrubbing brush to remove any potential pests or their eggs.

3. Herbaceous perennials will probably need dividing, discarding the centre and then replanting two or three sections from the outer part of the original plant. Trees and shrubs will almost certainly be very pot-bound, with roots wrapped tightly around the root ball.

4. Use a knife to cut away up to a third of the roots to prevent the tree from strangling itself. This will encourage the plant to put out fresh roots in the new season.

5. Fill the container with new potting compost (or whichever type of compost you used previously) and repot the plant, ensuring that it is firmly in the compost, just below the top of the container.

6. Water the plant thoroughly after planting. Alternatively, you could pot it up into a larger pot if you want a larger plant, as long as you are happy with the extra space and weight if you regularly move it.

In the years when you're not repotting your plants, they will benefit from a top dressing of compost on the surface of the roots.

Overwintering

Depending on where you live, there is a chance that some of the more tender plants in the garden will need protection during the colder months of the year. A gardener will often listen regularly to weather forecasts to hear if cold spells or frosts are predicted and, if so, take action to safeguard any vulnerable plants.

There are numerous slightly tender plants that could need protection if left outside over winter. And it's not always the obvious plants such as bananas, palm trees and tree ferns. Dahlias, for example, are one of the most popular garden plants and yet, depending on where you live in the country, they will probably need protection over the winter months.

• Depending on where you live, dahlias may need lifting out of the ground in autumn and storing before planting out again in spring.

OVERWINTERING DAHLIAS

In heavy clay dahlias should be brought indoors over winter to prevent them from rotting.

1 As the foliage starts to fade from mid to late autumn, dig up the tubers with a fork, taking care not to damage them with the prongs. Cut the foliage back to about 10cm from the crown.

2 Either tie the plants upside down by their remaining dying foliage in a shed or greenhouse or place upside down in a tray to allow excess moisture to drain away for about a week. Otherwise, there is a risk the dahlias will rot.

3 Turn the dahlias the right way up and place in a box or tray of sand, vermiculite or coir, and place them somewhere cool, dry and frost-free for the winter months, such as a greenhouse or shed. Regularly check the tubers over to ensure they're not rotting or drying out. Remove any rotting tubers immediately.

4 Once the risk of frost is over, they can be replanted outside. To bring them on earlier, they can be planted in pots in a greenhouse and then planted out as soon as the risk of frost is over. This will provide you with flowers a month or so earlier than planting tubers directly in the ground from winter storage.

• To protect plants from frosts or to extend the growing season they can be covered with a fleece or grown under cloches.

Winter Protection

Ideally, only choose larger trees and shrubs that are hardy enough to survive outside because it isn't possible to bring them all indoors in the same way that dahlia tubers can be protected. If you are happy to take the risk, only the more tender and exotic-looking plants will need protection. The most common method is to cover them with fleece or bubble wrap to help them make it through the winter months. With tree ferns, it is usually just the crown (where the fronds are growing out) that needs protection by packing it with bubble wrap or fleece. Don't worry if the fronds die back over winter, new ones should hopefully sprout once the weather warms up. Other plants, such as bananas, may need even more insulation and care.

INSULATING A BANANA PLANT

1 Cut back the banana plant to about a metre high. Place four bamboo canes around the plant, one in each corner.

2 Wrap chicken wire around the plant and attach to the four canes.

3 Stuff straw or bracken into the wire cage, pushing it right down between and around the stem of the banana plant.

4 Finally, place plastic sheeting over the top and pin it down. This will hopefully prevent the straw becoming wet and rotting.

Making Compost and Leaf Mould

Compost heaps might not be the prettiest feature in a garden, but they are probably one of the most important. Making your own compost is a great way of recycling garden waste rather than having it removed, and in addition the resulting compost adds loads of goodness to your existing soil.

Even in the smallest of gardens, a small plastic compost container can be tucked away in a corner and filled with garden and kitchen waste. For those with more space, two or three compost heaps are ideal; one for filling up with current waste, one in the process of decomposition and a third ready to be used in the garden.

Making Compost

The simplest way to make compost in your garden is to have a free-standing compost heap. However, if you want to keep the compost tidy and contained, it is worth making a structure. All you need are some pallets. Select three pallets of equal size, place them on their edges and nail or screw them together to make the back and two sides of the compost heap. You're then ready to add your compost ingredients.

There are three key ingredients that go into the process of making good compost in the garden:

- Carbon-rich materials, such as newspaper, wood shavings, old pet bedding, straw, cardboard, fallen leaves.
- Nitrogen-rich materials, such as grass clippings, herbaceous material such as annual weeds, stems and fresh leaves, kitchen waste.
- Air.

If there are too many nitrogen-rich materials in the compost heap, it will end up being a damp, soggy and smelly mess. Too much carbon and it will be dry and un-rotted and the decomposition process will be very slow. Generally, a good ratio of nitrogen to carbon is 60 nitrogen to 40 carbon.

If the material is dry, add water or let the rain percolate through to help with the composting process. Avoid adding perennial weeds to the compost heap as they will quickly spread. Perennial weeds include nettles, bindweed, ground elder, mare's tail and knotweed.

Ideally, compost heaps should be turned every few weeks, placing the material from the top at the bottom and vice versa to ensure that plenty of air is reaching all the compost. However, if you don't have time or the energy then turning it once a year is fine, it just doesn't break down as quickly. Worm farms are also very popular for small gardens and use kitchen waste.

• Fallen leaves are a key ingredient of good compost.

• Compost bins for placing your green waste in will provide you with wonderful compost in just a few months.

MAKE YOUR OWN LEAF MOULD

Leaf mould is made from leaf litter dropped by trees in autumn. Although it is low in nutrients, it is a great soil conditioner and will help retain moisture within the soil as well as helping to improve drainage. It will also encourage earthworms, which will also aerate and improve the soil. Best of all, making leaf mould is easy and it is a free resource and a by-product of having to remove the leaves off the lawns and flower beds anyway.

1. Rake the leaves off the flower beds and lawns in the autumn using a plastic rake.

2. Running a rotary mower over the fallen leaves to shred them and collect them in the collection box helps speed up the process of decomposition.

3. Place the leaves in bin liners, old compost bags or gardening bags.

4. If the leaves are dry, add some water and then poke holes in the bags to allow air to enter. Then tie up the bags and leave them in a place out of the way for a few months to rot down.

5. Occasionally over the next few months you can give the bags a shake or open them and mix up the leaves to speed up the decomposition.

6. Within six months to a year, you should have lovely dark leaf mould, which can either be dug into your borders or used in potting mixes when planting up containers as it has great moisture retention qualities.

Mulching

Bare soil is prone to dry out quickly and becomes full of weeds in just a few days, which is why gardeners use mulches to try to overcome this problem. There are lots of different types of mulches that can be used but almost all have the same intention, which is to suppress weeds and retain moisture in the ground.

• Wood chip or bark is an effective mulch for suppressing weeds and retaining moisture around trees and shrubs.

There is a range of different types of mulch that gardeners can use. Some are organic, made from natural products such as animal and plant material, and others are made from inorganic material.

Organic Matter
The most commonly used mulch is organic material such as wood chip or straw. Others include sugarcane and rotted animal manure. It improves the quality of the soil and will eventually rot down into the topsoil, which will improve the rooting zone for most plants. It will encourage worm activity, which aerates the soil, and the organic matter will also provide some macro- and micronutrients, although not as much as organic and inorganic fertilisers will. Garden compost is particularly useful as it is readily to

hand and is free since it is made in the garden. One disadvantage is that home compost heaps rarely get hot enough to destroy weed seeds. To apply organic matter around plants, it should be placed around the root area of each plant or shrub to a depth of about 5cm. Take care that the mulch doesn't sit directly against tree trunks as this can cause the tree to rot at its base. Instead, make a doughnut shape with about a 5cm gap around the trunk. This gap will also help channel the water to the roots below the trunk after planting rather than it washing away over the surface.

Organic mulch can be applied all year round. If using manure, make sure that it is well rotted as fresh manure can burn the roots. Do be careful what compost you use, though. If the compost hasn't been rotted down properly, you may inadvertently bring weeds into your garden if the material is riddled with viable weed seed.

Wood Chippings

This is a popular mulch, particularly in woodland gardens. If you have your own wood chipper or shredder, it is a great way of using up garden waste and recycling it on the flower beds. It is important the wood chips are rotted down before applying them as a mulch, though, because fresh ones can lock up the nitrogen in the soil. Wood chippings are great for suppressing weeds and for moisture retention, but they have very little nutritional value. Sometimes a weed suppressing membrane is laid on the ground first to prevent the wood chippings from rotting down into the soil too quickly.

OTHER OPTIONS

Other natural materials that are used by gardeners as a mulch to cover bare ground include gravel, colourful pebbles, shells and sheep's wool. Cardboard and straw are also good alternatives.

Weed-suppressing Membranes

Fabric such as weed-suppressing membrane can be laid over the ground to prevent weeds germinating. This is really useful if there is lots of bare ground and it's going to be a while before anything is planted. Sometimes it is used around trees, and although it is useful for the first year or so, it can create problems later if trying to underplant with bulbs or when adding more plants. It also prevents moisture and oxygen getting to the soil and kills beneficial microbes. Old carpet has been used in the past but does not allow oxygen and moisture into the soil. It is also extremely hard to remove later.

• Garden shredders and chippers are handy for reducing prunings to wood chip, which can be used as mulch on the beds.

PROBLEM SOLVING

Creating a garden is a lengthy process. First, you measure, draw and design the space and then you tackle hard landscaping. Soil is improved ready for the plants to arrive, and once installed, they soften hard edges and provide colour and movement. After all that hard work, you don't want your precious plants to succumb to pests and diseases. The good news is that by looking after your plants, many of these issues can be avoided. Catering to their needs, whether it's water, nutrients or light, will greatly reduce potential problems. Regular and careful observation will help you keep on top of any pests that sneak in under the radar, and early intervention can prevent them from spreading. If you do find yourself tackling an outbreak, there is a wide range of tools at your disposal, including weedkillers and pesticides, biological control and physical barriers. Finally, encouraging birds and other wildlife into your garden not only provides entertainment, but our feathered friends will also take on many plant pests.

Pests and Diseases

Garden plants are susceptible to a range of pests and diseases with the potential to harm your ornamentals and reduce crop yields. But take the time to wander around your garden on the lookout, because by spotting them early you may be able to nip these problems in the bud.

The organisms that cause problems for plants are many and varied. At the top of the size scale are hungry herbivores such as possums and rabbits, while microscopic bacteria and viruses can be equally damaging. The term 'pest' is usually taken to refer to animals that feed on plants, including mammals, birds, insects and other invertebrates like slugs and mites. Some eat plants wholesale, others pierce stems and leaves to extract sap or concentrate their attacks on particular plant organs, such as roots or seeds. Diseases are often the result of attack by fungi and fungus-like organisms, but bacteria and viruses also cause their share of outbreaks. The key to combating these interlopers is to identify them, so carefully inspect sickly specimens for the pest or infectious agent, and also take note of the type of damage caused.

What to Look For

Pests and diseases can affect all parts of a plant, so don't just scan the surface, but inspect the bark, under leaves and inside flowers for signs of trouble.

• Look under leaves for sap-sucking aphids and wipe them off with your fingers.

Whole plant General collapse is usually a symptom of drought, but if the plant has plenty of water it could indicate a disease such as wilt.

Roots can be affected by rots, including Phytopthora. The first symptoms you are likely to see are a yellowing and wilting of foliage followed by dieback. Improving drainage and adding organic matter to the soil is helpful. As they're below ground, you may only notice when the whole plant keels over, so regularly lift pot plants to check the roots. White curl grubs (or cockchafer) are also problematic.

Stems Fruit trees can harbour diseases like canker and scab, while woolly aphids and some other sap-sucking pests cause stem damage.

Leaves Problems are usually easy to spot, though some pests hide on the lower surface. Note the type of damage and also gather fallen leaves. Holes in leaves, distortion and powdery or sticky deposits are all common symptoms.

• Keep watch for slugs on leafy vegetables and pick them off regularly.

• Inspect leaves and stems for white, fluffy mealy bugs and their eggs.

• Cover ripening grapes with netting, to prevent birds spoiling the crop.

Flowers Many leaf pests can also affect blooms. Specific flower pests such as earwigs and thrips can damage petals, cause distortions or discoloration or reduce flower density.

Fruits Many edible fruits are targeted by insect pests, which cause holes or other injuries. Birds and fungal ailments can then exacerbate the damage. Hungry animals can also target fruit and seed crops, leaving little evidence behind.

CONTROL METHODS

There are many ways to protect your plants and to help them once a pest or disease attack has started. Integrated pest management (see pages 140–141), chemical controls (see page 142) and harnessing beneficial creatures (see pages 138–139) are discussed elsewhere. Prior to using such methods, it's worth trying this handful of quick and easy physical controls.

• First, consider quarantine for any new plants, both those you have bought and those that are gifted. Inspect them thoroughly for pests and diseases, not forgetting to check the roots, then keep them in a sheltered spot or cold frame away from the main garden. If they still look healthy after a few weeks, plant them out.

• Barriers can keep many pests and diseases at bay. Plastic sheeting erected in autumn will keep peaches and nectarines free of peach leaf curl fungus (this can be treated by applying a Bordeaux spray in late winter when the trees have just come into bud). Horticultural fleece can exclude carrot flies from carrots and parsnips (these can also be deterred by applying plenty of compost and planting companion plants, such as spring onions, with carrots). Rings of crushed shells, bran or copper tape can protect plants from slugs and snails; traps can also be successful and include sunken pots filled with beer and scooped-out melon and grapefruit halves.

• Finally, the easiest way to deal with pests is to remove them from the infected tissues by hand. Strip aphids from tender shoots with your fingers and collect molluscs in a bucket for disposal. Prune out diseased leaves and stems, always cleaning the blades of secateurs between plants to avoid spreading the disease. Gather fallen leaves and flowers from ailing plants and don't be tempted to compost them – put them in the bin.

Identifying Pests

Given the great diversity of garden pests, it can seem daunting trying to identify your plant's problem. Gather infested material or take photos, then visit the website of the Royal Horticultural Society, which contains information on recognising and controlling a huge range of pests and is a good one-stop shop. Here, we highlight ten common pests, to get you going in the right direction.

Pests	Plants Affected
Aphids	Most plants.
Caterpillars	Many plants can be affected. Brassicas can be severely damaged.
Gall wasp	All citrus, especially lemons, native limes and grapefruit.
Leaf miners	Many plants including allium, beetroot and chrysanthemum.
Mealy bugs	Many greenhouse and houseplants, including cacti and succulents, orchids, citrus, New Zealand flax, grapevines, etc.
Possums	A wide variety of plants, including roses, camellias and fruit trees.
Scale insects	Many plants, both indoors and out, including citrus, orchids, camellias, fruit trees and wisteria.
Slugs and snails	All plants.
Spider mites	Many indoor or greenhouse plants, including capsicums, tomatoes, citrus, orchids.
Vine weevil	Leaves of rhododendron, bergenia, hydrangea. Roots of heucheras, sedums, strawberries and vegetable crops, especially container plants.

Main Symptoms	Physical Control	Chemical Control	Biological Control
Pests clustered at shoot tips, sticky deposits, poor or distorted growth.	Remove by hand or flush with a hose.	Apply sprays containing pyrethrum, fatty acids or systemic pesticides such as lambda cyhalothrin.	Encourage ladybirds, lacewings, hoverflies and birds outside.
Holes in leaves with frass (fine powdery refuse produced by insects and their larvae).	Remove caterpillars and eggs by hand. Use fleece or netting to exclude adult butterflies.	Apply pyrethrum or deltamethrin, though carefully follow package limits when using on edible crops	Predatory nematodes can control caterpillars on brassicas
Stem swellings caused by a tiny Australian native wasp that implants its eggs within the stem tissue.	Before the end of winter, prune branches with galls that don't have the pinprick holes and dispose of them.	From mid-August hang in the tree yellow sticky traps with a chemical lure to catch emerging wasps.	There are natural parasite predators in northern parts of Australia. Predator release also occurs in Queensland.
Larvae excavate tunnels within the thickness of the leaf, leaving pale areas that later turn brown.	Remove damaged leaves or crush the pest inside. Cover crop plants with fleece. Gather fallen leaves from larger plants and destroy.	Leaf miners are protected within the leaf and so are hard to treat with chemicals. Systemic acetamiprid may give some control.	There are no biological controls, though birds may eat leaf miners.
White waxy secretions, sticky deposits and sooty moulds.	Remove bugs using a cotton bud. Dispose of heavily infested plants.	Apply systemic acetamiprid on houseplants. Use a winter wash on deciduous trees and vines.	A predatory ladybird (Cryptolaemus) and several parasitic wasps can be released in greenhouses.
Foliage eaten, as well as shoots, fruits and berries.	Gardeners can net effected plants or apply guards around the trunk of trees.	Repellent sprays (including those made from chilli and garlic) can deter possums if applied regularly.	Possums avoid predators, so employ your pet dog to patrol the perimeter.
Brown, helmet-shaped bug, usually immobile. Sticky deposits and sooty mould are common side effects.	Remove bugs using a cotton bud. Dispose of heavily infested plants. Use a winter wash on deciduous trees and vines.	Apply deltamethrin, lambda-cyhalothrin or cypermethrin or acetamiprid.	Several parasitic wasps can be released in greenhouses.
Irregular holes in leaves, often with slime trail. Holes in potato tubers.	Collect molluscs at night. Use barriers and traps. Choose more resistant potato varieties.	Apply slug pellets containing ferric phosphate or metaldehyde.	Predatory nematodes can control slugs and snails in warm weather.
Yellow mottling or white spotting on leaves, which fall early, webbing between leaves and stems.	Remove fallen leaves and badly infested plants. Increase humidity.	Use frequent applications of plant oils or fatty acids, or the systemic pesticide acetamiprid.	Adding compost and mulch can encourage predatory mites.
Irregular notches in leaf margins caused by adults. Wilting and death of plants caused by larvae.	Collect adult weevils at night. Lift pot plants and remove larvae.	Drench compost with acetamiprid (only suitable for container plants, not for use on soil or edible plants).	Predatory nematodes can control this pest on both edible and decorative crops. Effective both in pots and open soil.

Identifying Diseases

Unlike pests that move around, diseases sneak up surreptitiously, so always keep a watchful eye for changes in your plant's appearance. Look for altered colour and texture or the emergence of toadstools or other growths. The onset of symptoms can be sudden, as with clematis wilt, or slow as with many viral conditions. Remove infected material rapidly to prevent spread, but keep samples in sealed bags to aid identification.

Diseases	Plants Affected
Club root	Brassicas, including swede, radishes, cabbages, sprouts, wallflowers.
Damping off	Seedlings of most species.
Downy mildew	Many plants including brassicas, peas, onions, pansies, busy lizzies.
Honey fungus	Many plants including roses, apples, pears, privet, lilac, rhododendron.
Blight	Potatoes, tomatoes.
Powdery mildew	Many plants including roses, peas, courgettes, honeysuckle, bergamot.
Rust	Many plants including hollyhocks, fuchsias, leeks, pelargoniums, mint, broad beans and pears.
Scab	Apples, pears, olives, avocados, oranges, mandarins and cotoneaster.
Viruses	Many plants including cucumbers, tulips, sweet peas, daffodils, tomatoes and strawberries.
Wilt	Many plants including tomato, peony, roses, maples, capsicum.

Main Symptoms	Physical Control	Chemical Control	Biological Control
Stunted growth, sometimes wilting. Roots grossly swollen.	Control weeds and choose resistant varieties. Practise crop rotation.	None available. Adding lime to increase soil pH can help.	None available.
Seedlings collapse and die. White mould sometimes present.	Only use commercially produced seed compost and new or sterilised pots and trays. Reduce watering and improve ventilation.	None available. Only use mains water as collected rainwater and grey water are not sterile.	None available.
Discoloured patches on upper sides of leaves, with mould on lower sides. Leaves may fall, some plants die.	Control weeds, avoid dense planting and choose resistant varieties. Practise crop rotation. Remove and destroy infected leaves and plants. Avoid overhead watering and watering in the evening.	None available. Downy mildews are especially common in wet summers.	None available.
Premature death, often preceded by heavy flowering, fruiting or early autumn colour. Dead roots with white fungal growth beneath bark.	Remove and destroy infected plants and install plastic root barriers to prevent spread.	None available.	None available.
Foliage turns brown and collapses. Tubers begin to rot.	Destroy infected material, Earth up potatoes. Employ crop rotation. Grow tomatoes in a greenhouse.	None available. Choose resistant varieties, though changes in the fungus can make these less effective.	None available.
White powdery deposits often visible on leaves, flowers and fruits.	Remove and destroy infected material. Reduce susceptibility by watering to prevent water stress, then mulch.	The fungicide tebuconazole can be used on ornamentals, and plant invigorators can be used on all plants.	None available.
Pustules form, usually on the lower sides of the leaves, releasing spores. Infected leaves yellow and fall.	If spotted early, remove infected leaves and destroy. Avoid excess fertiliser applications.	The fungicide tebuconazole can be used on ornamental plants but not edibles.	None available.
Dark lesions on leaves, yellowing and leaf drop. Black, aborted flower buds. Dark lesions (scabs) on fruits.	Destroy infected material. Prune trees to improve airflow through canopy. Choose resistant cultivars.	The fungicide tebuconazole can be used on ornamental plants but not edibles.	None available.
Streaking or discoloration of leaves and flowers, distortion.	Destroy infected material and plants, disinfect pruning tools. Choose resistant varieties.	None available. Viruses are often transmitted by aphids and other pests, so control these too.	None available.
Sudden wilting of whole plant. Death of whole branches. Brown patches on leaves, flowers fail to open.	Destroy infected material, improve plant health by mulching, disinfect tools, avoid moving contaminated soil.	None available.	None available.

Cultural Problems

A myriad of pests feed on garden plants, causing a range of troubling symptoms, but sometimes an ailing plant is not under attack. When not provided with the appropriate quantities of light, water and nutrients, plants will often appear sickly and the only solution is to improve your growing practices. In extreme cases, you may be forced to replace the plant with something better suited to your plot.

When a plant is unhappy where you have placed it, this is usually because it originates in a very different habitat from the one you have provided. Plants from the Mediterranean Basin, such as rosemary and lavender, will not thrive in shade or on wet soils as they are used to full sun and dry roots. In less extreme cases, however, it is possible to perk up your plants by carefully altering the amounts of light, water and nutrients they receive. Careful cultivation is at the heart of gardening and it is crucial to know how to read the signs of sickness.

Light
The sun provides the energy that plants require to create food via photosynthesis, but species differ in the amounts of light they need or tolerate. Plants from shady habitats, such as ferns, hostas and Japanese maples, will not thrive in full sun, and their leaves may scorch and wither when overexposed. In contrast, plants from sunny climates, like herbs, vegetables and many conifers, will produce sparse, often elongated growth when grown in the shade. These are the extremes and many garden plants sit somewhere in between; check your plant's preferences before you purchase and don't forget that overhanging trees and nearby buildings may cast shade on an otherwise sunny garden.

• Mediterranean lavender needs full sun and a well-drained soil to thrive.

• The leaves of some plants will scorch when exposed to direct sunlight.

• Greenhouse plants can suffer in the heat if not well ventilated.

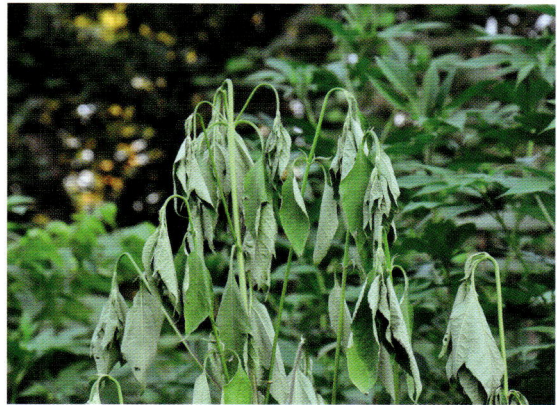

• Regular watering should prevent plants from wilting in dry weather.

Heat

Temperature is another important factor and plants exposed to extremes of heat or cold can suffer. Bedding plants and tender veg such as tomatoes will often show purple mottling on their leaves and a lack of vigour if planted out too early in the season. Extreme heat during Australian and New Zealand summers can cause physical damage, including leaf burn. Protect plants with shade cloth ahead of heat waves. Winter frosts will turn some natives and exotics to mush and defoliate others, so be prepared to protect such plants before temperatures drop.

Water

Gardeners can respond to light and temperature levels, though they have little control over them, but while Mother Nature is in charge of rainfall, soil moisture is very much dependent on the activities of gardeners. By adding soil supplements, we can improve drainage or moisture-holding capacity, and we can supplement natural precipitation using hoses or drip irrigation systems. Most plants will tell you if they're thirsty by wilting, but excessive water can be tricky to spot. Plants from dry climates generally suffer first, so watch Western Australian natives, lavender and other herbs. When excessive water in winter interacts with freezing temperatures, it can kill sensitive plants which might have survived if kept dry.

Container Culture

With their roots confined, container plants are dependent on gardeners. They cannot spread roots into the soil to seek additional moisture and nutrients, so they are among the first casualties in a hot summer. Furthermore, even when it's pouring with rain, little finds its way into the compost. Careful preparation at planting time can reduce the risks of desiccation. Choose the largest container you can accommodate, as it will hold more moisture, then add slow-release fertiliser and moisture-retaining gel to the compost. Pick plants that tolerate some drought and avoid trees, climbers and plants with large leaves, as all are very thirsty. Where possible, install drip irrigation on an automatic timer, as this uses water more efficiently and stops you having to remember to water.

• Plants in pots depend on gardeners for most of their water.

Weeds

A commonly cited definition for weeds is that they are merely plants growing in the wrong place, so why do they vex us gardeners? Firstly, their rapid growth can often outcompete that of our chosen plants, smothering them with less attractive foliage. They also steal a portion of the water and fertiliser we apply and can harbour pests and diseases that attack our plants.

Annual or Perennial?

Garden weeds are classified according to their life histories, either annual or perennial. Annuals complete their life cycles in a single year, often in shorter periods, and include purslane (*Portulaca oleraceae*), winter grass (*Poa annua*) and groundsel (*Senecio vulgaris*). Perennial weeds live for many years and can be herbaceous, as in soursob (*Oxalis pes-caprae*), three corner garlic (*Allium triquetrum*) or common plantain (*Plantago lanceolata*), or woody vines and shrubs, like blackberry (*Rubus fruticosus*) or ivy (*Hedera helix*). Annual weeds are generally easier to eradicate than perennials and different strategies are needed to control them. Whether annual or perennial, all weeds are fast-growing and reproduce readily, often by both seed and vegetative methods.

Physical Barriers

A good place to start when looking to control weeds is to prevent them from entering your garden in the first place. Inspect all new plants, both purchased and gifted from other gardeners, and remove any weeds you find. If weeds are invading under the garden fence from next door, use a plastic barrier, such as those designed to control bamboo, to keep them out. Of course, you will never exclude all weeds, as seeds float on the breeze or are delivered in the droppings of birds. Weed membranes can control perennial weeds as they exclude light. However, they prevent air and water getting to the soil and discourage microbial activity.

• Lay permeable membrane between crops to reduce the need to weed.

• Apply weedkillers on dry, still days and always follow pack instructions.

Weeding

Annual weeds are best pulled by hand, ideally before they produce seeds. Regular hand weeding will greatly reduce them and a thick mulch will prevent remaining seeds from sprouting. Annual weeds can be composted, but don't put flowering plants on your heap as they may pollute your compost with weed seeds. Perennial herbaceous weeds are much more challenging to control by hand as any roots left in the soil can re-sprout. For this reason, avoid using power tillers and cultivators as they cut up the weed roots and spread them throughout the soil. If digging, carefully remove as many roots as you can find and be prepared to return for additional sessions.

Chemical Control

Weedkillers, or herbicides, can be an effective method of weed control providing you closely follow the pack instructions. Contact herbicides kill only the parts of the plant they touch and are most effective on annual weeds and seedlings. Systemic herbicides are absorbed by the plant and transported around its body, killing the roots as well as the stems and leaves. These are the most effective chemicals for use on perennial weeds. When spraying, choose a dry, still day as rain will wash away the chemical, while wind can cause it to drift onto decorative plants. Keep children and pets away from the sprayed area for 24 hours after application. Where perennial weeds are growing through your garden plants, choose a systemic herbicide that can be painted onto the leaves, as this reduces the risk of damaging valued plants. For woody perennials, cut plants down to the ground, then apply systemic herbicide to the stumps, to kill the roots.

WEED DISPOSAL

Do NOT compost perennial weeds as they can survive and reinfest the garden. Woody perennials can be cut and pulled by hand, or trimmed with a strimmer. Larger woody weeds, including trees, are best removed by a professional. Take woody weeds to the tip, rather than composting them at home. As a final resort, convert weedy patches to lawn; after several years of regular mowing, even the most vigorous weeds will be gone.

Choosing Healthy Plants

Plant problems should not be considered only after planting. While designing your garden and choosing the plants to grow, it is essential to consider their future health. At the nursery or garden centre, only pick those in fine fettle and, where possible, opt for disease-resistant varieties. Furthermore, in your design consider only species that will thrive in your area as unhappy plants are more prone to ill health.

• Only purchase plants with healthy root systems, avoiding poorly rooted or pot-bound specimens.

Right Plant, Right Place

Selecting the right plant begins not at the nursery, but at home. Should you choose a plant that is not happy in the environment you can provide, you will have to cope with a whole suite of additional problems. Carefully assess your garden, looking in particular for the basic plant needs: light, water and soil. Once you're familiar with your own plot, visit neighbouring gardens and local parks, to see which plants thrive near you. With your own garden in mind, begin to look for plants in gardening books and online, taking note especially of their native habitats. Plants from woodlands will likely do well in shady areas with rich soil, while those from arid scrub are well suited to sunny locations with sandy soils. Build a list of possible picks, then head to the garden centre or find a good mail order or online retailer.

Check for Health Issues

If shopping in person, look for plants that are free of pests and diseases, show no signs of wilting and have well-established root systems. Don't be afraid to carefully remove the pot to check your plant has a well-developed crop of roots. Those with more compost than root, or so many roots you can barely see the compost, should be avoided. If something catches your eye, but you're uncertain of its requirements, check the label or ask the staff – always best to avoid impulse purchases! In some plant groups, where diseases are prevalent, breeders develop disease-resistant cultivars. Good examples are roses and fruit trees, and these cultivars can potentially save you a lot of problems in future.

Be Climate Aware

There will always be many popular plants that are not really suited to some areas of Australia and New Zealand. Plants that thrive in cool inland alpine areas of New Zealand's South Island, for example, will not cope in the Australian tropics, while plants that thrive in the Mediterranean climate of south-west Western Australia often struggle on Australia's east coast. If you are tempted by climatically inappropriate plants be prepared to devote the extra care they will need to survive. This can include providing frost protection in winter or sun protection and extra water in summer or amending the soil to improve drainage.

• With such great diversity readily available, there's a plant suited to every situation.

Crop Rotation

In the vegetable garden, plants are chosen based on what food they'll produce, rather than what conditions they need. Most veg want full sun and rich, well-drained soils to crop well, but how you arrange your plants can improve their health. Crop rotation involves growing veg in different areas each year. If you stick to the same patch for your potatoes, then potato pests and diseases build up in the soil and this can condemn future harvests. Instead, plant an unrelated crop, such as beans or onions, in the potato bed, as they're not susceptible to most potato problems. Leguminous crops (beans and peas) bind atmospheric nitrogen into the soil, so plant hungry veg such as brassicas on your bean beds the following year; they'll grow great guns absorbing the fixed nitrogen, which may reduce the need for pest control and result in healthier plants.

Beneficial Creatures

While it may seem like there's no end to the parade of pests looking to attack our plants, some animals actively help to control these nuisances. Garden birds are indefatigable insect predators, while blue-tongue lizards and frogs keep slug numbers down. It's also worth remembering that some of our less popular garden residents, such as wasps, spiders and beetles, are often effective hunters of other bugs, while bees pollinate flowers and crops.

Organic gardeners have for many years relied on Nature's hit squad of hungry creatures to control garden pests. With a little encouragement, various birds, mammals, reptiles, amphibians, insects and other invertebrates will make a home in your garden and reduce the need for using potentially harmful chemicals. Welcome them into your outdoor space by providing food, shelter and nesting materials. Once in your garden, keep them safe by reducing the use of pesticides, offering safe shelters and controlling inquisitive household pets.

• Attract beneficial creatures into your garden by providing a reliable water source.

• Many gardeners actively feed wild birds, purely for the pleasure of viewing them, but once attracted into your garden, they will often forage for bugs to feed their young. Installing nest boxes and providing nesting materials, such as feathers and cloth, will also draw them in.
• Leaving fallen timber and leaf litter provides habitat for insects and reptiles who will scoop up pests, including slugs and snails.
• A compost heap is the perfect home for scavenging mice and rats, and sometimes snakes, so be careful when turning it!

Plant Protectors

Provide plenty of flowers in your garden and many pollinating insects will follow, including the bees that fertilise the flowers of crops such as apples and tomatoes.

- Pollination is not the only benefit; hoverflies are pollinators, but their larvae feed on pests such as aphids.
- The caterpillars of nectar-feeding red admiral butterflies consume weedy stinging nettles.
- Plant protection need not only rely on animals; some companion plants actively prevent garden pests. The fragrance of herbs can deter bugs; summer savory (*Satureja hortensis*) can protect broad beans from aphids, while hyssop (*Hyssopus officinalis*) deters cabbage white butterflies from brassicas.
- Grow French marigolds (*Tagetes*) or basil to protect tomatoes and cucumbers from whitefly.
- Some easy-to-grow annuals can act as sacrificial lambs; lettuces on the veg plot readily draw in slugs and snails, thus sparing more important crops, while nasturtiums (*Tropaeolum majus*) are chosen over brassicas by hungry caterpillars.
- The vigorous herbs mint and tansy (*Tanacetum vulgare*) can take over if not grown in containers.

Build a Pond

Providing a reliable water source year-round is the best method to attract frogs and aquatic insects. Adding small native fish helps with mosquito control. The best wildlife ponds vary in depth and are planted with a mix of plants that provide food and shelter for tadpoles and frogs. Ensure the water is topped up over summer, ideally using collected rainwater to refill, and in winter float a ball on the surface, to provide a hole in any ice that forms.

• Caterpillars are usually considered pests, but some species will eat weeds for you, such as this red admiral caterpillar munching on a nettle.

Integrated Pest Management

Originating in agriculture, integrated pest management (IPM) aims to reduce our reliance on chemical pesticides. Rather than looking to eradicate pests entirely, such schemes seek to manage pest populations, keeping them at acceptable levels using a variety of tools. When gardeners incorporate IPM principles into their own landscapes, they benefit as using fewer chemicals not only protects the natural environment but also saves money.

• Hang sticky traps near susceptible plants to monitor pest levels; if they become excessive you may need to employ suitable controls.

Horticulture is not the only discipline to incorporate IPM; it's also proved successful in agriculture, forestry, museum specimen care and domestic pest control. This success comes as a result of taking a scientific approach. Pests are identified, their populations evaluated and any resulting damage is monitored. Subsequent control measures are proportionate to the damage caused. Also, instead of reacting to individual outbreaks, IPM focuses on the entire ecosystem, as by keeping plants healthy, they are less likely to succumb to pests and diseases.

Standing Guard

A key tenet of IPM is to monitor pest populations. This can involve hanging sticky traps in the greenhouse, pheromone traps in fruit trees, or simply wandering round your garden on a regular basis looking for trouble. In many cases, if you catch a pest or disease early enough, you can remove the offending bugs or infected leaves by hand without needing to resort to chemicals. It's worth keeping notes on what you discover and regularly reviewing the success of your efforts, as with especially troublesome pests you may need to up the ante.

'Prevention is better than cure' is another important aspect of IPM. Seal up cracks in greenhouse glazing and net open windows to stop bugs getting inside.

• When buying new plants, check for hitch-hiking pests and weeds or quarantine new acquisitions prior to planting.
• Regularly remove weeds that may harbour pests and keep the garden clean, disposing of dead and diseased tissues rapidly.
• Clean shears and pruners regularly, as they can harbour disease.
• Finally, healthy plants are happy plants, so ensure you give yours adequate water and fertiliser. Both too much and too little can cause stress, making plants susceptible to disease. For example, excess

fertiliser causes plants to produce soft growth that is especially attractive to pests. Learn to recognise when your plants have had enough or not. With careful monitoring and preventative measures, you'll be able to reduce outbreaks of pests, diseases and weeds.

Biological Control

Encouraging beneficial creatures (see pages 138–139) will help in the fight against pests, but sometimes you'll need a bit more assistance. Biological control is the use of predatory or parasitic organisms to target plant pests. It's especially effective in enclosed greenhouses and conservatories where whitefly, scale, mealy bug and mites can all be controlled. Outside, minute worm-like nematodes can be applied to the soil to control vine weevils, slugs and carrot fly. Biological control will not eradicate all pests, but will reduce their populations.

• Set up slug traps baited with beer around vulnerable crops such as lettuce.

Last Resort

If you've exhausted all other methods of control, IPM does allow for carefully controlled use of chemicals (see page 142). Avoid spraying widely and frequently, as this can have unexpected consequences. In some cases, pests that survive are more likely to be immune to the chemical and future populations will grow from these hardy bugs, so future infestations will be even more difficult to control with chemicals. Even where this is not the case, as with slugs and snails, it's always worth choosing the mildest chemical that will do the job and applying it over the smallest possible area as they may adversely affect biological control predators, not to mention bees and other wildlife. When controlling slugs and snails, start by searching the garden and collecting them by hand. Make sure to check popular haunts such as under rocks and at the foot of walls. Employ barriers like crushed shells or copper rings around especially vulnerable plants. For round two, try using traps baited with beer or bran, or upturned melon or grapefruit halves. If you're still having problems, resort to a chemical control, such as slug pellets, but always follow the manufacturer's instructions.

Using Chemicals

A range of chemicals is available to control weeds, pests and diseases. Using them is safe, providing all package instructions are followed, but it is possible that they can negatively affect the environment and many gardeners choose not to use them at all or only in times of great need.

Whenever using chemicals in the garden, it is essential (and a legal requirement) to read and follow any instructions. The package generally also includes a use-by date, after which any remnants should be disposed of, plus safety instructions should you accidentally spill the chemical or splash it on your skin or eyes. Never dispose of unwanted or expired chemicals by pouring them down the drain – contact your local council to find an approved disposal site. Store chemicals in a safe location, away from children and pets, and wear protective clothing when applying them. Most garden chemicals can be bought in concentrated form, requiring dilution in water, or as ready-to-use packs. Use concentrates when applying over a large area, while ready-to-use packs are ideal for small applications.

Pest and Disease Control

Chemicals are available to control insects (insecticide), slugs and snails, and fungi (fungicides). Most are sprayed directly onto the plant, though slug and snail products are typically in pelleted form. As with weedkillers, they are best applied on dry, still days, and you should avoid spraying flowers directly, as the chemicals can affect pollinating insects. Keep children and pets away from sprayed areas for around 24 hours after application and avoid contaminating ponds and other water sources. Insecticides can work in several different ways, combating pests directly or in a systemic fashion, whereby they're absorbed by the plant and transported throughout its body, damaging any insect that feeds on the plant. Plant invigorators promote healthy growth and discourage sap-sucking insects. Organic pesticides are becoming more readily available, though they often require more frequent applications. Online and other resources sometimes recommend the use of washing-up liquid, rhubarb-leaf extract, baking powder or vinegar as pesticides or herbicides, but take care when using 'unofficial' compounds as their effects can be unpredictable.

• Spray a winter wash over fruit trees to kill pests and their eggs.

Lawn Repair

A neatly clipped, verdant sward forms the perfect foil for blooming borders, but all too often, your lawn lets you down. Whether it's brown patches, fungal infestations or you have more weeds than grass, lawns are susceptible to a variety of problems that can leave them looking less than perfect. Many of these problems are cultural and can be solved with better lawn care, but direct action is often needed to control weeds and diseases.

Lawn problems are many and varied and solutions usually depend on the cause. Perhaps the most common symptom is discoloured patches, and these can result from pests and diseases, drought, excessive chemical application and even urinating dogs. Mower blades may also scrape the turf, especially if there are humps or hollows, or along the edges. Weeds, including clover and plantain, are another common lawn problem, though they may have some benefits. Clover leaves typically stay green through dry periods, even after the grass turns yellow, while the flowers of dandelions, clover, English daisy and many others are popular with bees and other pollinating insects.

• A verdant lawn sets off your blooming borders, as long as it's healthy.

• Rust fungi can affect longer grass in late summer or early autumn, though powdery mildew, first seen around autumn, is more common here

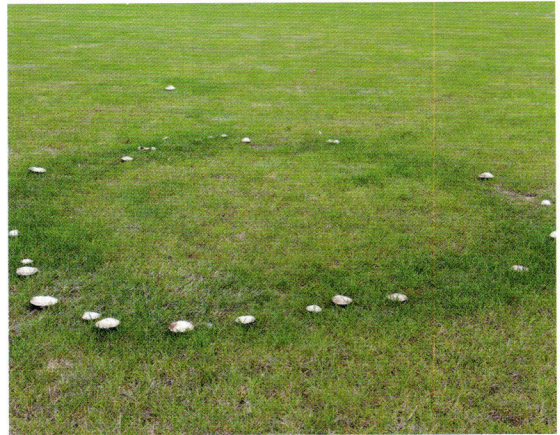

• Fairy rings are circles of mushrooms. They can cause adjacent grass to die.

• Dog urine kills grass, leaving irregular brown patches on the lawn.

• Summer drought can leave your lawn looking brown and faded.

Patch Up

Yellow, brown or bare patches can scar the perfect lawn, but there are many possible causes. It is important to identify the source of the problem before finding a solution.

• White curl grubs and cutworms cause dead patches to appear, often attracting hungry birds. They can be controlled using predatory nematodes watered onto the grass.

• Fungal diseases of grass include red thread, rust, fusarium and take-all patches, and these commonly begin as red or yellow patches that turn brown as the grass dies. There are limited options for chemical control of lawn fungi, but regular mowing and improving turf aeration will help prevent infestations. Removing clippings after mowing can prevent a build-up of thatch, which encourages fungal growth. However, clippings can act as a mulch, reducing the need to water the grass in summer.

• Fairy rings are hoop-like clusters of toadstools and they often cause the grass adjacent to the ring to die. The only method of control is to excavate the ring to a depth of 30cm, though this is heavy work. It is perhaps better to simply fork the dead areas and reseed, an approach that will also help repair damage caused by insect larvae and other fungi.

- Lawn damage due to dog urine can be cured by watering the grass immediately after the dog does, though any spots you miss may need to be reseeded.
- Chemical damage is easily avoided by following package instructions; be aware that spilled mower fuel and oil can also harm the grass, so take care when topping up.
- Physical damage to the turf commonly occurs when a mower runs over a hump or slips off an edge, scalping the grass. Try to even out humps and hollows by carefully lifting the turf with a spade, removing/adding soil until level, then replacing the grass. Damaged lawn edges can be repaired in similar fashion; cut a square around the damaged section, then lift and turn the turf so the outer edge faces inwards. You'll have a clean, straight outer edge and the damaged section can be repaired by seeding.
- Summer drought can lead to the entire lawn turning brown. Most healthy lawns will recover once the rains return, but you can help by raising the cutting height on the mower and leaving the clippings on the soil to act as a mulch. Better this than watering your lawn in high summer, which is very wasteful of water.

Weeds and Moss

For some gardeners, a patchwork lawn with daisies, clover and dandelions mixed in is an attractive feature, but for others, only a uniform carpet of grass will do. If you prefer to remove the weeds, there are several methods available.

- Keep the grass healthy by feeding, forking and raking, as this will ensure it is vigorous and able to outcompete the weeds.
- Raising your mower blades can also encourage grass at the expense of weeds.
- Many weeds can be removed by hand using a trowel, while specialist lawn weedkillers can be applied in spring and summer.
- Moss (also liverworts, algae and lichen) is often symptomatic of damp, shady lawns with poor drainage. Improve the health of the grass by feeding, forking and raking up the moss.
- Consider clearing overhanging tree branches to allow more light onto the lawn.
- Top-dress with a sandy mix in autumn and apply lime in areas with acidic soils.
- Choose a lawn fertiliser that contains a chemical weed and moss killer.

• Heavy growths of moss can indicate poor soil drainage and insufficient light.

PRODUCTIVE GARDENING

Growing fruit and vegetables can be one of the most rewarding aspects of gardening. For many, there is an unparalleled pleasure in growing, cooking and serving produce that has just been picked. With crops like sweetcorn, tomatoes and apricot, the difference in taste is often remarkable, but everything that makes the short journey from garden to kitchen retains maximum freshness and nutritional benefit. Longer-lasting crops that can be stored are conveniently nearby in leaner months, broadening choice and saving time spent at the supermarket.

Whatever space is available, there will always be room to cultivate some sort of edible crop. Sprouting seeds, herbs, lettuce and microgreens will grow happily on a sunny windowsill, and many vegetables and fruit trees produce excellent crops in pots on a balcony or outside the kitchen door, even more so as new varieties are increasingly coming to market specially bred for this purpose.

Most traditionally, an area of the garden is put aside to grow a variety of crops. The vegetable patch is usually square and slightly hidden, while fruit bushes and orchard trees are given their own space. Plots, too, are designed on the same lines. In modern gardens, though, the boundaries are becoming blurred. Vegetables like chard, artichokes and runner beans are often given pride of place in the ornamental garden, being wonderfully attractive plants in their own right, and fruit trees, with their delightful spring blossom, grace many a garden without seeming out of place.

Growing Fruit and Vegetables

The satisfaction of growing something from seed, nurturing it and then being able to harvest and cook it is so rewarding. For a gardener, it requires the full ambit of horticultural skills, including knowledge of propagation techniques, soil preparation, pruning of fruit trees and an understanding of a huge range of different crops.

One of the wonderful aspects of growing fruit and veg is that they can be grown almost anywhere. Ranging from the huge suburban back gardens, to community plots or tiny balconies, there is an opportunity for almost everybody to grow their own food. Herbs can be grown in window boxes and hanging baskets and even fruit trees can be grown in pots on a balcony or small patio.

With a little bit of horticultural skill and knowledge, it becomes possible to cheat the seasons and produce your own crops either earlier or later than usual. In fact, a really skilled fruit and veg grower can produce food all year round if using the right protective equipment.

• Even the smallest garden space can grow some exciting and interesting veg, such as wasabi and vanilla beans.

• Growing your own produce is a wonderful and rewarding hobby, often resulting in beautiful and delicious vegetables.

New Avenues

Growing your own food opens up a whole new raft of different foods to try – produce that you would struggle to find on the supermarket shelves. Crops can include such items as cucamelons (a cross between a cucumber and a melon), cuttuce, an ancient Chinese lettuce that is also used as a celery or the delicious oca (New Zealand yam). Alternatively, even traditional veggies can be grown just as a different shape or colour, such as round carrots or purple cauliflowers. You can also push the boat out by trying traditional ornamental crops such as the tubers of dahlias, the flowers and buds of day lilies and the young shoots of hostas or bamboo.

Health Benefits

Your own home-grown fruit and veg is good for your body, as you will probably end up eating lots more nutritional meals as you harvest your crops. You may also become fitter and stronger, as cultivating the soil rewards a gardener with just as good a workout as any gym could offer, and of course it is an opportunity for breathing in the great and healthy outdoors. Being outdoors among plants and growing vegetables has been shown to be very therapeutic, increasing a person's mental well-being and happiness.

Beautiful Produce

Finally, just because you're growing fruit and veg, this doesn't mean that it can't be as beautiful as a traditional ornamental garden. There are many examples of stunning kitchen gardens and potagers that are as spectacular to look at as the crops are to eat. A citrus tree flowering and fruiting in a pot is just as impressive as any ornamental tree, while the textures provided by foliage and stems and the range of colours from flowers and fruit can be a feast for the eyes as well as the stomach.

• Vegetable gardens can be just as beautiful as ornamental gardens, and there are health benefits, too, from growing your own.

Soil Preparation

Soil preparation is key to growing vegetables successfully in the garden. Although vegetables are mainly annual crops, they are often demanding in that they require lots of nutrients and fertility to keep cropping. Fruit trees and perennial vegetables such as asparagus and rhubarb will be in the ground for longer than most other vegetables, so preparing the soil before planting is even more important.

Before sowing seeds or planting seedlings and plants, the soil needs to be prepared to give the vegetables the best chance of establishing and to enable them to maximise the size of yields they can provide. Sometimes radical clearing may be needed before starting. This is often the case when taking on an abandoned community plot, or sometimes a back garden full of building rubble.

Clearing Weeds

In the case of an overgrown plot, the area can either be cut and then weeded, or if you're not organic a systemic weedkiller can be applied to kill the roots of any pernicious perennial weeds.

If spraying perennial weeds, wait until there is maximum leaf cover to ensure the weedkiller is absorbed through the foliage and taken back down into the roots. After spraying, leave the foliage for a couple of weeks to give the weedkiller a chance to take effect. It may be necessary to do a second or even third spraying with really pernicious weeds.

• The trick to growing vegetables successfully is good soil preparation, including removing all weeds prior to planting.

Even if you're just hand-weeding, it will probably help to cut first if the site is really overgrown to make it easier to reach the soil and roots. Ideally, this should take place before annual weeds have had a chance to set seed because otherwise they will quickly spread, creating a similar problem either later on in the season or the following year. Most annual weeds should come out quite easily, just being prised out with a border fork. Perennial weeds, though, will need far more work as some roots can go down as far as a metre. When digging them out, try to remove as much of the root as possible, and don't add them to the compost heap, but instead either dispose of them or leave them to dry out in the sun on a rack or fence until completely desiccated, before composting.

If you're lucky enough to take on a fairly well-maintained garden, it may just need a light hoeing to remove annual weeds prior to digging and adding organic matter.

Digging Over

Once the weeds have been removed, the area should be dug over to a depth of 30cm, with organic matter such as garden compost or well-rotted manure added. Digging over the soil will make it easy for planting and enable the roots to develop and spread. Once it has been dug over, it should be raked level and, if there's time, left to settle for a few days prior to planting or sowing. If the ground is going to be left for a while before planting, it is worth covering it up with another top dressing of organic matter to prevent weeds germinating in the bare soil.

Green Manure

Green manures are plants sown by gardeners into vacant ground between sowing vegetable crops. The main reason for doing this is that their roots fix nitrogen from the air when growing in the spring and summer, increasing the fertility of the soil. Green manures are also used for covering bare soil, preventing weeds from germinating – a bit like a living mulch. They also protect the soil from erosion and provide additional interest in the garden, rather than leaving bare ground to look at. The best time for sowing them is in late summer or autumn, and some, such as clover dalkeith, even continue growing throughout winter. Green manures are usually cut down in spring and left on the surface to desiccate. A couple of weeks later, the material on the surface and the remaining plant material in the ground can be dug into the top 25cm of soil. Allow it to compost in the soil for a further two weeks before planting or sowing.

Green manures can be perennial or annual. Types worth trying include mustard, lucerne, comfrey, fenugreek, buckwheat and clover.

• Fenugreek (*Trigonella foenum-graecum*) is a fast-growing green manure that is ready for digging 10 weeks after sowing.

Planning Crops

Being able to plan is just as important as having good horticultural skills and knowledge when it comes to working out where and when crops are going to be grown. There's a plethora of different vegetables that can be grown, all with different sowing and cropping times, so many gardeners like to write plans and plot it all on paper first.

• Beans leave a fertile soil thanks to their nitrogen-fixing qualities.

Planning Where Everything Will Go

Unless you have a huge garden and lots of labour available, you are probably going to have to restrict yourself as to which crops you grow due to space and time available. Winter is the best time to start planning as most of the beds are usually empty, and you often have more time on your hands.

When planning the kitchen garden, firstly plan your structure with regards to where paths, beds, compost bins, and sheds are going to be placed. You may also want to consider whether you have room for a greenhouse or small polytunnel. Next, work out where fruit trees and perennial vegetables such as asparagus, horseradish, globe artichokes, Jerusalem artichokes and rhubarb will go. This is because these are usually kept in the same place, so once they're planted you have to work around them for a few years. Once this is done, you are ready to work out which vegetables will go where, and at what time they need to be sown, harvested and removed to make way for other crops.

Your Favourites

Unless you are growing for somebody else, the best method to start with is simply to list your favourite vegetables and the ones you definitely want in your garden. After all, there is no point in

• Carrots are a popular root crop and prefer a deep but light, stone-free soil to grow in.

filling the space with food you don't particularly like. Another criterion for choosing what to grow is whether you can get it easily at the supermarket, and if so, is it cheaper to buy? An example could be maincrop potatoes. They take up lots of space on the plot, yet are easily available and cheap when purchased from the shop.

CROP ROTATION

Once you have made your list of annual vegetables to grow for the year, you can plan where to plant or sow them. Most kitchen gardens use a system called crop rotation. This involves avoiding growing the same plants in the same soil in successional years. This is to reduce the risk of pests and diseases in the soil, which target specific crops. Instead, a different crop is grown in the bed after it has been harvested, and the previous crop is grown in another bed. Most gardeners divide their crops into four categories for crop rotation, and use four beds to rotate them in.

The rotation pattern is usually as follows in each bed: potatoes and tomatoes, followed by root vegetables with onions and garlic, followed by peas and beans in year three, followed in the fourth year by brassicas and the cabbage family. Other crops, such as pumpkins, squashes, cucumbers, sweetcorn and lettuce, tend to have fewer problems and can be just slotted in wherever there is space.

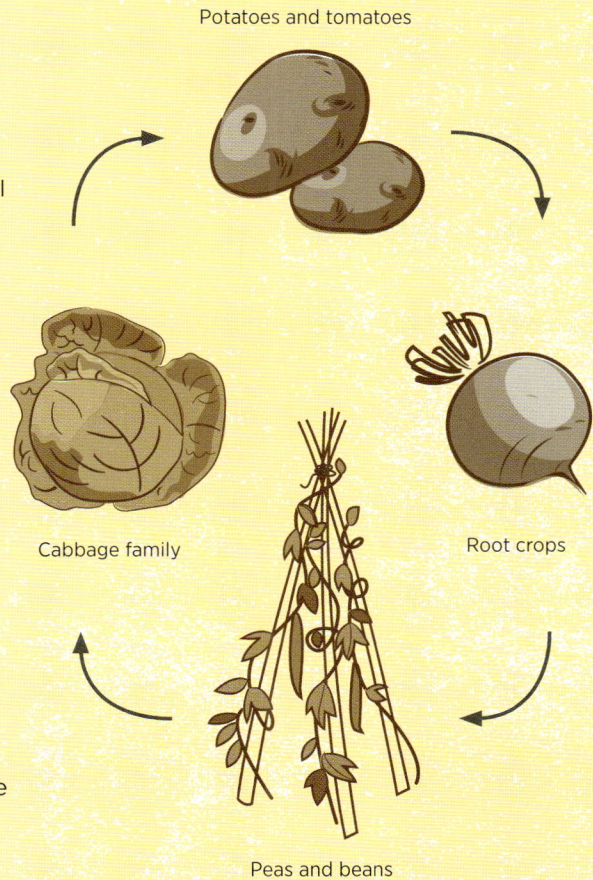

Potatoes and tomatoes

Cabbage family

Root crops

Peas and beans

Crops that either take up a lot of space or are cheap to buy or easily bought (so you may not want to grow them if short on space) include: cabbages, cauliflowers, potatoes, carrots and onions.

Crops that are hard to find in the shops but are easy to grow include heritage varieties of tomatoes, pumpkins and beans.

• Marrows are basically larger versions of courgettes, but specific 'marrow' varieties will taste much better than overgrown courgettes.

• Tomatoes can be grown outside.

Sowing Vegetable Seeds

The majority of vegetables to be found in the productive garden are raised from seed. Each crop has its own special cultivation requirements but the basic guidelines for successful sowing are similar in almost all cases.

Buying Seed

Good-quality vegetable seed is available from many reputable suppliers. Buying fresh, well-stored, vacuum-packed seeds will certainly help successful germination once sown. The variety of seeds on offer can be bewildering as suppliers compete to breed bigger, better, more disease-resistant varieties, although there is now a growing trend for reverting to the old heritage crops. It is best to concentrate on choosing cultivars for taste, reliability in a specific set of conditions and pest or disease resistance.

The majority of seeds are sold by the packet, either just as they are or sometimes with a coating to make them easier to handle or to improve germination rates. Certain seeds are also available embedded into tape to ensure ideal spacing. Once bought, they should be stored in a cool, dry place away from pests such as rodents. Difficult seeds, such as parsnips, can be pre-germinated indoors on a piece of damp kitchen paper a week or two before sowing.

• Broad beans are one of the hardiest vegetables and can be sown directly into the soil even in cooler temperatures.

Seed Sowing into the Ground

There are several techniques for sowing seeds outside, either directly where they will grow, in trays or pots or in a dedicated seedbed where they can be transplanted later on into their final positions. There are some crops that should not be transplanted, mostly root crops, as the process will disrupt the straight growth of their tap root; and some that grow so quickly they will be harvested before any need to transplant. Others, though, can be started elsewhere until space becomes available to move them on. In a rotation system, this is very helpful.

Seeds of whatever size and shape should only be sown in properly prepared ground. Well-dug soil should be raked to remove large stones and debris until a fine 'tilth' is achieved. This is soil that is made up of evenly sized crumbs, neither too dusty nor too full of heavy clods. If the soil is wet, it is best to stand on a board to avoid damaging the nearby soil structure.

Most seeds need a soil temperature of above 7°C (45°F) to germinate successfully and need constant moisture during the germination process.

Seed Sowing into Pots or Trays

Sow seeds of most summer crops in pots or trays four to six weeks before you want to plant them in the ground and place in a warm, well-lit spot and keep moist.

Thinning Out

Most crops require a certain space to flourish so seedlings sometimes have to be 'thinned out' before their closeness causes a problem. Use a pair of scissors to cut off the plant above ground if seedlings are delicate and closely spaced, or gently pull out the weakest seedlings by hand to leave evenly spaced, stronger plants to grow to maturity. Sometimes the thinnings can be eaten, so are not necessarily wasted.

DRILLING SEEDS

The most common method of seed sowing is to take out a 'drill'. Using a string line as a guide, make a small, straight channel with a hoe or trowel, at the correct depth. As a rule of thumb, the bigger the seed, the more depth it will require. With larger seeds, it is often recommended that they are sown at a depth of two or three times their size. However, packets of seeds always offer advice on seed depth. Sprinkle or space seeds evenly along this channel, making sure not to sow too thickly. Cover and firm gently before watering.

Crops that will be harvested young or that can tolerate growing close together can be sown in wider drills or broadcast-sown, where squares of soil are raked to a fine tilth and the seed is scattered evenly over the whole area before being raked over lightly once more and gently watered.

Larger seeds, such as beans, can simply be pushed into the soil by hand at the correct depth and spacing.

• Some seeds will benefit from being sown in seed trays before being pricked out and potted on.

Raised Beds

As the name suggests, raised beds are simply beds for growing vegetables or ornamental plants that are raised up from the ground. There are numerous benefits of growing vegetables in this way and they are becoming increasingly popular for people who suffer with bad backs or have poor or even no soil in their garden.

• There are lots of benefits to growing vegetables in raised beds such as better drainage and less back-breaking work.

Raised beds can be any shape and size, although ideally they shouldn't be so wide that it is necessary to climb on them to maintain them as this compacts the soil. It is recommended that the centre of the bed shouldn't be over 1.2m from an edge of the raised bed, so that plants can be reached and maintained from the side. They can be built either directly onto patios or concrete, or on top of existing beds.

Benefits of Raised Beds
Added height Growing plants in a raised bed automatically raises them to a new height, meaning they offer a more sensory experience as they are closer for touching, smelling and picking. The extra height can also provide additional seclusion and privacy from neighbours or other sections of the garden.

Comfort Raised beds are at a far more comfortable height for planting, sowing, maintaining and harvesting crops. This is also a good solution for people in wheelchairs, or those with bad backs or other limitations.

Keyhole Gardening

An increasingly popular type of raised bed is called a keyhole bed. The idea originated in Africa, and is now a system being used more widely. It consists of a raised bed, traditionally made out of whatever free materials were available from the surrounding landscape, most commonly rocks. The beds are round, but there is a cleft in the side of the bed (hence the name 'keyhole') leading to the centre, where materials to be composted are piled. The compost bin is filled with garden waste, and as the material gradually breaks down, it leaches into the surrounding soil in the bed. The theory is that the constant leaching of nutrients and moisture from the compost bin should reduce the need to feed and water any vegetable plants growing in the raised bed.

Style Raised beds can be made out of almost anything, but can be designed to look very chic and fashionable. They provide an overall structure to a garden design, on what could otherwise be a flatter space.

Drainage Because the beds are raised off the ground, it improves drainage. This is particularly useful on an existing site with poor drainage or soil or at the bottom of a slope.

Warmer A raised bed will usually warm up faster in springtime than one in the ground, which will be more prone to coldness and dampness. They're also less likely to be affected by a ground frost.

Soil to suit what you want to grow A raised bed can be filled with suitable soil for the plants. If you want to grow blueberries or even cranberries, you can fill it with ericaceous compost to suit their requirements for acidic conditions. If ericaceous is simply added to the ground, it can quickly leach away, leaving the plants in the wrong conditions.

• Keyhole gardening is a type of raised bed with compost in the centre which leaches into the soil, increasing its fertility.

Salads and Leafy Crops

Most salads and leafy crops are fast-growing and easy to grow. They generally don't take up much space, either, so can be grown in window boxes and tubs and containers. They're ideal for people living in flats or who only have a small garden. They'll even tolerate a bit of shade, so can be grown in a porch or used to brighten up a dappled, shady area of the garden where other sun-dwelling vegetables might not be so happy.

Not only do salad leaves offer a delicious, crunchy, flavoursome addition to sandwiches and salads, the range of colours and textures can also look spectacular in the garden. In potagers, you often see a tapestry of leaf colours and patterns created as a feature that is just as good to look at as it is to taste.

The key to growing leafy crops is to sow and harvest 'little and often'. This will help to avoid gluts because unfortunately salad leaves don't keep long once they're picked and can quickly run to seed if left in the ground for too long and especially in hot weather. They are quick to germinate, so it is better to sow every couple of weeks and to harvest regularly. This will ensure you always have an abundance of fresh leaves. The other beauty of growing salad leaves is that they can be grown as catch crops, sowing them between slower-growing vegetables and harvesting them before their neighbours have grown to full size and matured.

Varieties of Lettuce to Try

There are lots of different salad leaves to try. The most common is lettuce and there are a few different types:

- Crisphead types include the most popular lettuce: iceberg. Crispheads are ball-shaped, producing tightly packed, large, crisp and crunchy leaves with a large central heart.
- Romaine (or Cos) types have a looser arrangement of crispy leaves than the crispheads, with more of an elongated or loaf shape.
- Butterheads generally have a loose head of leaves with a buttery, mild but sweet flavour. Butterhead lettuces usually last longer than the other types if kept in the fridge.

• Bok choy, also known as pak choi or bok choi, is a tasty Chinese lettuce.

• Rocket is a fast-growing salad leaf with a peppery flavour.

Some salad leaves are 'cut and come again', meaning that you can harvest the fresh new growth with scissors and they will keep sending out new leaves to be harvested again a week or two later.

Other Salad Leaves

Other popular salad leaves include spinach, which has varieties suitable for either autumn or spring sowings. Rocket has a strong, hot flavour and is hardier and easier to grow than spinach. The leaves can be picked as and when they are required for salad. Silverbeat is also easy care and tolerant of most conditions. Chinese cabbage is sometimes sold as Chinese leaves and their heads can either be steamed like cabbage or eaten fresh like a lettuce. Oriental vegetables such as Japanese mustard spinach, mibuna, mizuna, Chinese mustard greens and pak choi are all becoming increasingly popular to grow, and most can be either added to salads and eaten fresh, or steamed, or added to flavour stir fries, soups, stews and many other dishes.

Sowing Lettuce Seed

Salad leaves don't require much depth of soil. As little as 10 to 15cm is usually adequate, but they must have drainage. They prefer to be in sun or dappled light, but they can often struggle with summer heat, so may need shade in the middle of the day. Rake the soil to a fine tilth and then take out a thin drill using a cane or finger. Lightly sprinkle seeds into the drill, cover over with the soil, and water. If they are to be grown as 'cut and come again' they don't need thinning out, but if they are to develop as fully grown, hearting lettuces, they will need thinning out when they're about 2.5cm high to an eventual spacing of 30cm apart (smaller types such as semi-cos can be closer).

• Romaine (or Cos) lettuce has an elongated shape and loosely packed leaves.

• Mizuna is a Japanese leafy vegetable with attractive dissected leaves and a peppery flavour.

• Pick spinach when young or leave to mature for a stronger flavour.

• Iceberg lettuce forms a round ball of tightly packed, crunchy foliage.

Fruiting Vegetables

Although botanists would refer to most of these crops as fruits because they contain their seeds inside the flesh, in the gardening world they are considered very much part of the veggie patch and are mainly used in savoury dishes in the kitchen.

Fruiting vegetables will need to be grown in a warm, sunny spot and in cool areas might need some protection from the cold in the form of a greenhouse or polytunnel when young seedlings. Greenhouses and polytunnels can also be used to extend the season of summer vegetables. Crops in this group of vegetables include tomatoes, eggplants (aubergines), cucumbers, capsicums, chillies, courgettes, marrows, pumpkins and sweetcorn.

Tomatoes

Tomatoes should be sown in punnets about five to six weeks before you want to plant the seedlings in the ground and this should only be done when the daytime temperature regularly tops 20°C. Most tomatoes are grown as cordons (sometimes called 'indeterminate' types), which need a training system to support their growth. As the plant grows, some people believe that pinching out sublaterals encourages fruit production. It also stops the plant becoming too dense, which can encourage disease. However, some tomatoes have a bush habit (called 'determinate') and require little or no support. The 'tumbling types' of tomatoes can even be grown in hanging baskets. Watch out for tomato blight and choose varieties with resistance if it is a regular problem each year in the area. Avoid planting tomatoes in the same place two years running as this can cause problems with pests and diseases. Blossom end rot (when dark patches appear at the blossom end of fruits) is usually caused by inconsistent watering. Maintain consistent watering practices and plants will also need a weekly feed rich in potassium (such as

• Tomatoes are easy to grow but need a long growing season, so should be sown early in the year under cover.

a tomato feed) once they have started to form trusses. Indeterminate tomatoes are prolific fruiters from January until the onset of cold weather.

Cucurbits

The cucurbits (pumpkins, cucumbers, courgettes, marrows) should be sown in pots or in compost mounds over the soil in mid to late spring after the risk of frost is over. The cucurbits have large seeds and are often sown on their side to prevent water sitting on the surface and rotting the seed. When they're planted out, give each one lots of space and add plenty of organic matter into the planting holes and surrounding soil as they require plenty of

nutrients and moisture to enable them to develop to their full size and produce lots of fruit. They may also need feeding with a tomato feed every couple of weeks once they start to flower.

Most of the cucumbers grown in Australia and New Zealand are outdoor varieties and many are "burpless" with thin, non-bitter skins that don't require peeling. All outdoor cucumbers can be direct sown in spring once the risk of frost is over, or they can be sown indoors in winter and transplanted. Being a sprawling vine, they can be left to spread on the ground or trained up netting or a trellis to conserve space.

Capsicums (Bell Peppers) and Chillies

Capsicums and chillies are heat-loving vegetables that (especially chillies) require a hot, sunny spot. Those in cool climates might need to at least start them in a greenhouse or polytunnel and then plant them out once the risk of frost has passed. Otherwise, sow

• Cucumbers have a climbing or sprawling habit and need plenty of space to grow either.

them in trays outdoors in late spring and transplant once they are mature seedlings.

Eggplants

Eggplants also like hot, sunny conditions and, while they are treated as an annual in cold, frosty climates, they are a perennial in warmer areas. Direct sow seeds (in spring and summer) in warmer areas or in trays in cooler areas and transplant once they are mature seedlings.

Sweetcorn

The plants are wind-pollinated and should therefore be planted in a grid shape at about 40cm apart. The grid should be at least 4 x 4 plants for it to be effective, although a bigger grid is better.

Cabbage Family

The cabbage family, also known as brassicas, includes many well-known vegetables like Brussels sprouts, kale, cauliflower, broccoli and, inevitably, cabbage. Turnips and swedes are also members of the same family but are usually included with the rest of the root crop group, as is the less well-known kohlrabi. They are all easy to grow and collectively one of the healthiest and most nutritious of all the different vegetable groups.

This family grow best in cool weather, from late autumn to mid spring, when there is little else left to harvest in the kitchen garden.

All brassicas like similar conditions and tend to suffer from the same pests and diseases, some of which can be relatively serious. They are best grown in a different place each year to avoid too many problems. It is normal to sow brassicas in a seed bed before transplanting them out later, which can also help pest control.

Brassicas generally need firm, fertile soil with plenty of nitrogen and regular watering to do well. Lime is usually added in the autumn before planting to prevent the worst of the diseases, club root, and the soil must be firmed properly before planting to prevent wind rock and loose heads forming.

• Brussels sprouts provide a useful winter crop when little else is available.

Kale and Brussels Sprouts

The hardiest of the brassicas and most tolerant of heat and drought is kale. Brussels sprouts need to be planted in summer to allow enough growth for the sprouts to develop in winter. They should be staked as well as planted firmly or the individual sprouts are likely to 'blow', opening up like a flower, but kale is a little more easy-going. Red and

• Kale is a flavoursome winter crop.

• Calabrese is one of the faster growing members of the brassica family and is often sown directly into the ground.

• Cauliflower is one of the trickier members of the brassica family to grow.

black kale cultivars are also available to spice up this rather coarse vegetable.

Broccoli

Broccoli is a useful and productive plants to grow. Broccoli, including purple sprouting broccoli, is planted in spring and allowed to grow at its own pace before the spears are harvested early the following spring. It can be harvested 9 to 10 weeks from transplant.

Cauliflower

The fussiest of the flower-head brassica crops is the cauliflower. It performs very badly if conditions are not exactly right, requiring plenty of water and food, but the challenge is worth it to produce a creamy white, tight head. Cauliflower seedlings bolt in the heat so, in warm areas, plant the seedlings in late summer and autumn.

Cabbage

Cabbage do best in cool weather but some varieties are slower to bolt than others and have better resistance to caterpillars. The cabbage season begins with 'spring greens', sown the previous autumn and encouraged to grow loosely. These are then followed by spring-sown summer cabbages and later cabbages that can be harvested through autumn well into winter. Many winter cabbages can withstand frost, including the dark, crinkle-leaved savoy, and can stay in the ground until required.

As the cabbage family is a food source for pigeons, caterpillars, root flies and whitefly, they require plenty of attention and preventative protection, including collars round their roots and netting or mesh to keep out unwelcome diners.

• Cabbages can be grown practically all year round. Watch out for pests such as cabbage white caterpillars.

Perennial Vegetables

Perennial vegetables require space and a suitable site as they will remain in situ for many years. They can sometimes be slow to establish but will eventually produce a regular crop for anything up to 20 years without the constant annual preparations that other vegetables require.

Rhubarb

This is an invaluable addition to the productive garden, providing fruity tartness in the early part of the year when nothing else similar is available.

Rhubarb is normally planted as a bare root during the dormant season, at intervals of 1m (3ft) or so. It requires well-drained soil with plenty of rich organic matter. A sunny site is best but rhubarb will tolerate a slightly shadier site that may not be so good for other crops.

Rhubarb should not be harvested in its first year, and only a few stems should be picked in the second. Once fully established, it can then be picked regularly. By planting both summer and winter varieties rhubarb can be harvested all year round. Only the stems are edible as the leaves themselves contain a toxin. At the end of each season, remove all old leaves before mulching with manure or compost. It is relatively trouble-free but should be protected from slugs and snails.

Forced rhubarb is something of a speciality, with its early, sweet flavour. Simply cover the crown with a container that blocks light a few weeks before the season commences for skinny, sweet, pink stems.

• Rhubarb is a vigorous perennial plant producing lots of juicy and succulent stems.

Asparagus

A short but prolific season makes asparagus a luxurious joy if space can be found for it.

It requires a very well prepared bed in a sheltered, sunny position. Ruthlessly weed before digging out a trench and adding plenty of organic matter. Asparagus is usually planted as bare root crowns, which are spread out on individual mounds at least 30cm apart before being covered with soil and watered, ut it can also be planted as seeds and plants.

Allow the plants to build up strength in the first two years, and resist the temptation to harvest until the third year. Thereafter, the spears should be cut off just below ground level as soon as they are of eating size; the more they are cut, the more will grow. After midsummer, the ferny foliage can be allowed to develop. Maintenance is easy. Cut down dying foliage stems in winter, mulch and apply fertiliser in spring. Asparagus especially enjoys a seaweed mulch.

All male varieties are the most productive.

Artichokes

Despite the shared name, the two types of artichoke commonly grown are not related. Globe artichokes grow thistle-like large silver leaves and flower buds that are harvested around midsummer. They, like asparagus, are usually grown from root cuttings or offsets planted in the dormant season in a sunny, sheltered site with plenty of organic matter. They are large plants that can easily shade out other crops, so site appropriately.

Jerusalem artichokes are grown for their edible tubers. As long as they are in a sunny spot they will grow happily in poor soil, producing a mass of tall sunflower heads in late summer. They have a tendency to spread, so careful control is needed. In order to do this, dig up the patch each year. Harvest plenty of the nut-tasting tubers in late autumn and replant a few to keep them in check.

Less well-known perennial vegetables include French sorrel (*Rumex acetosa*), which must be differentiated from sheep sorrel, which is a weed.

Peas and Beans

These are staples of the vegetable garden, producing heavy crops throughout late spring to late summer, full of useful protein and relatively easy to grow. They are collectively known as legumes, with some able to tolerate cooler conditions while others have arrived here from much warmer places and need a little help at the start.

All the legumes are usually planted in a sunny site in very enriched soil, preferably newly manured or composted, although they can produce their own nitrogen in nodules on their roots. All legumes need regular watering, even though feeding is less essential. The climbing varieties need something to twine up and wrap their tendrils around, either a wigwam of canes or some sort of supported netting or sticks.

Broad Beans
Broad beans from Europe are delicious when young and freshly picked but are tough enough to be planted and survive through winter. Sowing from April means you can avoid leggy growth, but later sowings are equally successful and can spread the season right through summer. Taller varieties will require supporting, but there are dwarf cultivars available. In spring, the tops should be pinched out once enough pods have begun to form, to encourage a better crop.

• Peas usually need shelling prior to cooking, unless you try sugar snaps or mangetout which are eaten in the pod.

Peas
Peas are a cool weather crop that prefer deep loams. The taste of a young pea fresh from the pod is unsurpassed for delightful sweetness and flavour and is quite addictive. Twiggy brush and sticks are ideal for growing most peas on but taller varieties may prefer a firmer support.

Peas should be harvested regularly and young before the sugars turn into starch, unless floury peas are required. Once cropping is finished, cut the stems off at ground level and leave the nitrogen-fixing roots in the ground to feed the next crop.

• Broad beans can be sown early on in the year and so are often one of the first crops to harvest in the garden.

As well as the standard pea, mangetout and sugarsnap peas are also available, where the whole pod is eaten.

Runner Beans

A classic sight in a traditional summer vegetable patch, the runner bean is both beautiful and highly productive, almost too productive, as the more the beans are picked, the more new pods will grow. Support for runner beans needs to be strong and tall. They climb strongly and can be very heavy when laden with so many long green pods.

Runner beans originate from South America and are perennial, dying back in autumn and reemerging in spring. Sow direct into the ground in spring. They thrive in rich, moisture-retaining soil, preferably in a previously prepared trench filled with uncomposted kitchen waste, as long as they are watered regularly, especially when flowering. They can be damaged by black bean aphids.

French Beans

This group includes both climbing beans, such as borlotti, and dwarf varieties that rarely reach more than half a metre high, making them perfect for pots. They are fast growing annuals that can be direct sown once risk of frost has past. Purple and yellow varieties are available as well as the standard green.

• French beans shouldn't be planted out until the risk of frosts has passed, but can be sown indoors to get them off to a good start.

• Runner beans (right) should be picked every few days to keep the plant cropping regularly throughout the season.

Onion Family

Food would be much blander without this group of vegetables, which provide taste and savour to a wide variety of dishes in the kitchen. They have a reputation stretching back centuries for boosting good health and vitality but, whatever their status as a medicinal wonder, they are easy and rewarding to grow.

• Onions are more easily grown from 'sets', although they can also be grown from seed.

Both onions and shallots like a sunny spot, with rich, well-drained soil. Good airflow will help prevent rust, the most common of the onion diseases, which weakens the plants though rarely kills them. Other members of the onion family include spring onions, fast-growing small onions for salads, perennial onions and chives.

Onions

Onions, the staple of cookery, can be grown from seed or, increasingly popularly, from sets, which are baby onions already partially grown. Seeds can be direct sown and then thinned or sown into punnets and the seedlings transplanted in spring. Separate completely for the largest onions or leave to grow on in small clumps to save space, although the bulbs will be smaller. Onion sets can be planted out later in spring as they need less time to grow on and are usually planted in drills, pushed gently into the ground until only the tips show. Protect newly planted sets from birds, which often pull them out.

Both brown and red onions can be grown, with red onions being considered the sweeter. Water when dry and weed carefully around the shallow-rooted bulbs until the leaves begin to bend over in summer. At this point they can be harvested. Lift carefully and dry for several days, preferably in sun, to improve their storage.

• Shallots are grown in a similar way to onions.

•After harvesting, onions should be left out to dry in the sun for a few days before cooking or storing.

Shallots need a longer season than onions and are normally grown from sets. Each set will gradually form a clump of new shallot bulbs, which can be harvested just a little earlier than onions but in similar fashion. French shallots, with their elongated torpedo shape, are considered to have a finer flavour than the round varieties.

Leeks

They like moist conditions and are one of the few vegetables that enjoy heavy, more acidic soil, but will thrive anywhere as long as they have rich, moist conditions. Leeks are sown in punnets in spring to early autumn before being transplanted out into deep holes to ensure a good length of white stem. Later, they can be sown directly into drills, especially if they are to be harvested young as mini-veg. Left to grow on to full size, leeks can be harvested from autumn through to the following spring.

Garlic

For maximum flavour, nothing beats garlic, an onion family member associated with the Mediterranean but which grows well across the different climate zones in Australia and New Zealand as long as the right varieties are planted. Supermarket cloves don't do well because they are often sprayed with an inhibitor to stop them sprouting, so it is always best to buy specialist bulbs from a horticultural supplier. Garlic needs a cold period followed by a long season of sunshine to do really well. Plant individual cloves tip up in autumn in a rich, moist, but well-drained and sunny site, and water in dry spells. Garlic can be eaten fresh while still green, for a mild kick, or left until the leaves yellow before being lifted and dried for storage.

• A popular winter crop, leek seedlings are planted in deeply to blanch the stem and therefore make it more tender.

Root Crops

Always following behind the greedier vegetables in the productive garden, root crops are a mixed bunch, coming from a variety of families but nearly all sharing a dislike for fresh manure, which will make the roots distort and divide with often grotesque results, as will stony ground. They also tend to need space and time to grow, so are perhaps best suited to a larger plot.

Turnips and Swedes

These are more of a speciality crop and not that common. Being members of the cabbage family, these can cope with slightly richer soil. They are not to everyone's taste but turnips are enjoying something of a revival, especially when young. Baby turnips can be harvested after only six weeks, given moist, rich soil, but should always be harvested within three months or they will become woody and unpleasant. You can direct sow the seeds. Swede takes much longer to grow and is sown directly into the ground in spring to mature in the winter months. Thin out carefully to avoid unnecessary disturbance.

• Swedes are a popular wintertime crop but need a long growing season so should be sown directly in spring.

Parsnips

Parsnips are better regarded and more classic in their root crop requirements. A light, stone-free soil that has been deeply dug will suit them best, along with plenty of sun. The seed can be sown directly into the ground. Thin out but do not overwater, and harvest from late summer onwards, although they can be left in the ground for longer, being frost-hardy. It is claimed that their flavour improves with a touch of frost.

• Turnips can be harvested as 'baby nips' after just six weeks from sowing and have a tender, sweeter flavour.

• Parsnips are a popular winter root crop that need a long growing season, so are often sown in early spring.

CARROT FLY

Carrots are very prone to attack by the carrot fly, which lays its eggs in the roots. The larvae can burrow throughout, causing unsightly damage. Any disturbance will release a scent that attracts the flies but they can be successfully dealt with by fencing the carrot bed with fine mesh as they are unable to fly higher than 60cm.

Carrots

Carrots, top of most people's list of tasty roots, can almost be treated as a salad crop. Regular sowing will ensure crop after crop of small baby vegetables throughout summer, while some can be left to grow on until winter. Carrots prefer light, sandy soil, cleared of any stones, with reasonable fertility in order to produce long, straight roots, although ball-shaped varieties are available for heavier soils. The seeds are very fine so thinning is usually necessary. Cutting the tops off with a pair of scissors will prevent too much disturbance but thinnings removed from the ground can be eaten as baby carrots, so wasting less. Water regularly to avoid splitting.

Beets

The beet family is also normally included in this group, largely due to the characteristics of beetroot itself, although other beets are grown for their leaves only.
Beetroots are full of flavour and health benefits and can be sown from spring through to early summer and harvested around six weeks later for the sweetest, most tender crops. Golf-ball size is perfect as bigger roots tend towards woodiness. Increasingly, non-purple beetroots are available to grow.

Potatoes

In a garden with plenty of space, potatoes are often given a bed all to themselves, but if not they are usually lumped in with this group for obvious reasons. Not technically a true root crop as the tubers, not the roots themselves, are eaten, potatoes are grown from 'seed' potatoes, small egg-sized tubers that are often encouraged to start producing shoots before planting in spring, a technique known as 'chitting'. This starts them into growth and encourages earlier cropping. Planted in rich soil, potatoes are traditionally earthed up over the growing season before being harvested when their flowers open, in the case of early potatoes, or left to the end of summer.

• Beetroots can be sown successionally every few weeks to provide a regular supply of tasty roots throughout the season.

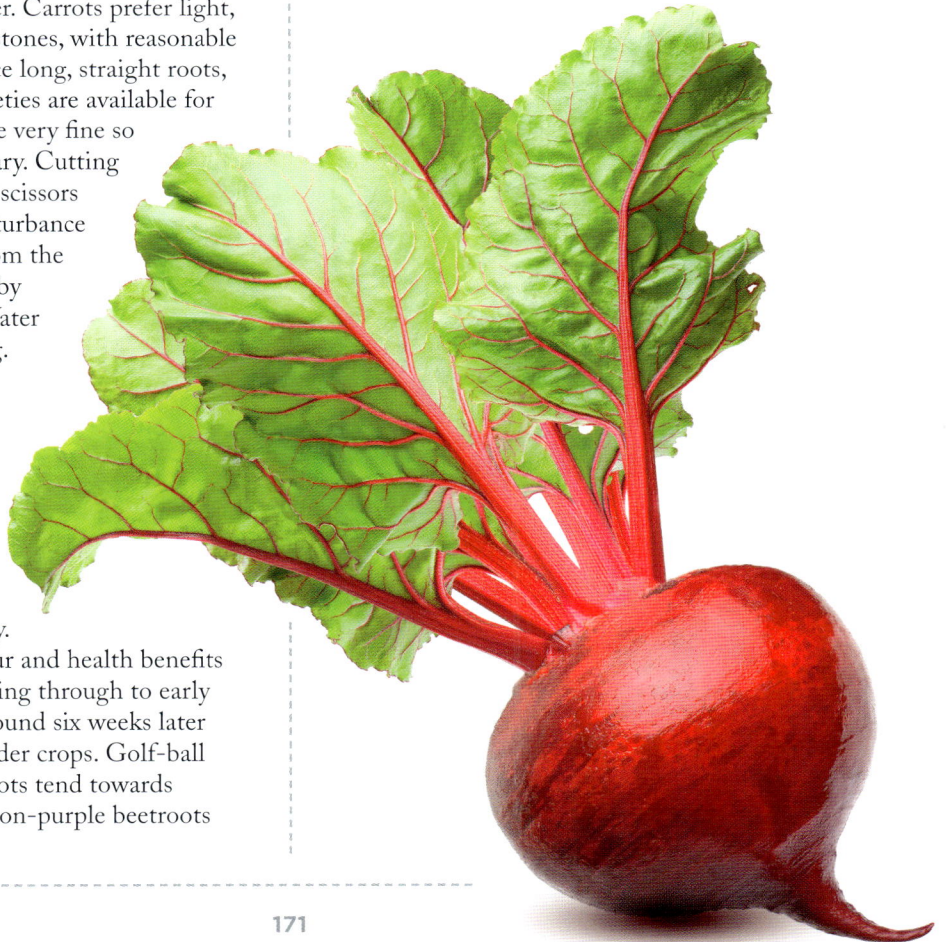

Growing Herbs

Even if you are not planning to grow your own fruit or vegetables in your garden, herbs are such a garden mainstay that you will probably find them working their way on to your planting lists without even realising it. Who can plant a garden without at least considering rosemary, sage, thyme and mint?

Gardeners can have a lot of fun with herbs. Fantastic results can be achieved with very little effort in beds and borders, containers, hanging baskets, troughs and windowsills. All that is needed is well-drained soil (dig in lots of horticultural grit if you are not sure) and plenty of sun. Commonly, herbs are grown together as they all require similar growing conditions, but if you feel confident enough, try mixing them into ornamental displays.

Formal herb gardens can look very good if you have the space. Traditionally these are edged and compartmentalised with low shrubs, clipped to shape, to create interesting patterns and to define the beds. The edging plants play quite an important role, because they maintain the structure and interest of the beds in winter, when most of the herbs are dormant. For smaller or less formal gardens, herbs can be planted through gravel or in tight spaces between paving stones on a sunny patio.

• Thyme can be planted in light, well-drained soil but can just as easily be grown in a container for easy harvesting.

CREATING A HERB BED

To set up a new herb bed, dig in 5kg (11lb) of well-rotted organic matter per square metre to raise fertility levels. After this, herbs will rarely need feeding, and after an initial few weeks of watering to help new plants take root, watering will no longer be necessary either. Regular picking and trimming will keep your herbs in good shape, and remove any dead material on sight.

Where to Grow
If you like to use herbs in your cooking, then it really helps to have them growing close to the house, ideally near the back door in a special trough, container, window box or raised bed. It will have to be a sunny position that gets at least six hours of sun per day in midsummer; any less and your herbs will struggle and may lose their flavour.

Herb	Full Sun	Partial Shade	Soil	Moisture	Hardiness	Height (cm)	Spread (cm)	Sow	Harvest
Chives (*Allium schoenoprasum*)	Full sun preferred		Loam, Chalk, Sand, Clay	Moist but well-drained	H6	40	30	Sept–Mar	Nov–May
Coriander (*Coriandrum sativum*)	Full sun preferred	Partial shade preferred	Loam, Chalk, Sand	Moist but well-drained	H5	40	25	Sept–Apr	Oct–May
Dill (*Anethum graveolens*)	Full sun preferred		Loam, Chalk	Well-drained	H4	90	30	Mar–Apr	Sept–Oct
Bronze Fennel (*Foeniculum vulgare*)	Full sun preferred	Partial shade preferred	Loam, Chalk, Sand, Clay	Moist but well-drained	H6	150	50	Sept–Dec	Dec–Jan
Mint (*Mentha suaveolens*)	Full sun preferred	Partial shade preferred	Loam	Moist but well-drained	H5	100	150	Aug–Sept	Oct–Mar
Oregano (*Origanum amanum*)	Full sun preferred		Chalk	Well-drained	H3	10	50	Sept–Nov	Nov–May
Parsley (*Petroselinum crispum*)	Full sun preferred	Partial shade preferred	Loam	Moist but well-drained	H4	45	45	Jun–Dec	Sept–Apr
Rosemary (*Rosmarinus officinalis*)	Full sun preferred		Loam, Chalk, Sand, Clay	Moist but well-drained	H4	150	100	Sept–Nov	All year
Sage (*Salvia officinalis*)	Full sun preferred	Partial shade preferred	Loam, Clay	Moist but well-drained	H4	100	100	Sept–Nov	Nov–Jun
Sweet basil (*Ocimum basilicum*)	Full sun preferred		Loam, Sand	Well-drained	H1C	45	40	Sept–Feb	Nov–Apr
Thyme (*Thymus vulgaris*)	Full sun preferred		Loam, Chalk	Moist but well-drained	H6	45	45	Sept–Nov	All year

Situation
- Full sun preferred
- Partial shade preferred

Soil Type
- Loam
- Sand
- Chalk
- Clay

Watering
- Moist but well-drained
- Well-drained

Hardiness
On a scale of 1 to 6

• Herbs can be grown in containers and kept just outside the kitchen window so they can be picked easily when required for cooking.

PLANTING A HERB TROUGH

Before you start, choose a selection of herbs that complement each other well. For a Mediterranean mix, for example, try chives, sage, thyme, tarragon and rosemary.

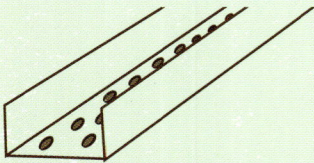

1 Ensure that the trough has holes in its base for drainage.

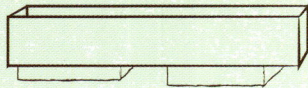

2 Position the trough where you want it to go, raising it off the ground slightly using bricks or flat stones.

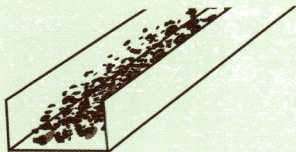

3 Line the bottom of the trough with a layer of grit or gravel.

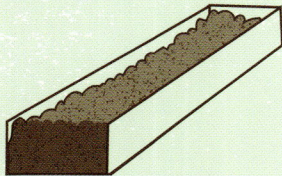

4 Fill the trough with soil-based compost, leaving a 1cm space between the top of the compost and the rim of the trough.

5 Arrange the plants until you are happy with the way they look. Water each plant in its pot, then remove each one by turning it upside down and easing it out.

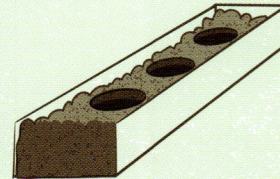

6 Dig a hole in the compost large enough for the root ball of the plant, and place the plant in it.

7 Firm the compost around the plant using your fingers.

8 Plant the rest of the trough in the same way, then level the compost and water in well, giving the trough a good soaking.

9 Top off the compost with a layer of gravel or grit. The purpose of the grit is to keep the leaves clean from compost, but it is also a nice ornamental touch.

• If you're short of space in the garden, a range of herbs can be grown in vertical herb troughs attached to walls and fences.

How to Grow

Herbs tolerate most soil types, but if you have a sandy, free-draining loam, you are already halfway there. Wet and heavy soils, particularly those with a high clay content, are best avoided, as are acidic soils. In such cases, the best solution is to grow herbs in a container or raised bed filled with a well-drained soil-based compost.

When to Harvest

The best time to harvest herbs is on a warm, sunny day, just before they start to flower. Use a sharp knife, and try to take material from all over the plant so that the shape is kept balanced. Do not worry about frequent harvesting – herbs have evolved to cope with such treatment. However, do not cut back into the older woody growth.

Soft Fruit

There are lots of different soft fruits that are grown in kitchen gardens and plots, with a wide range of colours and flavours to excite and tantalise even the most discerning of taste buds. Soft fruit doesn't take up too much room and most of them can be grown in pots. Strawberries can even be grown in hanging baskets.

Raspberries

Raspberries prefer slightly moist and acidic soil in full sun. There are two different types and their method of cultivation and pruning is different, so it is important to establish which one it is. Firstly, there are the autumn-fruiting raspberries, which bear fruit from late summer through to early winter. Then there are the summer-fruiting types, which produce fruit from early to late summer, depending on the variety.

Summer varieties produce the fruit on canes produced the previous year. To prune them, the old fruiting canes should be cut down to ground level after they have finished fruiting. The new canes

• Raspberries are either summer or autumn types: the type determines how they should be pruned.

(produced in that year) should then be tied in, leaving a spacing of about a hand's width between each one. Any other surplus canes can be cut back to ground level.

The autumn-fruiting varieties produce all their fruit on canes formed in the same year. They are very easy to care for. Simply cut the entire plant down to ground level in late winter or early spring, which will encourage new, vigorous, fruit-bearing crops the following autumn.

• Strawberries are mainly summer-bearing types that crop in midsummer or ever-bearing types that fruit throughout the season.

Gooseberries and Redcurrants

Gooseberries are delicious if the fruits are thinned out and the remaining fruits left to allow their flavours to ripen on the bush. Redcurrants look beautiful when in fruit, with the bush almost looking like it is dripping with red translucent berries. Gooseberries and redcurrants have a very similar growth habit and are often trained and pruned in the same way. They can be grown as open-centre bushes, stepovers or upright vertical cordons, standards or fans. They will both tolerate shade, so are useful plants for growing as fans on north- or east-facing fences and walls.

Both gooseberries and redcurrants fruit on older wood and at the base of the previous year's growth. To prune a gooseberry or redcurrant as a bush, clear any suckers or growth coming off the short central leg the bush sits on. Select five or six branches that are facing outwards and remove growth coming up through the middle so it is 'open-centred', like a goblet on a short stem. In subsequent years, the new growth on the branches should be pruned back to a couple of buds between late autumn and late winter, except for the leaders of each branch, which should be cut back by a third. Keep the centre of the bush free from other shoots. They grow best in cool, well-mulched soil and they need a winter chilling.

Blackcurrants

Blackcurrants have a different growth habit to redcurrants. They fruit on young shoots produced the previous year. They are grown as stool bushes, whereby they are planted more deeply than usual so that the top of the root ball is several centimetres below the surface of the soil, which encourages a multi-stemmed habit from the base. Due to their growth habit, they are not suited to growing as cordons, fans or open-centre bushes.

Blackcurrant pruning is easy. Simply use a pair of loppers to remove about a third of the thicker, more mature wood at the base of the plant between late autumn and late winter. Always remove any wayward shoots that may rest on the ground once laden with fruit. They grow best in cool, well-mulched soil and they need a winter chilling.

Strawberries

There are two types of strawberries commonly grown in the kitchen garden. The most common are the summer-bearing types, which bear large fruits from late spring through to midsummer. There are also ever-bearing or perpetual types, which fruit for most of summer and early autumn, but don't produce such large fruits as summer types. Both types are traditionally grown in strawberry beds, spaced about 30cm apart in rows 70cm apart. Straw is placed under the foliage as the fruit develops to stop the berries rotting on the ground. Strawberries can also be grown in hanging baskets, planters and growing bags, all away from ground level where slugs and snails will find it harder to reach the fruit, though beware of birds.

Strawberries produce runners on the main plants, which should be removed while the plant is growing to channel all its energy into the production of fruit. Runner plants can be potted up, though, and planted out the following year to increase stock. Strawberries are usually grown for two or three years before being dug up and replaced with new plants. If space allows, the replacement plants should go in a new bed to reduce the chance of pest and disease infestations.

Tree Fruit (Apples and Pears)

Apple and pear trees offer at least two seasons of interest, with glorious blossom in spring and attractive fruit in late summer or autumn. Even in winter their bare, gnarled trunks and branches can bring an impressive architectural and structural quality to a garden.

Both apples and pears have similar growth habits and can therefore be treated the same. For the trees to bear fruit, they need pollinating from another fruit tree nearby, which must be of a different variety but flower at the same time.

Garden centres and nurseries have devised a system of categorising fruit trees into pollination groups to ensure that trees will have adequate pollination when planted. If there is a tree in a nearby garden, this may well suffice, but if not it may be necessary to buy two trees in the same group. It is best to get expert advice from a specialist nursery regarding pollination groupings, to avoid later disappointment.

ROOTSTOCKS

Apple and pear trees are also grafted or budded onto rootstocks, which determines their eventual height.

Apple rootstocks
The most commonly found apple rootstocks are as follows:

M27 Extremely dwarfing – suitable for stepovers, growing in containers and free-standing tree. Grows to 1.2–1.8m x 1.5m (4–6ft x 5ft).

M9 Moderately dwarfing – suitable for stepovers, cordons, growing in containers and free-standing tree. Grows to 1.8–2.4m x 2.7m (6–8ft x 9ft).

M26 Dwarfing – suitable for fans, cordons, espaliers, growing in containers and free-standing tree. Grows to 2.4–3m x 3.6m (8–10ft x 12ft).

MM106 Semi-dwarfing, the most popular rootstock – suitable for fans, cordons, espaliers, growing in containers and free-standing tree. Grows to 3–4m x 4m (10–13ft x 13ft).

M111 Vigorous – best grown as a free-standing tree. Grows to 4–4.5m x 4.5m (13–15ft x 15ft).

M25 Very vigorous – best grown as a free-standing tree, but probably too vigorous for most gardens. Grows to at least 4.5m x 6m (20ft x 15ft).

Pear rootstocks
Quince C Dwarfing – suitable for cordons, espaliers and free-standing tree. Grows to 2.5–3m (6–10ft).

Quince A Semi-vigorous – suitable for fans, cordons, espaliers and free-standing tree. Grows to 3–4.5m (10–15ft).

Tree Shapes

Apples and pears are particularly versatile and can be trained into many different shapes, making them attractive features in the garden. The most common shapes are shown below, but in some historic and contemporary gardens there are even more elaborate and impressive shapes, which can be created with a bit of imagination and pruning know-how! The shapes below are known as 'restricted forms' because they are regularly pruned to a desired ornamental shape, as opposed to growing into a free-standing shaped tree.

Pruning Apple and Pear Trees

Free-standing trees are pruned mainly in winter. This includes removing crossing branches and thinning out laterals to ensure the canopy isn't too dense and the sunlight is able to reach most of the tree. On open-centre trees, any branches growing into the centre should be removed.

Restricted forms of fruit trees are pruned in late summer after they have finished growing. A method called the Modified Lorette system is used, which involves pruning back the new growth to one or two buds. In winter, any dense clusters of spurs can be pruned out.

• Pear trees should be pruned at least once a year to keep them in shape and to ensure new growth.

TREE SHAPES

Oblique cordon

One of the most commonly seen shapes in the garden. It consists of a central trunk with a system of short spurs and laterals coming off them. It is grown at an angle of about 45 degrees to slow down the vigour of the plant and encourage better flower and fruit distribution along its trunk.

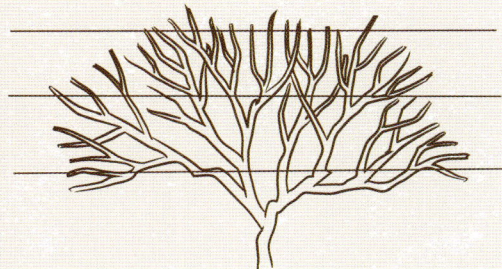

Fan

A very attractive method of training fruit trees onto a wall or fence. Trees are grown on a short trunk and then branches are spread out in a fan shape and tied on wires attached to the fence or wall.

TREE SHAPES

Espalier
Probably the most ornate method of pruning an apple tree. It is suitable for training against a wall or fence or on a system of wires strained between two upright posts. It has a central stem or trunk, with numerous tiers of horizontal branches trained out on either side of it. Along these horizontal branches are short fruiting spurs and laterals. There is usually about 25cm between each tier. There can be as many tiers as the vigour of the tree can cope with, but it is usually three or four.

Central-leader/spindle trees
Grown with a central leader and a 'Christmas tree' style of shape, with tiers of branches narrowing towards the top of the tree This shape ensures that the higher sections of the tree cast minimal shade on the lower branches.

Stepovers
Quite simply a single-tiered espalier. They are a popular and ornate method of edging pathways or vegetable beds. They're usually grown on M27 or M9 rootstocks as other rootstocks are too vigorous. The first tier is about 40cm off the ground, meaning that they can be 'stepped over', hence their name.

Free-standing trees
Bush tree grown on a single trunk with a goblet or open-shaped structure above.

Stone Fruits

There is a wide range of stone fruits that can be grown in the garden, all belonging to the genus *Prunus*. They're all easy to grow, and look just as wonderful when covered in spring blossom as they do when covered in fruit.

• Apricots are traditionally grown under cover.

Stone fruits require a certain number of chilling hours to set fruit, so they are best suited to cooler and more temperate climates. One of the key aspects to remember is not to prune them in winter, as this leaves them susceptible to diseases. Instead they are usually pruned in spring or midsummer. For the same reason, avoid pruning trees in this group when it is raining or in damp conditions.

Plums

Probably the most popular of all the stone fruits. Plums are prone to over-cropping, so it is essential that their fruits are thinned as they start to swell to avoid branches snapping, to a spacing of every 5–8cm or a pair every 15cm. Plums don't respond as well to pruning as apples and pears do, and therefore it should only be carried out to help shape the tree, remove crossing, dead or diseased wood, or to thin out a dense canopy.

Peaches and Nectarines

Very closely related, and grown in the same way. They both require a warm, sheltered site to ripen well, and are usually grown as free-standing trees. Their swelling buds may need protection from the rain with a plastic cover in early spring, as this can cause the fungus peach leaf curl to manifest itself. They fruit on wood produced the previous year, so pruning should involve removing some of the older wood and tying in newer shoots. It is important to

thin the fruit to get them to ripen fully. When they are the size of a hazelnut they should be thinned to 10cm apart and when the size of a walnut to 20cm apart.

Apricots

These have a similar growth habit to plums. Their fruit should be thinned out to 5–8cm apart when hazelnut-sized. They bear their fruit on growth made the previous year (like peaches) but also on short spurs from the older wood, like plums. Pruning is therefore best done as a combination of some replacement pruning and some spur pruning.

Cherries

There are two different types of cherries, sweet and acidic (sour) ones. Unfortunately, they have different cropping habits and therefore the pruning and training is different. Sour cherries (such as morello) bear fruit on wood produced the previous year and so pruning entails removing some of the older wood to give new shoots room to grow. Sweet cherries produce fruit on an older system of spurs, and therefore pruning should entail shortening some of the branches to encourage fruiting spurs. Pruning should take place from early to midsummer.

Cherries are usually grown as free-standing trees. Sweet cherries require more sunlight and should be grown on a south- or south-west-facing wall, but acidic cherries will tolerate some shade. They can also be grown as free-standing trees.

• Cherries are either the sour types that fruit on the previous year's wood, or sweet cherries that crop on older spurs.

Other Popular Fruits

There are simply thousands of different fruits to try growing in the kitchen garden. Some of the more popular ones are listed below, but do look out for other exciting or perhaps unusual ones in plant catalogues or nurseries. After all, one of the pleasures of growing your own fruit is being able to eat something you might not readily find in a shop.

• Blueberries are easy to grow but require acidic soil. If this isn't possible, grow them in pots in ericaceous compost.

Hybrid Berries

Given enough space and a cool winter there are lots of hybrid berries worth trying, including loganberries, jostaberries, loganberries and non-weedy blackberry varieties. They are generally vigorous plants, being related to the bramble, and many have thorns so care is needed when pruning them. However, most of them produce delicious fruit. They have a similar fruiting habit to summer raspberries, producing fruit mainly on growth produced the previous year. Prune them after fruiting, removing the older fruiting canes by cutting them at the base, and tying the new growth onto a system of wire or trellis. These new canes will produce fruit the following year.

Blueberries

Blueberries are a delicious soft fruit, but require acidic soil of 5.5pH or lower in order to thrive. If these conditions aren't possible, they can be grown in containers or raised beds filled with ericaceous compost. If planting in the ground, they should be planted at 1.2m apart in full sun, in moist but well-drained soil. If growing in a container, they should be watered with rainwater to avoid increasing the pH levels. They should be pruned by removing about a third of the older wood towards the base of the plant. This is to encourage younger shoots, which will produce the berries. The best time to prune is early spring just as the buds are beginning to swell. This is to help identify if any branches are dead so that they can be removed at the time of pruning.

Kiwi

This is a climbing, sprawling plant and therefore needs some support when growing it in the garden. Most kiwis need both male and female plants to produce fruit (the fruit appearing on the female) and it is estimated that one male plant will pollinate up to eight females. Plants should be planted about 4m from each other. In smaller gardens with limited space, self-fertile varieties can be grown, meaning only the single plant is required. They require a warm, sunny site and may need protection from frost in springtime by being wrapped in a fleece. Pruning takes place in winter by cutting laterals back to about three or four buds beyond the final fruited shoot. In addition, about one-third of the oldest laterals should be cut back to about 5cm from the main trunk, which will encourage new shoots the following year. They may need a summer prune as well to keep their rampant growth in check.

• Kiwis usually require a male and female plant to produce a crop, although there are self-fertilising varieties available.

Fig

With its luxuriant, glossy foliage, there is no other plant that can conjure up a Mediterranean or exotic theme in the garden like the fig. If left to its own devices, it will develop into a large sprawling bush or small tree, but probably not producing many edible figs. Pruning can take place in late summer or spring. Remove some of the older wood and tie in new shoots. Because figs produce fruit in the tips, some of the new shoots can be cut back to encourage more tips to form, which will in turn produce more fruit.

Introduction to Protected Cultivation

Gardeners can exercise a great deal of control over their gardens but there will always be one factor that, by and large, remains outside their sphere of influence. Weather and climatic conditions play a huge role in the success or failure of every garden activity, influencing almost everything from the germination of seeds and the success of cuttings to the length of the growing season, the range of plants and even the type of maintenance required.

For centuries, gardeners have searched for methods and equipment that will allow them to manipulate and alleviate the influence of the seasons and climate, and modern gardeners now have a range of possibilities available to them, something that may become ever more important as climate change takes hold. While traditionally the use of protection for plants has largely been about extending the growing season or growing specialist exotic plants, it may also allow our gardens to cope better with extremes in the future.

Greenhouses

The greenhouse enables some gardeners to have warm season crops such as tomatoes and basil all year. They are also used to house succulents and other warm-weather collections by some gardeners in cool areas. They can also play a useful role in plant propagation. It is quite possible that the greenhouse can trace its history as far back as the Roman Empire.

Cold Frames and Cloches

There are, however, other, less costly types of protection available. In the vegetable garden, it is common to see cold frames holding trays of newly germinated and pricked-out crops, cloches protecting newly planted seedlings or polythene tunnels covering lines of produce that appreciate a little extra warmth. Vegetable growing is an area where gardeners can influence conditions surprisingly well through the use of some sort of protection, and in the case of commercial production protected cultivation has become a highly technical, efficient means of maximising the value of a crop.

• Carrot plants being grown under a cloche.

• Greenhouses can protect your favourite tender potted plants from the worst of the winter weather, especially if heated.

Cold Frames, Cloches and Tunnels

Cold frames and cloches are most often employed to protect germinating seeds and seedlings, while tunnels provide shelter, warmth or sometimes shade when plants are growing.

Cold Frames

There are a number of uses for a cold frame. If space is limited it can be treated as an unheated greenhouse to overwinter half-hardy plants and autumn-sown seeds or to shelter plants that dislike the damp, such as alpines. Most commonly, though, it is a useful piece of equipment for plants initially grown in a more protected environment to get used to outside conditions, a gradual process known as 'hardening off'.

A standard cold frame is made up of clear sides, either glass or plastic, with one or more top frames known as 'lights'. The most inexpensive versions are made from lightweight aluminium, making it possible to move them easily around the garden. They provide the maximum amount of light for plants but are not as strong as other types and may have to be pegged down in strong winds. They are also less good at insulating the plants within from the cold, although this can be remedied by adding layers of insulation such as bubble wrap or old carpet if necessary, bearing in mind that this will need to be removed in the day to let light and air in.

Brick and wood frames are also possible, though expensive unless home-made, and will retain warmth much better.

'Lights' should be either sliding or hinged to allow gradual and proper ventilation, while the choice of glass or plastic should depend on the risk to others. If children and animals might be in danger, plastic is a more sensible option, even if it does not transmit light quite so well.

• Cold frames are useful, especially in springtime, to harden off young seedlings before planting out in the ground.

Cloches

The word 'cloche' covers a number of different shapes and styles of protective coverings, which are mostly seen in the vegetable patch, although they can be equally useful elsewhere in the garden. Any plant that requires a little extra warmth will welcome a cloche.

At its most basic, a cloche for an individual plant can be made by cutting off the end of a plastic bottle. Ready-made cloches such as the bell cloche, usually made of glass, are considerably more attractive.

For larger groups of plants or taller plants, tent or barn cloches are more suitable. Made of either glass clipped together or cheaper but less effective plastic, they can be placed over plants to provide extra protection and warmth in winter or to speed up the start of the growing season in spring.

• Growing plants in a tunnel will provide extra protection to slightly tender plants and get seedlings off to an early start.

Tunnels

Tunnels, like cloches, both protect and warm the plants and the soil underneath, encouraging earlier cropping. Whether rigid or flexible, they are made from a series of hoops supporting a length of either plastic or fleece. They can also be covered with shade netting to protect plants like lettuce that are prone to bolting in sun. A polytunnel works along exactly the same lines but on a much larger scale.

Greenhouses and Basic Requirements

A glasshouse or greenhouse, as it's often called, can be either heated or unheated. Either way, it is a useful addition to the garden, although it must be remembered that the plants grown in it are utterly dependent on the gardener for most of their basic needs, whether that be soil, water, light, nutrients, temperature or ventilation.

TIPS FOR CHOOSING AND SITING A GREENHOUSE

Pick a style that blends with the overall garden design and is suitable for the space available. There are a number of styles available, from the most common 'span' type to the curvy 'mansard'. Lean-tos are useful in limited space, as are mini greenhouses. Specialist styles, such as alpine houses, are also available but are designed for specific purposes rather than general use.

• Greenhouses should always be sited on firm, level ground or the frame may warp and the glass crack.

• Avoid siting in a wind tunnel or frost pocket but try to provide some shelter – a wall or windbreak is fine. Avoid large trees, which cast too much shade and could fall. A free-standing greenhouse should receive no more than a few hours of shade each day.

• Ensure good access so that wheelbarrows and other items can be moved and unloaded easily and safely.

• If possible, choose a site close to services such as electricity and water. Even if you are not making use of them initially, you may wish to make some additions further down the line.

• If planning to use the greenhouse primarily for overwintering tender plants or raising new plants in spring, orient it east to west to make the most of winter sunshine. If planning to use it mostly during the summer months, orient north to south.

• Lean-to greenhouses should be positioned in slightly more shade than free-standing greenhouses to avoid overheating.

• With good care, a greenhouse can greatly increase the range of plants that can be grown, while keeping out the extreme cold, wind and rain, and even without extra heat will warm up more quickly in spring to lengthen the growing season.

Shading, Ventilation, Heating and Watering

Successful greenhouse gardening requires getting the environment and conditions just right to suit the plants within. An unheated greenhouse is economical and suitable for growing summer crops such as tomatoes but cannot protect plants from the worst winter weather. Adding heating allows for a larger range of plants to be maintained and better propagation opportunities, but a warm greenhouse suitable for growing tropical plants needs a minimum temperature of 13°C (55°F) to ensure such plants thrive.

Heat is a key factor, especially for growing plants that are not suited to the outside climate, but, equally important, shading through the hottest days of the summer will also be required in the vast majority of cases, however much plants like the sun. Ventilation too is a vital factor to be considered and balanced against heat retention and humidity requirements.

Shading

Shading helps control the temperature and prevents vulnerable young plants from receiving too much sunlight, which leads to leaf scorch and dehydration. On average, shading should reduce light levels by around 50 per cent and this can be done by applying a specialist shading paint directly onto the glass or by installing greenhouse blinds, which have the advantage of being adjustable and can be automated for convenience. Plastic netting and mesh is also available, which will perform a similar function.

• Always remember to ventilate a greenhouse properly as this will reduce overheating and keep the atmosphere inside fresh.

Ventilation

Ventilation is essential even during the winter months to avoid a build-up of damp, stale air, which encourages disease, and to allow fumes from some types of heating to escape. In summer, it is also vital to control temperature. The sunshine that enters a greenhouse cannot escape back out through the glass so the heat must be dissipated through open windows, doors and even extractor fans if necessary. Automatic hinged windows that open when a specific temperature is reached are available if constant attention is difficult.

Heating

Any heating needs to be powerful enough to maintain at least the required minimum temperature for the plants inside. The cheapest and most reliable is electric heating, if a source of power is nearby. Mains gas is also a possibility. Stand-alone heating, normally bottled gas or paraffin, is available for greenhouses that are too far away from a mains supply or require less regular heat. These are less controllable, relatively expensive and need regular checking and ventilation, but may be useful on a small scale. Insulation such as bubble wrap should also be considered and will help to keep heating costs down.

• With extra heating a wider variety of plants can be grown, including more tropical specimens.

Watering

The type of watering system used will depend on the kinds of plants being grown. In a normal greenhouse, a watering can does the job as well as anything else, as each plant's needs will be slightly different. Automatic systems such as seep hoses and capillary watering (using an overhead reservoir) are practical for anyone who plans to go away for any length of time, but they still need to be checked regularly to ensure the plants are getting the right amount of water, as this can vary not only from plant to plant but from season to season.

For tropical plants that require extra humidity, the greenhouse must also be 'damped down' with extra water on the paths or benches, or else a spray mist system can be installed, which is especially useful for propagating cuttings. Damping down is also useful in hot weather to cool the temperature inside the greenhouse and increase humidity, which will help pollination, fruit growth and spider mite control. This is best done early in the morning, allowing the sun to evaporate the water over the course of the day.

• Automatic watering systems will ensure that plants receive a regular supply of water and help to keep cuttings healthy.

Growing Under Glass

Aside from managing the conditions, the biggest issue with greenhouse growing is often lack of space. Most greenhouses are used for a variety of tasks and have to be multipurpose to a certain extent, the only exceptions being specialist greenhouses that contain specific groups of plants, such as ferneries or orchid houses. This requires sensible organisation and maximising the space available.

• Staging and shelving can make a big difference to the amount of plants that can be grown in a greenhouse.

A typical greenhouse will need some space for plants growing directly in the soil or growing bags at ground level, space to display and store specimen plants or those that need overwintering, and space for seed trays and cuttings, as well as the equipment required for successful propagation and potting up. Usually this means having a central path with beds or staging, whether permanent or removable, on either side and at the end furthest from the door.

Staging is useful to bring plants up to a sensible height, making caring for them much easier, and can double as a work surface if the gardener requires. Quite often there are shelves for extra storage below the tabletop level, ideal for resting plants, equipment and anything that requires shadier conditions. For maximum efficiency, stand-alone staging can be used in winter and removed in summer to allow bigger plants to grow in the bed below, while permanent shelves are best used for display and propagation.

In a small greenhouse, a separate heated propagator will ensure more successful propagation without taking up too much space. In bigger, warmer greenhouses, fitting soil-warming cables and misting units on some of the staging will considerably increase propagation possibilities.

Investing in automated systems can reduce the workload considerably while ensuring continuous care for the plants, especially if daily checking is not feasible.

Typical Conditions for Growing Plants

Plant type	Minimum temperature	Ventilation	Shading
Seeds	7°C–24°C (44°F–75°F)	Low	Shade until germinated
Cuttings	7°C–24°C (44°F–75°F)	Low Extra humidity required	Shade until rooted
Overwintering alpine plants	No heat	High	No shading required
Overwintering tender plants	2°C (35°F)	Low	No shading required
Subtropical and tropical plants	13°C (55°F)	Low Extra humidity required	Shading required in summer
Bedding plants, flowering pot plants and summer crops	2°C (35°F)	Low	Shading required in summer
Cacti and succulents	2°C (35°F)	Low	No shading required

• Inside a small heated propagator these dahlia seedlings will flourish in the warmer conditions without using up too much space.

Greenhouse Care and Hygiene

Having invested in a greenhouse, it makes sense to ensure it remains in good condition for as long as possible, and safety-wise it is essential to make routine checks and repair any damage to avoid future problems.

Routine Maintenance

The best time to carry out routine maintenance is autumn, before it becomes too cold to leave tender plants outside. Dirt and moss can be gently scraped away from the exterior glass using a plastic spatula before it is cleaned with water and, if required, a specialist greenhouse cleaning product. Avoid too much pressure on the glass panes in case they crack. Any small cracks can be taped temporarily but broken panes should be replaced completely.

Gutters and downpipes can be cleared of debris and repaired at this point, as can any rotten wood and rusty fittings that may need attention. Wooden structures should be painted regularly to prevent rotting but aluminium structures usually require little attention.

Inside, all plants should be removed before the glass, structure and floor are cleaned. Brush or vacuum away all dirt and debris before applying diluted garden disinfectant to the structure, staging and floors but not the glass itself, which may be cleaned with water unless algae build-up is a problem. If so, the glass panes should be cleaned with a specialist algae remover while the plants are out of the greenhouse. Cleaning thoroughly will help reduce many future problems with pests and diseases. Lastly, check any fixtures and fittings such as ventilation windows, and repair or replace where necessary. Return the plants as soon as the repairs are finished.

• Keep a regular check on plants in the greenhouse to ensure that pests and diseases don't take over and damage your crops.

Greenhouse Hygiene

Good hygiene is essential in a greenhouse, where the specialist conditions are perfectly suited to pests like spider mite and whitefly and a variety of fungal diseases that can easily spread rapidly through plant stock. As a rule, prevention is better than cure and clearing away any debris or early signs of disease on a regular basis, as well as ensuring adequate ventilation, will certainly help.

Pest populations can build up extremely quickly unless caught early on, so vigilance is very important. There are chemical controls and fumigants that can be used, but for those who prefer a different method, biological pest control is also an option. To ensure that natural predators have enough food to survive and multiply, they should be introduced when the pest population is starting to expand. Once in place, they will hopefully keep the pest problem in check. Sticky yellow traps hanging from the roof are also effective and inexpensive to buy.

Good cultural practice is required for preventing fungus attacks. Any plant debris should be disposed of quickly to ensure that rot does not take hold, and the greenhouse should be well ventilated.

• Keeping the greenhouse tidy, clean and orderly will go a long way to reducing the possibility of pests and diseases.

Introduction to Plant Propagation

Raising new plants using a range of simple techniques is a cost-effective and satisfying activity. With reasonable grasp of the following methods and some basic equipment, gardeners can add considerably to the range and number of plants in the garden without spending a fortune on ready-grown plants, sell or swap anything surplus to requirements and even breed new varieties.

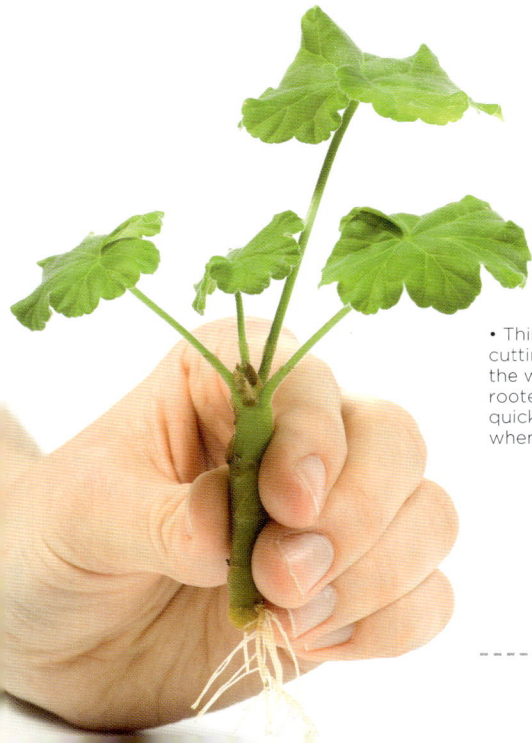

• This pelargonium cutting is already on the way to being well rooted and should quickly establish when potted on.

Plant Reproduction

Plants reproduce either by producing seed following fertilisation, sometimes in very large quantities, which is then scattered around to germinate and create new plants, or by replicating their own tissue (see page 50). Runners from parent plants, bulblets that grow round the edges of certain bulbs and tree branches re-rooting where they touch the ground are just a few of the examples of natural methods of increase and renovation that can be seen all around us. Understanding the principles of what is known as vegetative reproduction opens up a wealth of possibilities for the gardener.

Propagation Methods

Plants can often be propagated in more than one way but there is usually a method more effective than the others. In some circumstances, there will only be one possibility available. Rare, unusual plants may simply not be available in anything other than seed form, while certain hybrids have to be propagated vegetatively to ensure the offspring remain true to form. The most common method of vegetative propagation is to remove small pieces of tissue from the parent plant. The will to survive in plants is such that small lengths of stem, leaves or roots will eventually become an independent plant, given the right conditions. Taking cuttings like this is an excellent way to use a small amount of material to create many more plants.

Propagation can take place both indoors and out. Outside, hardy vegetables and annual flowers are often directly sown into the ground to germinate in the soil. Most sowing takes place in the spring after the risk of frost has passed and the soil has warmed a little, but autumn sowing is sometimes recommended for an earlier show the following year.

With protection, many more plants can be propagated, extending the season and range considerably. Seeds and cuttings often respond better to warmth and the results will be quicker and more successful. Windowsills, cold frames and greenhouses can all be brought into use for propagating purposes.

Propagation Tools, Equipment and Compost

Propagation requires a number of very simple tools and materials, easily obtainable, although more complex equipment can be obtained for professional propagation, which will certainly increase the range and success of the process.

• A wide variety of containers and pots are available for propagation purposes, depending on the technique being used.

Basic Toolkit for Propagation

• Pots and trays. A selection in different sizes is important to extend the range of plants grown and to maximise the usage of space. Trays are usually used for seed sowing, while pots are better for taking small amounts of cuttings or for bigger seeds, such as squash, which prefer to be grown individually. Trays containing individual modules are very effective and can be used for both seeds and cuttings, so that each individual baby plant has its own space to grow. Module-grown plants are also much easier to pot on.

• Compost. Despite its name, all-purpose compost is not ideal for seed sowing and cuttings, as it tends to be rather coarse and contains nutrients more suited to larger plants. Seed-raising mixes are blended specifically for this purpose. It contains much smaller amounts of nutrients to prevent seeds and cuttings putting on too much top growth too quickly, and is much finer. It also contains a higher proportion of fine drainage

material, such as sand; rot and mould are the big enemies of successful propagation. Other forms of growing medium are also available. Perlite and vermiculite and even sand can be used to cover seeds gently or even to root certain cuttings into.

• Labels and something waterproof to write with are essential to keep track of the plants you grow. It is very easy to forget which seeds have been sown and which cuttings have been taken if you are growing several different varieties.

• Secateurs and a sharp knife are needed for taking cuttings, and a watering can fitted with a rose for gentle watering will be required.

• Two specialist items for propagation are also needed. A dibber, a small pointed stick, is useful for pricking out seedlings and making holes to insert cuttings easily, while hormone rooting powder will speed up the rooting process and may help with more difficult plants.

• Small tools useful for propagation include secateurs for cutting plant material, dibbers for making holes and trowels for compost.

• Clear plastic bags kept in place with an elastic band can be used for covering small amounts of cuttings in pots and providing useful humidity. On a slightly larger scale, a propagator tray with a lid, whether heated or unheated, will perform the same function.
• Professional equipment available includes misting units, which help to keep the air humid and prevent too much water loss in the early stages, and some form of bottom heat to encourage faster rooting.

OUTSIDE SPACE

Outside, it is handy but not essential to put aside space for growing hardwood cuttings – somewhere out of the way but accessible, where such cuttings can be left for a year or so with a minimum of attention. A seed bed for raising plants from seed that can then be planted out elsewhere is also useful, especially for vegetables such as brassicas and leeks.

Watering and Hygiene

Plants are more vulnerable during propagation than at any other time of their life and need to be cared for properly. Tiny seedlings can be prone to drying out or rotting very easily if the conditions are unfavourable, while cuttings, depending on their type, must be monitored to ensure the optimum environment for them to 'strike' and thrive.

• The plastic bag over these dahlia cuttings will keep moisture in but can also cause rotting if left too long.

• These cuttings of rosemary (right) will benefit from careful moisture control to prevent rot.

Moisture Management

Whatever the method used, propagated plants usually need to be kept moist but not waterlogged, kept out of direct sunlight, but in a well-lit spot, and given adequate fresh air. A damp atmosphere with poor ventilation will encourage fungal diseases, and waterlogged soil will deprive young plant roots of essential oxygen.

Seedlings, for example, are prone to 'damping off', a condition that results from overcrowding and damp, ill-ventilated conditions and causes the entire tray or pot of seedlings to keel over and die off.

Cuttings, too, have their issues. The softer cuttings and those with more leaves are most at risk. Lacking roots initially, they must be prevented from transpiring too heavily and drying out as they are unable to draw up water from the compost. For this reason, they are covered with clear plastic or a lid to trap moisture inside, which helps keep

them turgid. The downside of this is that unless lids and bags are regularly removed, the stale air inside encourages mould and rotting. Turn plastic bags inside out at least once a day to allow fresh air in and prevent any build-up of algae or mould.

The optimal propagating environment is provided by a misting unit. This works by applying a fine mist of water over the top of cuttings to ensure the leaves are covered with a layer of water that prevents transpiration. Mister units supply a gently humid atmosphere while maintaining the free flow of air as plants do not need to be covered. Combined with some sort of bottom heat system, usually buried soil-warming cables, it is the professional choice for successful propagating.

Good Hygiene Practices

In conjunction with providing the right conditions for propagating plants, good hygiene practices should always be maintained. In greenhouses, the disinfecting and cleaning of tools, equipment and surfaces should be a regular occurrence, as should the prompt removal of debris and dead or infected tissue. Fungicidal solutions are also available, which can be applied to prevent many problems.

As many diseases and spores are carried in soil or water, great care should be taken to minimise the possibility of cross-contamination from boots, other plants and equipment. Tap water and bottled water are less likely to carry diseases and should be the preferred option unless the plant is particularly sensitive to chemicals and minerals, as in the case of carnivorous plants, for example.

It goes without saying that one should never attempt to propagate material carrying diseases such as viruses or other pathogens, as this will simply increase the problem. Any diseased plants that have been unwittingly propagated should be removed and carefully disposed of immediately the issue comes to light.

Propagation from Seed

The result of plant sexual reproduction, seeds are the most common method for reproducing a wide variety of plants. New trees, shrubs, perennials, annuals and vegetables are all available to grow from seed with a minimum of equipment and cost. Collecting seed from plants, usually in the autumn, is even more cost-effective, and ensures gardeners have a further supply of a favourite plant with the wonderful possibility of exciting diversity, since variation in our plant life is mostly a result of the recombination of genetics that takes place when a seed is created.

• Seeds can be sown individually into pots before being placed into a propagation tray to give them the right conditions.

• It is easy to forget what you have sown, so clear, informative labelling is always a good idea.

• A lid placed over seedlings in a propagation tray will help to keep essential moisture in during the germination period.

Seed Collection

To obtain fresh seed, it should be collected as soon as ripe, normally as the seed capsule begins to split. Apart from a few seeds that need to be sown straight away, such as walnuts and acorns (store acorns in the fridge to give them a cold snap before sowing), most can be stored after cleaning in a cool, dark, dry place in paper bags or placed in a refrigerator until the following spring. In all other respects, they can be treated in the same fashion as shop-bought seeds.

Seed Germination

Several factors are involved in successful seed germination: water, air, warmth and dark conditions, with the exception of a few plants whose seeds germinate in light.

- Under cover, it is important to sow seeds thinly in order to discourage damping off, so choose an appropriately sized pot or tray for the amount of seeds to be sown. Ensure that all equipment is thoroughly clean.
- Seeds should be sown on good-quality seed compost that has been gently firmed rather than compacted, as delicate roots need to be able to push through and to access air and water easily.
- Unless they need light to germinate, seeds should be covered lightly with compost or vermiculite. Shop-bought seeds will usually recommend a planting depth but, if you are unsure, the rule is that seeds should be covered to a depth once or twice their diameter. If in doubt, shallow sowing is usually preferable to sowing more deeply.
- Water gently with a fine rose on a watering can to avoid dislodging seeds, especially if they are fine, and place where they will enjoy some warmth. Germination can take anything from a few days to several weeks, depending on the plant, but usually takes on average around seven to ten days.
- Ensure germinated seedlings remain moist and receive plenty of light. Turn regularly to prevent them stretching out towards the light and becoming leggy, and pot up individually when true leaves, rather than seed leaves, have been produced.
- Plants that are destined for outside planting will need to be hardened off, a process that involves introducing them gently to outside conditions by placing them in a cold frame, for example, and gradually increasing their exposure.
- Seed sowing outside is a little easier. Seeds are normally sown in finely raked soil in rows or broadcast, i.e. scattered thinly, and need to be kept moist until well established.

Germination Problems

There are a number of reasons why germination might not be successful, even if all the environmental conditions are suitable.

- Unviable seed. Seed that is old or has been exposed to extremes of temperature is far less likely to germinate successfully. It is for this reason that bought seeds have a sell-by date and should be stored appropriately.
- Seed dormancy. Seeds sometimes have an inbuilt dormancy mechanism to prevent germination in unsuitable conditions. This may need to be broken in order to induce seedlings to grow. Hard coatings, which protect the seedling in the wild through unfavourable seasons, can be gently filed down or nicked to allow water to enter and germination to begin. Other seeds may need stratification, recreating the hot and cold conditions that trigger the appropriate reaction.

F1 and F2 Hybrids

F1 hybrids are seeds resulting from the selective crossing and recrossing of two parent plants with specific desirable features to achieve a uniform quality. They are more expensive to buy due to the amount of effort required on the breeders' part, but will produce more vigorous plants. The seeds of F1 hybrids, commercially known as F2 hybrids, will not come true to type, which is potentially disappointing for the gardener. Where uniformity is not an issue, F2 hybrid seeds are sometimes available and are less expensive.

• The wonderful colour and shape of this *Viola* 'Angel Amber Kiss' is a result of selective breeding.

Propagation from Roots

Taking cuttings from roots is one of the easier methods of vegetative propagation, requiring only a few steps and a minimum of aftercare to produce vigorous new plants. In the case of roots, a little can go a long way. A variety of plants can be propagated successfully this way, including trees and shrubs that sucker naturally, and in the case of a few herbaceous plants, most notably oriental poppies, it is the only method available.

- -

• Thick pencil-width root cuttings are inserted deeply into individual modules in early winter from plants that are dormant.

BASIC STEPS OF ROOT PROPAGATION

Primarily a dormant season activity, it can take place at a less busy time of year, and ideally root cuttings should be taken in late autumn to early winter. Plants suitable for root propagation include *Anemone japonica*, *Papaver orientale*, *Primula denticulata*, *Acanthus*, *Verbascum* and *Phlox* as well as *Chaenomeles*, *Syringa*, Robinia and hops.

1 Choose healthy, vigorous plants, lift when dormant and wash the roots clean. Ideally, choose roots that are as thick as a pencil, although herbaceous root cuttings can be a little thinner.

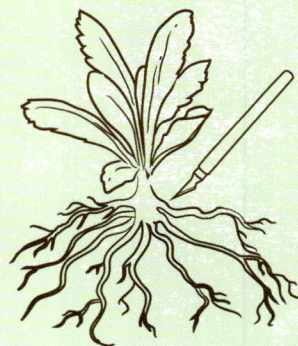

2 Cut the roots close to the crown of the plant, removing no more than a third at any one time before replanting the parent as soon as possible.

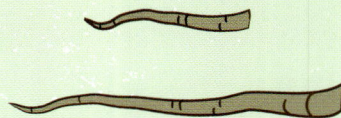

3 The minimum length for root cuttings should be around 2.5cm, although they will need to be larger if they are not being placed in a heated, protected environment. Normally 5–10cm cuttings will work well.

4 It is important to distinguish which end is which when inserting, so always cut the top horizontally and the bottom at an angle to be sure. New roots will only form on the end that was furthest from the parent plant.

5 Insert cuttings in a pot filled with very free-draining compost to which gritty sand or perlite has been added, as root cuttings need an open, free-draining compost to take successfully. Place each cutting vertically about 4cm apart so that the flat top is level with the surface of the compost.

6 Add a thin layer of gritty sand or perlite, water gently and place the pots where they will receive warmth or, if this is not possible, in a cold frame.

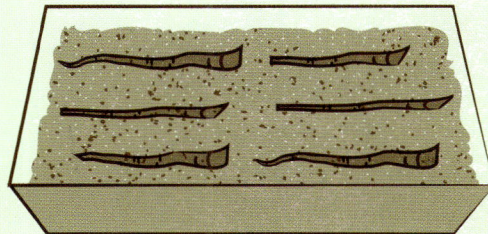

7 The cuttings should be growing well by the following spring and can be potted up when they have clearly rooted sufficiently. Grow them on before planting out.

8 If plants are too large to lift, dig down on one side to find a suitable section of root to cut away and follow the steps above.

9 Plants with roots that are too thin to be inserted vertically, such as phlox, need longer root sections to survive, so lengths of 7.5cm to 12.5cm are most suitable. These thinner cuttings are placed horizontally on the compost before being covered with a mix of compost and gritty sand.

Propagation from Divisions

Of all the forms of propagation, division is probably the easiest, taking advantage of an herbaceous plant's natural tendency to expand. It has other benefits, too; dividing plants that are congested will refresh and renew the look of borders and keep such plants heathy and vigorous for much longer.

• Suitable plants that respond well to division are ornamental grasses, hostas, asters, bergenias and iris, kangaroo paw, lomandra, dianellas, cannas and ginger, but almost all clump-forming perennials, as long as they have fibrous roots, can be treated this way.

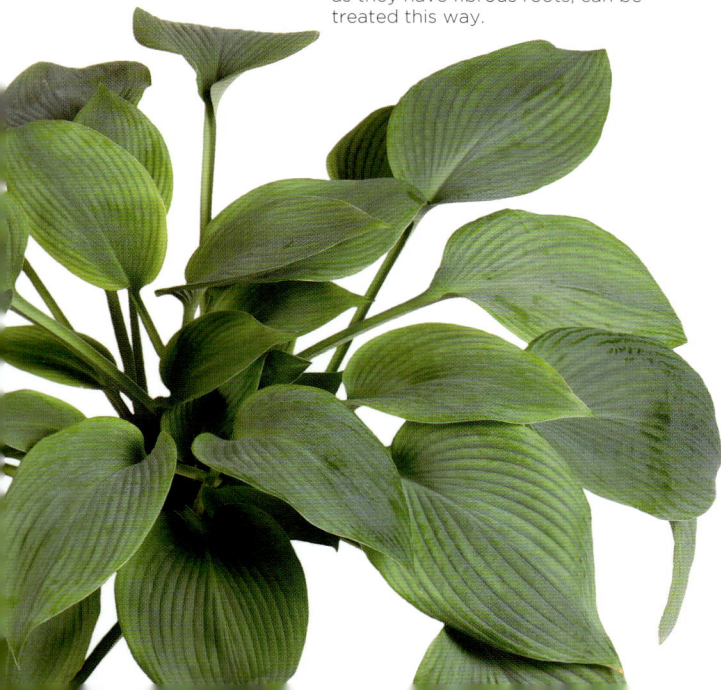

BASIC STEPS OF PROPAGATION BY DIVISION

Ideally, division should take place while the plants are not actively growing, but it can be done at any time as long as the divisions are watered well afterwards. As a rule, summer-flowering perennials are divided in early autumn or the following spring just before the new season begins, while spring-flowering plants are divided in summer as they produce new roots.

1 Lift suitable, healthy plants with a garden fork to avoid damaging the root ball, and shake off excess soil.

2 Smaller plants can be gently pulled apart by hand to make a number of smaller plants with their own roots.

3 If suitable, individual plantlets can be pulled away gently from around the edges to be replanted separately.

4 Larger, tougher plants may require a little more effort to separate. Two forks inserted back to back through the centre of the root mass can be used as levers to pull it apart before smaller sections are separated out.

5 In the most difficult cases, a knife, edging iron or spade may be required to chop through very tough woody or fibrous crowns and root balls. The divisions in this case should be a little larger to compensate for the extra damage.

6 Discard any old or unhealthy-looking pieces. Often this will be the centre of the original plant as the youngest, most vigorous growth tends to be on the outside of a clump.

7 All divided plants should be planted up or potted up as soon as possible and watered well.

Division of Rhizomes and Corms

Plants such as *Crocosmia* and *Iris*, which have storage organs as well as root systems, can also be divided successfully with a little extra care.

Crocosmia requires careful digging out before gently separating out the chains of corms. These can either be separated individually, if large numbers of plants are required, or split into smaller clumps but still keeping the chains intact, something they prefer.

Irises with rhizomes benefit enormously from being lifted regularly and split, as the central rhizomes become increasingly congested and weak. Simply lift the clump and cut away the outer, healthiest-looking fans with a portion of rooted rhizome attached. Trim roots and fan if necessary and replant as soon as possible, ensuring the rhizome protrudes just above the soil or compost level. Discard any weak, withered and old rhizomes.

Propagation from Stem Cuttings

Stem cuttings are a popular and effective way of increasing plant stock and in some cases can produce large amounts of new plants in a relatively small space. Many favourite plants are propagated this way. Pelargoniums, argyranthemum and suchlike are popular choices for this method of propagation, as are plectranthus, wormwood and Chinese lanterns. In some cases, where plants have been highly bred or are variegated, stem cuttings are the only way to ensure that the characteristics of the parent plant are maintained.

The various distinctions in stem cuttings refer primarily to the maturity of the material used, but the technique required is similar in all cases. Early in the growing season plant tissue is softer and greener, hence cuttings taken at this time are known as softwood and greenwood cuttings. The softest cuttings are taken from the growing tips of tender and herbaceous perennials as they wake from winter dormancy. Later on in the season, semi-ripe cuttings are taken, and finally, when plant tissue has fully ripened and become woody, they are known as hardwood cuttings. The earlier the cuttings are taken, the quicker they will tend to root, although there is an increased chance of rotting using soft material.

• Rosemary is an easy plant to propagate from stem cuttings, usually taken in late summer.

• Taking cuttings from geraniums means that fresh new flowering plants can be produced each year for seasonal displays.

While some plants are easy to propagate and unfussy about the time of year, others may be a little choosier. If in doubt, try cuttings at different times of the year to determine which works best or research the recommended method.

Some shrubs are best propagated when semi-ripe or fully ripe, with an extra cut or piece attached. Many prefer to be taken with a heel, which will come away from the main stem if a side shoot is pulled off gently. Evergreens and conifers are often taken more successfully this way. Others respond to wounding, which involves making a clean, shallow cut at the base of the cutting to expose more of the pith inside the stem.

If rooting succulents and cacti, cuttings must be dried out for a few days to callus over before being inserted into a medium that ensures very sharp drainage, such as sand or perlite. Although they need some moisture, they will quickly rot if the atmosphere is too humid.

BASIC STEPS OF PROPAGATION BY STEM CUTTINGS

1 Choose healthy, preferably non-flowering shoots and cut early in the morning, if possible, when the plant tissue contains more water. If there is any delay in preparing the cuttings, store them in a plastic bag in the fridge until ready.

2 Individual cuttings are usually prepared by first making a cut just below a leaf joint, or 'node'. This is where the plant's growth hormones are most concentrated and where new roots will form.

3 The length of a cutting depends on the size and attributes of the plant chosen, but is most commonly around five to six nodes long, or around 5–10cm. If required, cut to size just above a node, making a slanting cut away from the node to indicate which end is which. Hardwood cuttings are usually cut a little longer as they need more reserves of food, being taken at the end of the growing season and therefore taking much longer to root.

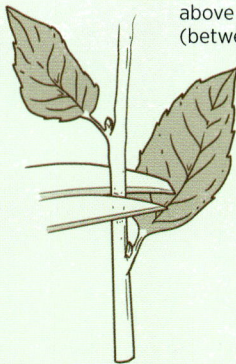

Nodal cut
Make a cut just below a leaf joint.

Internodal cut
Make a cut just above a node (between nodes).

4 Strip off the lower leaves to prevent them rotting in the growing medium, and trim by half any large upper leaves to ensure the cutting does not suffer too much transpiration loss before rooting can take place. Leafy cuttings still need to photosynthesise, but this has to be balanced with water loss while the plant is still rooting.

5 You can dip the cut end into hormone rooting powder and insert into a free-draining, good-quality pot or tray of seed compost, ensuring that the cuttings are not touching each other.

6 Water well and place somewhere light and warm but not in direct sunlight. Leafy cuttings benefit from a humid atmosphere so should be placed under mist or covered with a clear lid or plastic bag. Keep the plastic away from the cuttings with sticks or a frame. Hardwood cuttings are inserted more deeply, and require very sharp drainage. They are normally left outside in pots or trenched into the ground directly to allow for a longer, slower period of rooting.

Propagation from Leaves

Many popular house plants can be propagated using just a leaf or a leaf section, or even a section of leaf-like stem. Some can be cut into sections and placed in compost, other leaves will produce whole new plants from the leaf base, and a few with prominent veins will produce new plants if cut and laid flat on a suitable medium.

• One leaf, in the case of this begonia, can be cut into squares to make many more new plants.

Fleshy Plants

Whole leaves of fleshy plants such as African violet (*Saintpaulia*), may be removed from the parent plant with their stem attached. Choose healthy, fully grown leaves and trim the stem to around 3cm before inserting into individual pots of good-quality potting compost, watering carefully and covering with a clear lid or plastic bag. Leave in a warm place with good but not direct sunlight until baby plants form at the base. Remove the coverings and grow on until they are established enough to be separated from the leaf and potted on individually.

• African violets (*Saintpaulia*) are excellent plants to propagate as each one of their individual leaves can form a new plant.

• The prominent veins of this *Begonia rex*, if cut, will naturally produce new baby plants when placed into compost.

• These healthy succulent specimens are a result of propagating from just one leaf of the original parent plants.

Leafy Houseplants

Leafy houseplants with prominent veins, such as *Begonia rex*, can be used to make a number of new plants. Choose a good-sized, healthy leaf and remove it from the parent plant. Make short cuts across the strongest veins on the underside of the leaf and pin the leaf flat, cut side down, on a tray of compost so that it is in contact along its length. Roofing staples, paperclips or small pieces of bent wire will work well as pins. As before, water, cover and leave in a warm, light place until baby plants form, before uncovering and potting on. Alternatively, individual squares that include a strong vein can be cut out and pinned down in the same way.

Succulents

Succulents often also take well from leaf cuttings, using either whole leaves or even parts of the leaf in some cases, with the proviso that they need to callus over for a couple of days before insertion. *Sansevieria*, with its flattened leaf-like stem, is a good example. Remove a whole stem-leaf from the parent plant and cut across the stem to make 15–20cm sections. Insert these fairly shallowly, cut side down, into very free-draining compost and keep in a warm, dry place.

• The leaf of this *Sansevieria* can be cut into several sections to produce a number of new plants.

PLANTING DESIGN

More than at any time in history, design has become a critical feature of all aspects of daily life. Widespread access to media has brought an increased awareness to audiences, and information abounds about styles and trends in horticulture just as much as anything else.

Before contemplating aesthetic and design decisions, there are initially two essential practical considerations to take into account before ever pen is put to paper or a trip to the garden centre is attempted. The design process should begin with two questions: 'What will the garden be used for?' and 'How much time can be afforded to look after it?'

An honest appraisal is essential. Gardens should reflect their owners' preoccupations and lifestyle, as nothing will hide the shortcomings of a lack of care or inappropriate usage. Children and dogs will unintentionally create havoc if not given space; vegetable growing requires a certain commitment and will be a waste of effort if the produce is left to rot; neglected pots or shrubs shrouded in bindweed will impress no one.

Gardens can be high- or low-maintenance, depending on preference and resources. They must also have a clear sense of purpose.

Planning

In a way, a new garden is the easiest to plan as it will be very much a blank slate upon which almost any kind of scheme can be imposed, without the distraction of pre-existing features. It does, however, require a bigger element of creativity and usually more resources if it is not to look too immature.

In established gardens, there are other difficulties. As a rule, it is always worth observing an inherited garden for at least a year to see what seasonal changes may occur before choosing which parts to incorporate into future plans.

It is not always essential to produce detailed written or drawn plans, but they are useful to keep track of the overall objectives and prevent possible digressions and mistakes.

How to Plan

• The first step is to make a rough sketch of the individual elements required in the garden, including any existing immovable features. Sketching over a photo is an easy way of beginning the design process, drawing either bubbles or basic shapes. Forget colour or form at this stage, but do remember to include practical elements such as space for rubbish bins, washing lines, parking, compost heaps and sheds, and visualise how these may be hidden or disguised. Just as importantly, decide where paths should lead, and what route they should follow.

• This is a good time to check whether there are any conditions that will interfere with overall plans. Tree Preservation Orders and site-specific restrictions may be in place and the positioning of drains and services may have to be accounted for. Check also the condition of the soil – its quality and characteristics.

• Make a more detailed site plan with accurate measurements and schematics if needed, especially if there are hard landscaping features planned, which are usually installed before any planting takes place. Include details from any site surveys undertaken, noting cultivation factors such as frost pockets, prevailing winds, microclimates, soil type and pH. In short, anything useful that will inform the eventual scheme.

• Finally, decide on a particular style, and make notes of plants that will work and drawings of the look to be achieved, or research similar looks in magazines or digital media for inspiration. Think, too, about seasonal interest and the times the garden will be most used.

• Eventually, all these elements will inform more detailed planting plans further down the line.

• It's a good idea to make a detailed site plan with accurate measurements of a garden prior to starting a design or planting scheme.

Basic Design Principles

Good design is not necessarily complicated, as long as a few basic principles are followed. However, there are no hard and fast rules, and the only limit to what you can create in your garden is your imagination.

Sense of Place

Well-designed gardens and planting schemes always look as if they belong exactly where they are, almost as if they have designed themselves. They should fit, somehow, picking up the horticultural and social environment around them appropriately and retaining a suitable sense of proportion, whether they fit into the wider landscape around them or shut it out in favour of an exclusive and secret place. This is a difficult concept to define exactly and is best understood by looking at good examples elsewhere, either in the immediate neighbourhood or by visiting gardens of similar size further abroad that could provide inspiration. It should be the ultimate goal of good design.

• An old water pump in a courtyard provides a focal point for the area and gives a sense of place to the design.

Style

Style is very much a combination of personal preference and practical consideration. Informal or formal, low-maintenance for relaxing in or higher-maintenance for the plant lover who has time to concentrate on garden activities. Contemporary or historical, wildlife-friendly, child-friendly, wheelchair-friendly – the list goes on and on. The crucial factor is unity and cohesion. Haphazard and random style choices jumbled together will only suggest a lack of purpose and be challenging to the eye.

Scale

Gardens come in all shapes and sizes but a design that takes account of scale both overall and in individual features will look better than one where scale has been ignored. Each element of a garden should be in proportion to its surroundings. One small pot on a patio or a large lawn surrounded only by narrow borders will look empty and barren, but too much planting could be fussy and claustrophobic, especially if it grows too high. Vertical and horizontal elements should balance.

• Geometric shapes and structures such as these steps and topiary provide an appealing and orderly feel to the overall design of a garden.

Shape and Space

Straight lines, squares and rectangles can be very effective at making a garden seem larger by leading the eye along their length, and are easy to design with if proportions are maintained between the different elements. A simple rule is to divide areas into three, which is somehow far more pleasing than dividing by two, then combine thirds to make larger spaces. Using circles and curves in a design will feel more naturalistic and organic and create a sense of intimacy and informality.

All gardens need an element of space, a resting point for the eye, and good designs take account of this, using plants and features to frame and define restful areas of space rather than crowd space out completely or dissipate it.

Borrowed Landscape

Originally a Japanese concept, borrowing the landscape around a garden is a useful principle that can sometimes be employed to make the garden seem much bigger. Integrate features from outside the boundaries into the garden's design to make them seem connected. Hills, mountains, forests in the distance can all be useful. Even in the city, a tree in the distance can be framed by the planting inside to draw the eye further.

• Straight paths add a touch of formality to a design, while also leading the eye to focal points such as this bench.

Focal Points

Focal points are useful features that provide purpose to garden design. A path that leads nowhere or straight to a dead end is a frustration for the garden visitor. Far better to provide some sort of reward at the end – a piece of statuary, a specimen plant or a bench to draw the eye forward and create a deeper sense of perspective.

Navigation

Routes round the garden and accessibility are key features of design. Gentle meandering paths are informal and friendly, with elements of surprise possible, whereas straight pathways indicate a definite direction and a sense of formality.

Plant Forms and Their Functions

Plant selection is the most enjoyable part of garden design, where the gardener's tastes and preferences find their fullest expression. Even so, most garden designs will require a variety of plants to create the most pleasing outlook, unless the garden is determinedly specialised. Different plant forms are needed to perform a range of functions. It is the juxtaposition of the elements that makes for a cohesive design.

• Some trees can look dramatic in their own right with impressive structures and showy blossom displays.

Key Plants

In order to hold a scheme together, some plants should be considered as key plants to be repeated through different areas and within planting schemes to give a sense of continuity. Designs lacking this, consisting of lots and lots of different plants, can look fussy and lack cohesion.

Structure Plants

Plants such as trees and larger shrubs provide structure to a garden, adding vertical elements and height, a backdrop for smaller plants. They can also be used as hedges and screens to mask unwanted features or views. Tall, columnar trees provide the strongest vertical accents, while more spreading trees soften the line between ground and sky. They may also provide welcome shade.

Architectural Plants

Bold plants provide a strong statement in a design, drawing the eye towards them, breaking up softer lines and adding excitement and drama. They should be used sparingly, as a planting scheme full of showmanship would be exhausting to look at.

• Architectural plants in pots can be used as a focal point or to draw the eye to other areas of interest in an outdoor space.

• Using a fragrant plant, such as this jasmine, can conjure up a magical and evocative atmosphere.

• Garden design is often about understanding when a plant will be looking at its best and how it will combine with other plants.

Sensory Plants

Try to invoke all five senses. Scented plants, textured plants that beg to be touched, plants that move and rustle in the wind should all be considered as important features of your planting scheme.

• *Miscanthus sinensis* has dramatic flowering plumes and can make an impressive stand-alone feature.

Ground Cover Plants

Used to cover bare patches and around other plants, ground cover plants help to keep weeds down and, like taller filler plants, work quietly away, complementing better-loved plants. They are often the only option in difficult areas, such as under tree canopies.

Seasonal Plants

Seasonal plants include far more than the bedding plants and annuals that provide extra colour during the summer months. Many types of plants can ring seasonal changes in the garden. Trees and shrubs flower early in spring or put on a glorious autumn display of colour and berries. Bulbs herald the arrival of spring; coloured winter stems light up cold, dark days; perennials offer long seasons of interest and seed and flower heads that add fascinating silhouettes and shapes.

Filler Plants

Not every plant can be a star and many medium and small shrubs, as well as perennials and grasses, offer a gentler beauty that makes the star performers stand out even more.

• A variety of ground cover plants provides a contrast of colours and offers a backdrop to more dramatic plants.

Using Colour and Texture

More than any other facet of a planting scheme, colour can influence mood and atmosphere in a fundamental way. Our brains recognise and respond subconsciously to the visual stimulus provided by different hues of colour. Red is exciting, traditionally associated with danger. Yellows, oranges and bright pinks are also stimulatingly hot. They have the illusory effect of bringing the garden towards you. Blue, white, green and purple all have a calming influence and bring a cooler feel to the garden. Conversely, they extend the garden further outwards.

Texture

Texture is as important as colour in bringing a cohesive style to a planting scheme. It also allows for the combination of harmony and contrast that makes all the difference. Prickly upright stems, rough tree bark, flat flower heads, silver felted leaves and the shine of berries bring depth and an extra dimension to a planting scheme when combined and contrasted.

Grasses, for example, with their feathery plumes, add lightness to a planting scheme, while larger-leaved lamb's ears and salvias bring solid structure at a lower level. Contrast them with lighter, feathery ferns for a stylish shady area. Spikes against flattish clumps of daisy-type flowers are also a wonderful combination, but there are many to choose from.

• Planting schemes can either use contrasting colours, complementary colours or, as in this case, a single colour.

THE COLOUR WHEEL

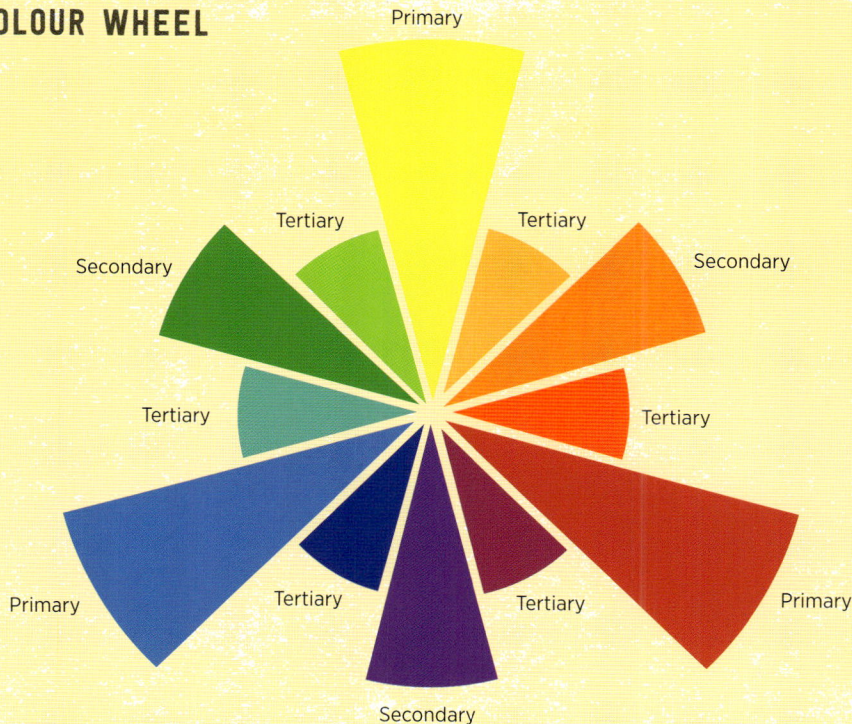

Primary

Tertiary

Tertiary

Secondary

Secondary

Tertiary

Tertiary

Primary

Primary

Tertiary

Tertiary

Secondary

The colour palette is often divided into a wheel, which helps determine the combinations of colour that fit well together. The wheel consists of the three primary colours, red, yellow and blue. Secondary colours are made by combining two primary colours – red and blue create purple, blue and yellow make green. A third set of colours can then be created by combining adjacent primary and secondary colours. Colours directly opposite each other on the colour wheel make for dramatic but pleasing contrasts that bring out the best in each colour. More subtle tonal arrangements can be achieved by combining colours adjacent to each other.

Simple Colour Combinations

- **Variations on a theme**. Plants with similar tones create easy, harmonious combinations that please the eye and create a subtle block of graduated colour that sweeps across a border.

- **Opposites attract**. Opposing colours create a sense of excitement, bringing out the best features in each other rather than jarring.

- **Three is the magic number**. This can work wonderfully well using colours that are evenly spaced round the colour wheel, the extra colour lifting the others in a sublime manner. Normally one of the colours is used a little less, to accent the other two.

- **Single and proud**. Although most single-colour gardens are actually a mix of subtle tones (since few plants are purely one colour), and occasionally contain a few accent and structural plants, they can look fabulously elegant and will certainly give the impression of a block of pure colour. They need extra care to be successful but the results can be stunning.

Arranging Plants

The art of arranging plants successfully takes account of all the design factors already explored. This can seem a daunting task, but with a clear idea of what the final look should be and a few simple rules to follow, it should become an enjoyable experience.

Informal Style

Style will play a huge part in the arrangement of plants. An informal look is best achieved by organising plants to look as natural as possible. The traditional herbaceous or mixed border, for example, is usually laid out to look spontaneous and flowing, although plenty of care goes into achieving this look.

Cottage gardens and gravel gardens are made up of flatter plantings in fluid, lozenge shapes, while the modern style usually referred to as 'prairie planting' takes this fluidity one step further, with larger, stretched-out drifts of grasses and flowers that make for a bold display with plenty of movement.

Height Order

Avoid a random and messy border by following simple rules. Larger shrubs, trees and plants are usually arranged towards the back, medium-sized plants in the middle and smaller plants towards the front, although this can be broken up by individual plants out of place for added interest. Repeated plants will add useful punctuation and provide a sort of rhythm, linking the border. It is also standard practice to plant only in odd numbers unless some sort of symmetry is specifically required. Similar rules apply to informal beds, with taller plants in the centre and smaller ones around the edge.

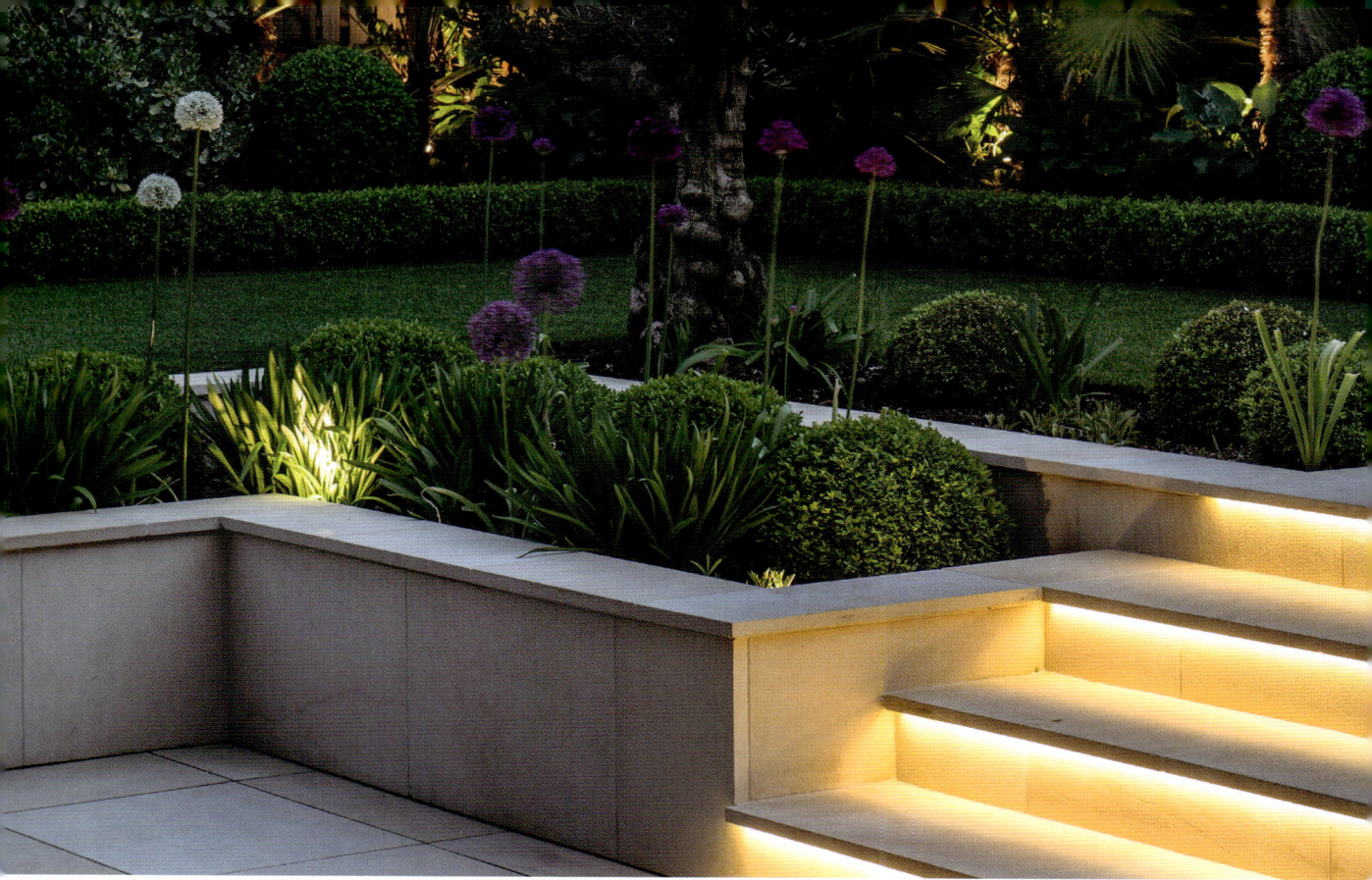

Formal Style

Formal gardens, by their nature, must look much more controlled. Here, symmetry is far more important, so even numbers are the order of the day. Clipped hedges define areas of planting, although looser planting within the hedges can be found. This, too, should be arranged in a subdued manner. Fewer varieties of plants are required and those that appear should have similar characteristics, such as height and growth rate, and be evenly spaced. This is also true of bedding arrangements, with the proviso that a greater quantity of plants might be required as there should be no perceivable gap between each bedding plant when fully grown.

Formal style is also evident in modernist garden design, especially in a sophisticated urban setting, but here the plant arrangements are sparse, architectural and asymmetric. Blocks of plants and a limited palette are appropriate for this kind of look.

• (Left) Traditionally, beds are structured with taller plants at the back and lower at the front.

• (Above) Following symmetrical patterns and shapes will often create a sense of formality and structure in a design.

• (Below) In a very favourable climate you may even be able to grow exotic-looking plants such as this bird of paradise (*Strelitzia reginae*).

Sustained Interest

Plants should be arranged to provide the maximum length of interest and seasonal variation, to be spread throughout the scheme. Maturity is also a consideration. It may take several years or even longer to achieve the final look, so try to arrange plants appropriately, spreading out quick growers and slow growers to achieve a balanced look.

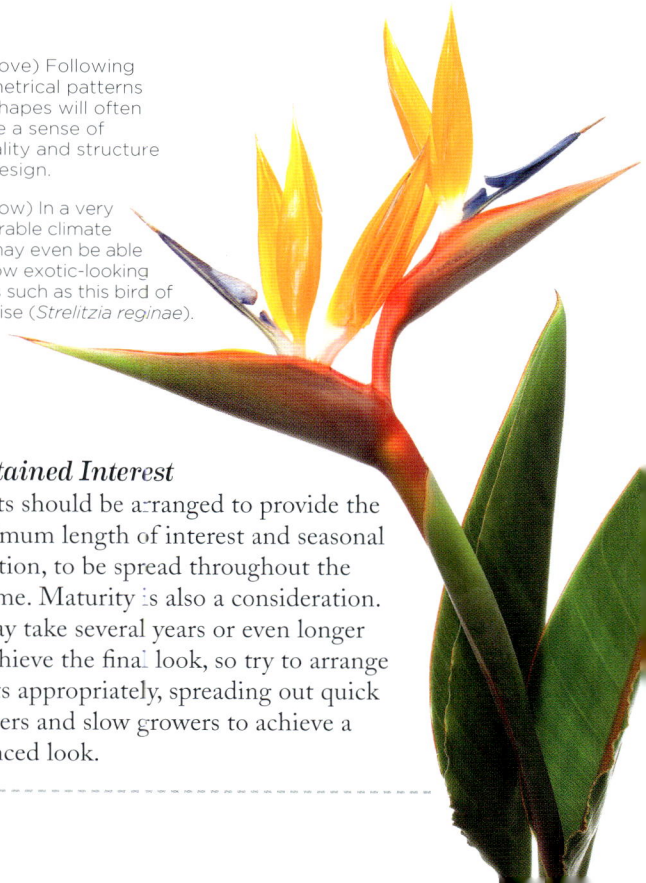

Planting Style – Formal

Formal garden styles focus heavily on symmetry and geometry. They exhibit a sense of proportion and balance and are usually rather restrained in terms of plant numbers and types. All in all, they should look as if nature is utterly under control.

Historically, formal gardens are associated with grand houses. Their grandeur and manicured look were a marker of culture and wealth. Inspired by classical culture and kept in perfect condition by an army of labourers, they remained largely the preserve of the upper classes for centuries. Today, the style still exists – referencing the past, albeit in a reduced form.

• Running water is a clever way of conjuring up movement in what would otherwise be a static planting composition.

Order of Layout

Formal gardens have a distinct order and pattern defined by hedges, walls and screens. These are arranged symmetrically or geometrically and give a feeling of balance at all times. The most extreme example of formal pattern is the knot garden or parterre, created using heavily clipped low hedges planted in intricate patterns and designed to be seen from the upper windows of the house. It is possible to create less complex designs for a modern garden using the same principles.

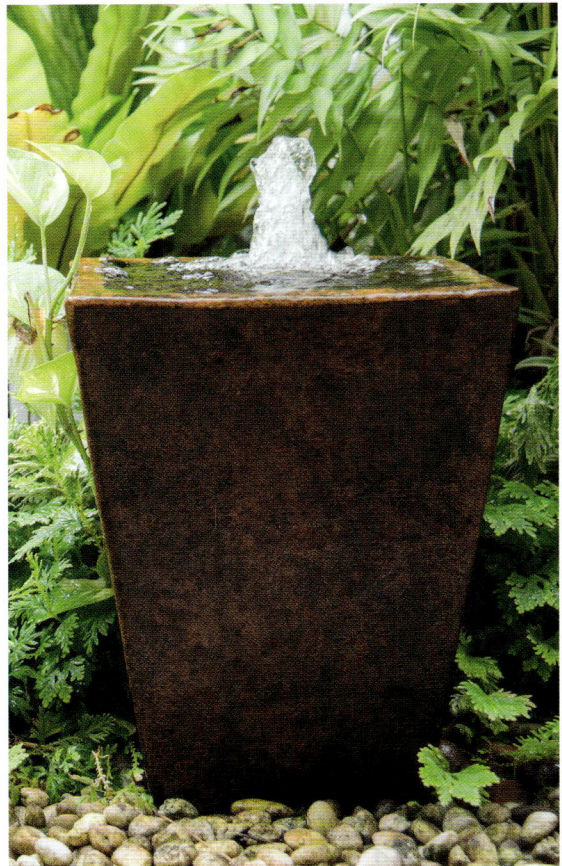

Topiary

Topiary is an important feature in formal gardens, enlivening the expanses of clipped green. Amid the control of a formal garden, clipped topiary can introduce a note of fun and whimsy, relieving the austerity of this style.

Water

Water features in a formal garden tend to be still, reflecting the sky and garden around them and emphasising further the balance and mirror symmetry of the design.

• Pairs of bay standards, such as this one, are often used on either side of an entranceway to draw people in.

• Clipped box hedges in stylised geometric shapes add structure, interest and elaboration.

Statuary

In keeping with the classical heritage, formal garden design often includes statues. They make excellent focal points for the long, straight lines that are characteristic of this style, but on a smaller scale, pots, urns or even blocks of stone will fulfil a similar function.

Avenues

The great formal gardens usually had enormous, often tree-lined avenues radiating away from the house. In today's garden, this can be recreated on a smaller scale with straight paths marked at intervals by smaller shrubs – topiary balls, lollypops, or even pleached trees for the brave.

Subdued Planting

A smaller range of plants will be needed for this kind of garden, although some looser planting helps to lighten the effect and may be welcome. Looser planting still needs to be contained and constrained by the more formal elements in order to provide proportional contrast.

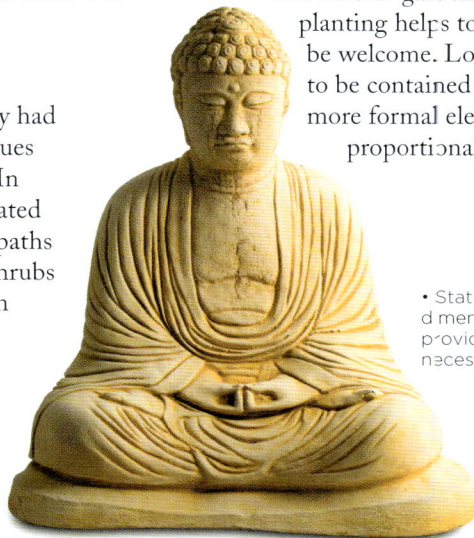

• Statuary adds an extra artistic dimension to a garden, and can provide interest when plants aren't necessarily looking their best.

Planting Style – Informal

Where formal gardens exhibit all the signs of complete control, informal gardens should resemble controlled chaos rather than complete disorder. They too, though relaxed and easy-going in style, take work to be successful. Even those who find themselves the owner of a wild space, such as native bush, may still need to perform certain tasks regularly, such as keeping paths clear or removing deadwood to prevent the wildness from taking over completely. Informality is helpful for families, where the damage caused by over-enthusiastic children may be less noticeable.

Curves and Contours

Gentle shapes, curves and contours are essential to an informal look. Unlike a formal garden, where lines purposely direct the eyes and feet in a clear direction, informal gardens are meant for meandering, for stopping at any or all points to admire a plant or simply to rest awhile. Curves are naturally restful and calming and not visually demanding in the way straight lines are.

Softening with Plants

In an informal garden, hard lines within the garden and unsightly features can be easily disguised using plants. Climbers can be left to smother walls, plants can spill out over paths, and ponds can be surrounded by marginal plants. Generally, planting should flow from one area to another.

Rustic Landscaping Features

Features of an informal garden should be in keeping with the overall theme, using materials that blend with and reflect the wider landscape. Natural stone and wood, as well as reclaimed and recycled items will add to a more relaxed atmosphere.

Exuberant Planting

Swathes of plants, although not essential, do help to encourage a more casual feeling. The great art of creating an informal garden is to make it look as if no human hand or brain has been involved in its creation. Colours are often deliberately mixed up and unsubtle, especially in cottage gardens, where the primary reason for growing a plant is its potential use, whether edible, medicinal or decorative. Growing vegetables and flowers together, potager-style, is possible even in a small garden. Even where colour combinations are more muted, they should look as natural as possible.

Relaxed Maintenance Regimes

Grass left long, annuals allowed to seed and spread, and shrubs that are only pruned for health both reduce the demands on the gardener and help to give a more natural feel to the garden. They also tend to be better for wildlife. Birds singing, bees busily visiting flower after flower, the snuffle and shuffle of a hedgehog in the dusk all contribute greatly to the atmosphere.

• Garden design often works best when it complements the existing natural features, such as in this case the rustic curves and slopes.

227

Planting Style – Contemporary

Contemporary designs are very much based on the garden as a living space, reflecting modern lifestyle choices. Entertaining in the garden, eating and drinking, relaxing after work, exercising, practising hobbies, spending time with children, growing your own food – modern gardeners have a variety of uses for their gardens, a world away from the traditional display of horticultural prowess that characterised the last century.

Distinct Areas

Contemporary designs tend to split gardens into a series of discrete areas – a place to eat and entertain, usually near the house; a place to relax, away from the pressures of modern life; a place to grow food and herbs; a play area for children. Even in a smaller garden, clever screening and planting can break up the garden into sections while still keeping the overall sense of place.

Garden Furniture and Structures

Contemporary gardens tend to have more furniture integrated into the initial design and structures, such as shelters or garden rooms that can be used to enjoy the garden all year round or provide inspirational spaces for creativity. Lighting and heating are also increasingly important.

• Even in small gardens, it is possible to define specific or distinct areas that make the space more structured and interesting.

• Garden furniture is an important aspect of design, as are unusual features such as the impressive wall planter in this contemporary garden.

Hard Landscaping Prominence

In an informal garden, much of the hard landscaping is disguised. Contemporary designs often emphasise the textures and forms of features such as walls and paving, bringing them to the fore. In very contemporary gardens, the plants complement the hard features, not the other way around. Walls painted in strong colours, the use of a variety of building materials and the juxtaposition of modern and old are all common themes.

Limited Planting and Palette

In keeping with modern pared-down design, planting colours are often muted and unified in tone. Fewer plants with more impact seems to be the trend. Shapes are architectural and dramatic in themselves, with colour a secondary factor. Colour comes in blocks, like a modernist painting, rather than in the combinations and contrasts of a more traditional garden.

• Less can be more, as in the case of this contemporary design using a simple palette of colours and limited planting for dramatic effect.

• Sometimes the plants take a back step and just provide a foil to a stunning architectural feature, such as this beautiful contemporary wall.

Designing for a Small Garden

More than ever before, people are living an urban lifestyle, where space is at a premium. Small gardens, balconies and shared communal spaces are increasingly the only access city dwellers have to outside space. Despite this, there is a trend for using what space there is for multiple purposes.

This presents a real problem in a small space, which can easily become cluttered and fussy without plenty of thought. Keeping to a style even in the tiniest plot will make the garden feel less cramped, generally, but there are many tips and design tricks that will make the most of what space there is.

• Breaking up a garden into clearly defined spaces or compartments creates a well-structured and pleasing aspect to the design.

Use Height

Most gardens have walls, fences or sides of buildings enclosing them, all of which can be utilised to either store essential equipment or host plants. Climbers and wall-trained shrubs, planters fixed up high, even vertical planting schemes will all help. Cupboards and shelves can be fixed outside as easily as indoors, keeping clutter away from the precious ground space. Mirrors on walls will bring extra light into dark places and also reflect the garden, making it seem bigger.

Compartments

Small gardens can be divided even further, creating secret spaces to explore and suggesting that the garden might be bigger than it really is.

• These upright planters take advantage of the vertical space by providing height and colour in an otherwise small garden.

Size of Plants

Do not be tempted to miniaturise all the planting because the space is small. Bigger plants can be expansive if used appropriately, drawing attention away from the size of the garden itself. Even a tree should be considered. It will provide shade as well as draw the eye upwards.

Colour

Use the characteristics of colour, planting hot colours near the house and blue colours further away to best advantage.

Furniture and Equipment

Choose furniture and equipment that can be folded and stored away when not in use to maximise the available space.

Paths

Pathways leading away from the house at right angles will draw the eye too quickly to the end. Diagonal pathways can prevent this from happening. Meandering paths in a small garden are likely to be too fussy and out of proportion to be successful.

• (Above) The generous planting helps to disguise the smallness of this space.

• (Below) Pots can be beautiful features in their own right.

Pots

A surprising number of plants can be grown in pots, including many vegetables. Rather than using lots of small pots, which will look and feel cluttered, use several large ones and make them a feature of the garden in their own right.

Making a Planting Plan

For individual planting schemes, a more detailed plan will be useful to help determine the correct placings for plants and the quantities that will be required. This is the final action to take before the pleasure of actually planting and watching the scheme develop.

If a detailed site survey has not been completed, begin by measuring out the space and making an accurate drawing of it on paper or using drawing software on a computer. Double-check the conditions – soil, aspect, sun – and check that the plants are suitable for the space.

Try to visualise what the plants will look like when in place. If sketching an elevation plan, or 3D view, is a step too far, use physical props to mark where plants are to be placed, keeping the proportions as accurate as possible. It is much easier to move things around now, before any money has been spent. Estimate the mature size of plants and allow for this in your final spacings – many gardening books detail the habits and growing conditions of Australian and New Zealand plants. When everything seems to work, begin to mark the plants on the plan, which is simply a 2D view from above.

Begin plotting trees and large shrubs on the plan before filling in with perennials and smaller plants. Make sure that everything is labelled correctly.

GARDEN DESIGN SYMBOLS

There are common symbols used in garden design that can be taken advantage of, although it is not strictly necessary to use them.

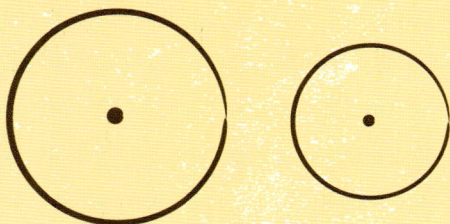

Shrubs are represented by proportionally smaller circles.

Wall shrubs and climbers are represented by a lozenge or triangle.

Trees are shown as circles with a mark in the centre to represent the trunk. They are drawn at their mature spread, not their initial size.

Perennials are represented as a series of connected circles.

Smaller plants and bulbs are represented by more amorphous shapes.

As the plan is to scale, it should be possible to estimate quantities fairly easily. Bulbs, annuals and perennials can be spread out or brought together during planting, as required.

All that is left now is to obtain the plants and plant them.

• A garden plan (above, top) and the final garden (above). An accurate plan helps to ensure the right amount of plants and landscape materials can be obtained for a perfect result.

THE GARDENING YEAR

There are gardening activities to be performed every month of the year, although some periods are busier than others. Many can only take place at certain times of the year; other activities have to be repeated over and over again.

A gardening calendar can never be entirely accurate as there are variations for many reasons that experienced gardeners learn to recognise – and now, of course, climate change is playing its part and will continue to do so for the foreseeable future, making accurate predictions of such matters as the beginning of spring and the arrival of winter almost impossible. Still, there is a natural cycle of gardening activity, even if it is delayed or brought forward a little.

Autumn is the real beginning, as this is when plans are made for the following season and preparations start. Winter can be a quiet time, and a miserable one if the weather is bad, but it can also be a time to get ahead of the workload.

Spring may start slowly but the workload soon increases and suddenly everything is happening at once. It can be overwhelming but in recompense the garden itself starts to flourish and put on a show. Summer starts much the same way but calms down towards March, giving a welcome respite and a chance to relax before the whole cycle starts again.

Early Spring

Early spring is a time of anticipation and new beginnings. As the days get longer and plants receive more sunlight, they are encouraged to begin preparation for growing. Bulbs start to come into flower in the precious light before bigger plants expand and days of sunshine will soon heat up the soil ready for early sowing of hardy annuals and vegetables, although in some areas there can still be a risk of frost. Be cautious, though – the soil should be warmer than 7°C (45°F) for at least a week in order for seeds to germinate successfully.

Gardens will be decorated with the early blossoms of almond and apricot trees, swags of purple echiums, pinpoints of colour from daffodils and other tiny bulbs and the first rich blooms of native frangipani and magnolia.

EARLY SPRING TASKS

IN THE GARDEN

- [ ] Clear the lawn of debris and begin mowing lawns on the highest setting.
- [ ] Prune flowering climbers such as wisteria and summer-flowering clematis.
- [ ] Prune hybrid tea and floribunda roses.
- [ ] Prune any shrubs that flower on new wood produced in the coming growing season. This includes shrubs such as buddleja, ceanothus and hardy fuchsias.
- [ ] Prune shrubs grown for winter stem colour, such as dogwood.
- [ ] Divide tired herbaceous perennials and replant young, healthy sections.
- [ ] Plant summer-flowering bulbs.
- [ ] Leave spring bulb foliage to die down naturally after flowering.

EARLY SPRING TASKS

IN THE GLASSHOUSE

- ☐ Take cuttings of overwintered tender perennials as they come back into growth.

- ☐ Sow summer annuals that need a warm start such as phlox, lobelia and snapdragons.

- ☐ Sow seeds of hardy perennials like campanula and delphiniums, which can be planted out later in the year.

- ☐ Start tuberous begonias into growth.

- ☐ Repot congested orchid plants using specialist compost.

EARLY SPRING TASKS

IN THE VEGETABLE PATCH

- ☐ Lift and separate tired clumps of rhubarb or plant new crowns.

- ☐ Sow asparagus, start propagating vegetable seeds you want to transplant in spring proper, harvest broad beans.

- ☐ Cut out all old summer-fruiting raspberry canes, tying in any loose new ones. Cut autumn-fruiting raspberries back completely.

Late Spring

A busy time of year for gardeners, when growth begins to speed up. The garden becomes green again as dormant trees and shrubs renew their leaves, providing a fresh backdrop for the performances of hyacinth, narcissus, tulips, ranunculus and veltheimia. Shrubs such as ceonothus, melianthus and wigandia are also in flower. You can expect to see the strong colours of camellias, viburnums and rhododendrons.

LATE SPRING TASKS

IN THE GARDEN

- [ ] Mow lawns more regularly, slowly reducing the height of the cut. Apply weedkiller and fertiliser.

- [ ] Prune any winter-flowering shrubs.

- [ ] Feed and mulch all roses and shrubs. Later on, begin spraying against blackspot or apply a foliar feed of seaweed extract to ensure their health.

- [ ] Tidy up herbaceous borders and stake plants that will need support later on before applying a mulch of compost or leaf mould.

- [ ] Clear away any spring flower beds and pots.

- [ ] Prepare and lay any new lawns.

- [ ] Sow remaining hardy annuals and plant out the summer-flowering bulbs started off in heat and any perennials and shrubs recently purchased. Keep them well watered.

- [ ] Sow biennials such as wallflowers and foxgloves.

- [ ] Towards the end of this period, plant out half-hardy annuals and bedding plants once all danger of frost has passed.

LATE SPRING TASKS

IN THE GLASSHOUSE

- ☐ Sow and plant tomatoes, capsicums, cucumbers, chillies and egg plants in beds or growing bags.
- ☐ Sow sweetcorn, beans and squash to be planted outside in summer.
- ☐ Take dahlia cuttings and leaf cuttings of houseplants.
- ☐ Prick out and pot up any seeds sown earlier. Begin to feed.
- ☐ Stop watering winter-flowering bulbs such as hippeastrum and leave to rest.
- ☐ Begin watering cacti and succulents after their winter rest.

IN THE VEGETABLE PATCH

- ☐ Plant new trees and fruit bushes.
- ☐ Weed fruit beds and mulch with straw.
- ☐ Dig over any remaining beds and prepare for planting.
- ☐ Plant artichokes, herbs, strawberries, sweetcorn, beans, cucumber, pumpkins and tomatoes.

Early Summer

In a typical garden, early summer is often the best time of year. This is when the first roses appear, bearded irises bloom and peonies and lupins start to come into flower. Behind and above them, philadelphus, lilac, weigela and the most extravagant of them all, the wisteria, put on a stunning show of colour and fill the warm, balmy air with fragrance.

Every part of the garden will now be growing rapidly and gardeners have to work hard to keep on top of the garden if they wish to avoid problems further on as weeds and grass, as well as garden plants, exhibit an unruly tendency to grow faster than can be coped with. In the vegetable patch, too, everything seems to be happening at once. Cropping, planting and sowing are all required to make the most of the lengthening days.

EARLY SUMMER TASKS

IN THE GARDEN

☐ Try to keep on top of routine tasks like weeding and mowing. Mowers should now be set to their lowest setting. It is always best to catch weeds early before they have set seed, so remove them or spray them religiously.

☐ Prune any shrubs that have recently flowered.

☐ Continue to spray roses in order to prevent disease taking hold.

☐ Remove suckers from plants on a rootstock, such as roses and plums, or with natural suckering tendencies, such as lilac.

☐ Deadhead any spent flowers to ensure another flowering frenzy.

☐ Plant out any remaining bedding plants and half-hardy annuals.

☐ Remember to water in dry spells. A good soaking once a week is essential for borders to look their best, and remember pots and baskets will require much more frequent watering.

EARLY SUMMER TASKS

IN THE GLASSHOUSE

☐ Feed and water plants regularly.

☐ Provide shade and ventilation to reduce temperatures and prevent the strong sun scorching leaves.

☐ Feed tomatoes as soon as the first truss has set and feed regularly thereafter.

☐ Prick out and pot up any remaining seedlings before acclimatising them to the outside.

IN THE VEGETABLE PATCH

☐ Continue to weed and thin around crops that have been sown directly, such as carrots and parsnips.

☐ Harvest asparagus, onions, plums, apricots, strawberrries. plant basil, capsicum, eggplant

☐ Plant out winter vegetables grown from seed.

☐ Begin cropping peas and watch for early strawberries.

Midsummer

There may be fewer trees and shrubs flowering but this is more than made up for by the arrival of large, blowsy clematis scrambling over walls and lavender flowers with their intense colour. They buzz with greedy bees and beguile the senses, while pots and hanging baskets of petunias and pelargoniums add a real wow factor to entranceways and patios. Growth begins to slow, leaving time to enjoy the garden a little more and to crop and enjoy the produce from the vegetable garden when peas, beans and potatoes lettuces are all ready to eat.

MIDSUMMER TASKS

IN THE GARDEN

- [ ] Continue to keep on top of weeds.
- [ ] In dry periods, raise the cut on the mower to avoid putting too much stress on grass.
- [ ] Deadhead roses and other flowering plants often. Bedding plants require extra attention to ensure they keep looking good for as long as possible.
- [ ] Prune ramblers as they finish flowering.
- [ ] Clip deciduous and evergreen conifer hedges.
- [ ] Water and feed plants in pots regularly.
- [ ] Take stem cuttings of shrubs.
- [ ] Plant autumn-flowering bulbs such as hardy cyclamen and nerine.

MIDSUMMER TASKS

IN THE GLASSHOUSE

- ☐ Keep feeding and watering plants in pots to keep them in tip-top condition.
- ☐ Watch for any signs of pests and diseases and take action quickly before the problem escalates.
- ☐ Pinch out the growing tips of egg plants and tomatoes when enough fruit has formed.
- ☐ Pot on any remaining spring-sown seeds.
- ☐ Take cuttings of subshrubs such as lavender, rosemary and santolina. Keep them warm but shaded from direct sunlight.

IN THE VEGETABLE PATCH

- ☐ Summer-prune espalier and cordon fruit trees.
- ☐ Continue to sow successionally. Carrots are good candidates.
- ☐ Ensure all crops receive plenty of water regularly to avoid splitting and suffering from water stress.
- ☐ Harvest and lift early potatoes and shallots and store in a cool, dark place.
- ☐ Turn and water compost heaps to speed up the process.
- ☐ Pick soft berry fruits as they ripen.

Late Summer

Herbaceous borders can begin to look tired at this point, especially if earlier deadheading was missed. There are always plants, though, that provide a stunning show. Hyssop, salvia, dahlia, crocosmia, cannas and coneflowers are all late-flowering. Dahlias are likely to be in full bloom and a second flush of roses is usually on show, too. Generally, the pace of the garden will have slowed but not stopped completely. More and more vegetables should now be ready to crop. As well as stalwarts like carrots and peas, summer vegetables such as courgettes and cucumbers should be ready for harvesting and will taste wonderfully fresh compared to shop-bought products.

LATE SUMMER TASKS

IN THE GARDEN

☐ Keep watering regularly, deadheading and removing weeds promptly. Begin to raise the height on the mower to reduce grass stress.

☐ Sow hardy annuals, such as cornflower, nigella and larkspur, to flower earlier the following year. Mark their position.

☐ Take evergreen cuttings, normally with a heel, and place in a cold frame for around six weeks to root.

☐ Plant early spring-flowering bulbs such as aconites and crocus.

LATE SUMMER TASKS

IN THE GLASSHOUSE

☐ Keep feeding and watering glasshouse crops and potted plants.

IN THE VEGETABLE PATCH

☐ Make new strawberry beds with the runners from older plants.

☐ Prune blackcurrants and summer raspberries after fruiting.

☐ Keep an eye out for caterpillars on brassica plants. Ideally, cover them with mesh before they arrive.

☐ Lift and store onions after drying them in the sunshine.

☐ Start picking early apples and continue to harvest vegetable crops. Freeze the inevitable surplus if necessary, or give it away.

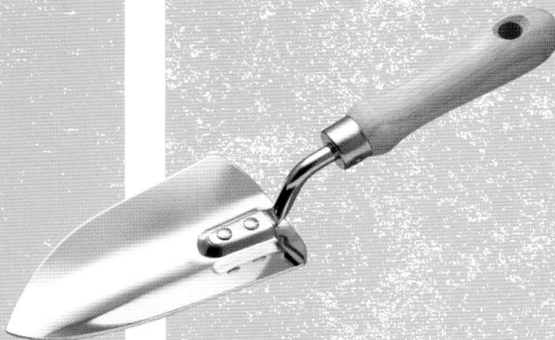

Early Autumn

Slowly but surely the garden begins to fade, developing rich autumnal hues of gold and red and glossy berries. Leaves begin to change colour and drop, sedums flower to ensure butterflies can continue to feed, and hydrangeas come into their own. The ultimate early autumn flower, though, must be the dahlia, but it has companions in the garden, late performers such as aster and chrysanthemum, Japanese anemones and the prairie flowers of rudbeckia and echinacea, which work so well with grasses. Now is the time that potatoes are lifted and maincrop carrots can be lifted wholesale.

EARLY AUTUMN TASKS

IN THE GARDEN

- [ ] A good time to prepare a new lawn as the weather starts to cool, ready for new turf or seeding. Cut grass only when necessary.

- [ ] Repair any damage to lawns from summer activities by over-seeding or patching with new turf.

- [ ] Tie in new shoots of rambling and climbing roses.

- [ ] Lift and divide overcrowded iris to refresh them for the following season.

- [ ] As summer bedding dies back, clear and prepare for winter displays.

- [ ] Keep on top of falling leaves and sweep or collect them to make leaf mould.

- [ ] Unless the autumn is very dry, this is an excellent time to plant trees, including indigenous tubestock, shrubs and roses, especially those bought bare-rooted.

- [ ] Begin planting daffodils and lilies but wait to plant tulip bulbs until later in autumn.

- [ ] Take cuttings of tender perennials such as argyranthemum, scented pelargonium, fuchsias and penstemons to pre-empt winter losses.

EARLY AUTUMN TASKS

IN THE GLASSHOUSE

☐ Check that heating is in good order.

☐ Clean off any shading paint and move shading netting to one side.

☐ Bring in any tender plants that have been outside for the summer.

☐ Repot cacti and succulents.

IN THE VEGETABLE PATCH

☐ Harvest capsicums, chillies and eggplants.

☐ Cover lettuces if cold weather threatens.

☐ Plant out spring cabbages. Check sprout plants and stake if necessary to avoid wind rock.

☐ Put grease bands around the trunks of fruit trees to stop winter pests crawling up the trunk.

☐ Sow green manure to suppress weeds and add nutrients to the soil in spring.

Late Autumn

Towards the end of autumn there will be clear signs of plants preparing for dormancy. Increasing numbers of leaves fall after an all-too-brief period of spectacular colour change, berries on trees and shrubs ripen, grasses fade and seed heads in all shapes and sizes bring birds galore to feast and stock up for winter. It is always worth making time to look for these autumn changes as one gale or storm will spoil the effect in an instant. This is a time of planning and in effect the beginning of the garden year. Now is the time to create new borders and beds as well as completing new lawns before the weather makes working in the garden too difficult.

LATE AUTUMN TASKS

IN THE GARDEN

- [ ] Finish laying new lawns when the weather allows.

- [ ] Apply weedkiller and autumn food to lawns. Only cut grass if required.

- [ ] Continue planting, especially bare-root plants and evergreens, and use this time to move any shrubs that are in the wrong place. Water regularly to ensure their survival and stake new plantings well.

- [ ] Plant climbers and biennials such as wallflowers, ready for flowering the following season.

- [ ] Look after any ponds, clearing out leaves and debris and thinning out aquatic plants.

- [ ] Keep collecting leaves to make leaf mould. Leave some out-of-the-way patches for insects and hedgehogs to enjoy.

- [ ] Prepare protection for any tender plants that cannot be moved under cover.

LATE AUTUMN TASKS

IN THE GLASSHOUSE

- [ ] Store lifted dahlias after the first frost has blackened them.

- [ ] Store lifted begonias and other summer-flowering bulbs.

- [ ] Remove summer crops once harvesting has been completed.

IN THE VEGETABLE PATCH

- [ ] Clear away summer plantings that have finished cropping, such as sweetcorn and beans.

- [ ] Harvest squash as they ripen.

- [ ] Dig over beds where possible.

Early Winter

Finally, all the leaves of deciduous plants should have fallen and any remaining herbaceous plants that clung on through autumn should have died back by now. Tidying when the weather allows – bearing in mind that too tidy a garden is bad for wildlife – is the order of the day, along with repairing hard landscapes and garden structures. If it is not too wet and cold, digging over beds and borders will keep the gardener warm and allow frost to break up heavy clods. There are few plants flowering now but their scarcity makes them all the more attractive. Witch hazels, mahonias and winter-flowering heathers will do their best to cheer the gardener up unless the weather is very inclement. Later on, evergreen clematis may appear. Grevilleas and some eucalypts will be in flower in some parts of Australia

EARLY WINTER TASKS

IN THE GARDEN

- ☐ Top-dress heavy, poorly drained lawns with organic matter.
- ☐ Finish clearing and tidying garden beds and borders.
- ☐ In colder areas, begin to prune roses.
- ☐ Check that vulnerable plants are well protected against frost.
- ☐ Plan and dig new borders, adding plenty of compost or manure, whenever the weather allows.
- ☐ Order next season's seeds and plants in preparation for the following year.
- ☐ Sharpen secateurs and shears and ensure that all machinery is given some annual maintenance.

EARLY WINTER TASKS

IN THE GLASSHOUSE

- [ ] Check forced bulbs and bring them out into the light.
- [ ] Remember to ventilate when possible.
- [ ] Check that stored bulbs and tubers are not rotting. Promptly remove any that are.

IN THE VEGETABLE PATCH

- [ ] Continue digging and improving the soil when the weather allows. Avoid digging or walking on wet soil.
- [ ] Finish pruning fruit trees.
- [ ] Lift leeks and parsnips and pick early sprouts.
- [ ] Plant parsnip and swedes, harvest coriander and rocket and brussels sprouts
- [ ] Check the pH of the soil. Lime if needed but do not mix lime and compost or manure. Limed beds can be improved with humus in spring instead.
- [ ] Clean and disinfect glasshouses thoroughly, along with pots and seed trays.

Late Winter

Short days and cold weather make gardening at this time of year a little more difficult, but there are always days when jobs can be started. Avoid wet, frosty days as more harm than good will be done by battling on regardless. It is still possible to plant shrubs and trees, to dig over beds and tidy away debris while keeping an eye out for the first bulbs and flowers to come out.

Winter-flowering iris will make an appearance at some point, while fragrance is supplied by daphne and winter-flowering honeysuckle. Hellebores and winter pansies will also provide extra flowering interest.

Inside, on the worst days, potatoes can be put to 'chit' and more cuttings can be taken of overwintering plants and chrysanthemums.

LATE WINTER TASKS

IN THE GARDEN

- [ ] Begin to clear herbaceous borders, removing weeds and forking over before mulching with compost or leaf mould.

- [ ] Continue clearing and tidying, planting and repairing whenever the weather allows.

- [ ] Keep checking vulnerable plants for frost damage.

- [ ] Prune dormant shrubs and trees, at least removing any dead, damaged or diseased material.

IN THE GLASSHOUSE

- [ ] As soon as the glasshouse has been thoroughly cleaned, sowing of annuals and hardy border perennials can begin. In warmer areas, seeds of glasshouse tomatoes and capsicums can be sown now as long as heat is provided.

- [ ] Take cuttings of chrysanthemums and overwintered plants.

- [ ] Pot up lily bulbs.

LATE WINTER TASKS

IN THE VEGETABLE PATCH

- [ ] Plant beetrot, lettuce, bok choi, carrots, harvest broccoli, cauliflower, spinach.

- [ ] Prepare beds ready for spring and cover with plastic or cloches to help the soil to warm up.

- [ ] Dig in green manures that have overwintered in vegetable beds – to give them time to decompose.

- [ ] Sow parsnips, shallots and onions in a prepared bed.

- [ ] Finish pruning soft fruit bushes, including autumn raspberries.

- [ ] 'Chit' seed potatoes to give them a better start. This needs to be done around six weeks before planting, so plan accordingly to take account of the last frost.

Further Resources

Books

- *100 Perfect Plants* by Simon Akeroyd (National Trust Books, 2017)

- *Allotment Handbook* by Simon Akeroyd (Dorling Kindersley, 2011)

- *The Australian Native Garden* by Angus Stewart and A.B. Bishop (Murdoch Books, 2016)

- *The Good Gardener* by Simon Akeroyd (National Trust Books, 2015)

- *RHS Lawns and Ground Cover* by Simon Akeroyd (Dorling Kindersley, 2012)

- *RHS Shrubs and Small Trees* by Simon Akeroyd (Dorling Kindersley, 2008)

- *The Complete Book of Vegetables, Herbs and Fruit in Australia* by Matthew Biggs, Jekka McVicar and Bob Flowerdew (Simon & Schuster, 2017)

- *RHS Practical Latin for Gardeners* by James Armitage (Mitchell Beasely, 2016)

- *RHS A–Z Encyclopedia of Garden Plants* (4th edition), ed. Christopher Brickell (Dorling Kindersley, 2016)

- *RHS Encyclopedia of Plants and Flowers*, ed. Christopher Brickell (Dorling Kindersley, 2010)

- *RHS Pruning & Training* by Christopher Brickell and David Joyce (Dorling Kindersley, 2017)

- *The Hillier Manual of Trees and Shrubs*, eds John G. Hillier and Roy Lancaster (RHS, 2014)

- *Garden Design: A Book of Ideas* by Heidi Howcroft and Marianne Majerus (Mitchell Beasely, 2015)

- *Planting: A New Perspective* by Piet Oudolf and Noel Kingsbury (Timber Press, 2013)

- *RHS Encyclopedia of Gardening Techniques* by RHS (Mitchell Beasely, 2008)

- *RHS Complete Gardener's Manual* by RHS (Dorling Kindersley, 2011)

- *The Vegetable Gardener's Bible* by Edward C. Smith (Storey Publishing, 2009)

Websites

- www.rhs.org.uk

- www.simonakeroyd.co.uk

- www.gardeningaustralia.com.au

- https://communitygarden.org.au/

- www.soilassociation.org

- www.organicgardener.com.au

Index

Picture Credits